MW01108364

Euro-Visions

Euro-Visions

Europe in Contemporary Cinema

Mariana Liz

Bloomsbury Academic
An imprint of Bloomsbury Publishing Plc

B L O O M S B U R Y
NEW YORK · LONDON · OXFORD · NEW DELHI · SYDNEY

Bloomsbury Academic
An imprint of Bloomsbury Publishing Inc

1385 Broadway
New York
NY 10018
USA

50 Bedford Square
London
WC1B 3DP
UK

www.bloomsbury.com

BLOOMSBURY and the Diana logo are trademarks of Bloomsbury Publishing Plc

First published 2016

© Mariana Liz, 2016

Library of Congress Cataloging-in-Publication Data
Names: Liz, Mariana, author.
Title: Euro-visions : Europe in contemporary cinema / Mariana Liz.
Description: New York : Bloomsbury Academic, 2016. |
Includes bibliographical references and index.
Identifiers: LCCN 2016005631 (print) | LCCN 2016007853 (ebook) |
ISBN 9781628923018 (hardback) | ISBN 9781628923025 (pbk.) |
ISBN 9781628922974 (ePDF) | ISBN 9781628922998 (ePub)
Subjects: LCSH: Motion pictures—Europe–History. | Europe—In motion
pictures. | BISAC: PERFORMING ARTS / Film & Video / History & Criticism.
Classification: LCC PN1993.5.E85 L59 2016 (print) | LCC PN1993.5.E85 (ebook) |
DDC 791.43094–dc23
LC record available at http://lccn.loc.gov/2016005631

ISBN: HB: 978-1-6289-2-301-8
PB: 978-1-6289-2-302-5
ePub: 978-1-6289-2-299-8
ePDF: 978-1-6289-2-297-4

Cover design: Jason Anscombe

Typeset by Newgen Knowledge wotk(s) Pvt Ltd.
Printed and bound in the United States of America

To my family, old and new

Contents

List of Illustrations and Graphs

Illustrations

Graphs

List of Tables

Acknowledgements

It would not have been possible to write this book without the help of numerous people. First, I would like to thank Katie Gallof at Bloomsbury Publishing for believing in this project. Thank you also to Mary Al-Sayed and Michelle Chen for their help while completing it. I would like to express my gratitude to FCT (Portuguese Ministry of Science and Higher Education) for their financial support towards the initial research that led to this book. Thank you also to everyone who spoke to me at the European Commission. A number of people read segments and earlier drafts of this book and provided useful feedback; these include Jan Palmowski, Sarah Street, Rob Stone, Paul Cooke and an anonymous reviewer. I am particularly grateful to Ginette Vincendeau for the guidance she provided, as well as for her endless patience and kindness. Olga Kourelou was an excellent colleague and friend throughout. Finally, I would like to thank my family for their constant support. I am especially thankful to Pete for his optimism and enthusiasm, without which I could not have finished this book, and to little Joaquim for smiling whenever I enter the room.

An earlier version of material included in Chapter 4 appeared previously as 'From Europe with Love: Urban Space and Cinematic Postcards', published in *Studies in European Cinema* 11: 1 (2014), and is reprinted by permission of Taylor & Francis Ltd, www.tandfonline.com.

Textual Note

Films are presented by their English titles, with the original title indicated the first time each film is mentioned. However, in order to facilitate reading, English titles alone are used in tables. A complete filmography can be found at the end of the book.

Introduction: Europe and European Cinema

What is Europe and how does European cinema portray it? These are the questions this book aims to answer. *Euro-Visions* is thus situated at the crossroads of two distinct yet related fields: Europe as a concept, especially as defined by the European Union (EU), and contemporary European film. To answer the first question we might begin by focusing on the event that inspired the title of this book: the Eurovision Song Contest. First held in 1956, Eurovision is an annual competition, which started as a television show and is now also broadcast online. Much of the discourse surrounding the contest replicates conventional ideas about the geopolitics of Europe. Commentators have questioned, for instance, the presence of Israel in an event originally developed in Europe, or joked about traditional alliances and divisions between participating nations – Spain and Portugal have, for years, awarded each other's act the maximum possible score: the famous *douze points*. The 2014 edition of the contest proved a particularly fruitful example of how Eurovision contributes to the debate about the meaning of Europe. This was especially because of its winner: Austria's Conchita Wurst, the 'bearded lady', as introduced by performer Tom Neuwirth. The drag act confirmed the commonplace that daring and often sexually charged content is typically produced (and broadcast) in Europe, which suggests that the continent's culture is more libertarian than cultures elsewhere. In her winning speech, a teary Conchita Wurst echoed this perception, as she dedicated her victory to everyone who believes in a future of peace and freedom. Europe emerged here tied to emotion, as well as openness, tolerance and democracy – key concepts in its political construction, and also central, as this book will show, to Europe's cultural definition.

Europe and the EU: In the news, but for the right reasons?

Europe is a central topic in today's public sphere. It is key to understand the early twenty-first century, its first decade offering a vivid picture of the disparity of responses Europe provokes and the dramatic changes the perception of the latter has undergone. In the early 2000s, the widespread enthusiasm for a project aimed at the democratic and peaceful integration of different peoples, in economic, political and cultural terms, was epitomized by the adoption of the Single Currency, the expansion of the Schengen area (effectively creating a borderless continent extending to a number of Eastern European countries) and the launch of the EU's Culture Programme with a budget of over €230 million. But at the time of writing, fifteen years later, Europe is increasingly questioned as the financial crisis and immigration (in public discourse) and accounts of Euro-centrism in a postcolonial context (in academic writing) are foregrounded as its strongest critiques, in political and theoretical terms.

There is massive evidence of the importance of Europe, not least in the work of the EU. Never has the EU been so present in public discourse as in recent years. If the euro-zone debt crisis that began in 2009 launched European politics into the top five of the most debated topics across the continent and potentially the world, in the United Kingdom (a traditionally Euro-sceptic country) the issue's prominence has been amplified by a governmental promise to hold an 'in/out' referendum on the EU in 2016. Demonstrating the ongoing relevance of European politics beyond Europe's borders, Barack Obama was in Brussels in March 2014 to attend a EU summit. This was his first official visit to Belgium since becoming US president in 2009. Regardless of its shortcomings, no political union in the world can be compared to the one developing in Europe. Its vitality can be observed both internally (as it proceeds with the negotiations for the accession of prospective members) and externally: represented by the president of the European Commission since 1981, the EU is the 'ninth' member of the G8 (the survival of the euro being the main issue at the meeting that took place in Camp David, Maryland, in the United States in May 2012), as well as a leading actor in the development of international legislation on areas such as climate change and human rights.

Attention to pan-European events has also been growing within popular culture. In addition to much branded sports competitions, such as the UEFA Europa and Champions League, the Eurovision Song Contest, mentioned earlier, has had an average of 125 million viewers every year. A record audience of nearly 200 million people watched it in 2015 – the year of its sixtieth anniversary – an increase of 2 million compared to 2014. EU initiatives aimed at the promotion of European citizenship also have an effect on individuals' perception of Europe. A good example is the Erasmus exchange programme, which was created in 1987 and allows students and staff in higher education to spend a fixed period of time in another European country, studying or receiving training. According to Umberto Eco, interviewed in January 2012 for the *Europa* series – a joint project developed by six European newspapers based in Spain, Italy, France, Germany, Poland and the United Kingdom – this initiative clearly reinforces European culture. For Eco, Erasmus constitutes 'a sexual revolution: a young Catalan man meets a Flemish girl – they fall in love, they get married and they become European, as do their children'. Arguing the programme increases European citizens' sense of belonging and identification with the continent, Eco goes on to suggest this 'should be compulsory [and] not just for students', as everyone should 'spend time in other countries within the European Union' (cited in Riotta 2012). Regardless of whether or not the impact of the Erasmus programme has been felt in the terms suggested by Eco, with the abolition of internal borders, the development of transport and communication and the re-localization of businesses and public institutions, more and more people not only travel within Europe but also change their residency from one European nation to another. The idea of Europe, especially for those who live in countries that adhered to the Single Currency, and/or travel without a passport within Schengen, is today experienced in practical terms, becoming an integral part of many people's daily lives.

However, at the same time as Europe generates positive interest, its significance is increasingly questioned. The debt crisis that began around 2009 (as well as criticism over the way it has been dealt with within the euro-zone), together with participation in the 2014 election of the European Parliament, which was the lowest ever across the continent, threatened not only the de facto continuation of the European political project, but also its public perception. The United Kingdom's popular press often alludes to the shortcomings of the European integration process. In their characteristically humorous tone, British tabloids have been responsible for a series of remarkable – and remarkably hostile – headlines on Europe, such as the notorious 'Up Yours, Delors!' (*The Sun*, 1 November 1990). The European Commission addressed a number of these attacks in a press release in 2012. Among the British 'EU myths' deconstructed (European Commission 2012) we find: 'EU plans to close thousands of British off-licences' (*The Sun*, 21 February 2005), 'Marmalade: EU regulates grandmother's recipe' (*Daily Telegraph*, 21 October 2003) and 'EU to rename Waterloo Station "Europe Station"' (*Daily Express*, 16 October 2003). Integrated Europe is here contrasted with national culture, as well as indigenous customs and traditions, which are perceived to be endangered. The tone is alarmist and the changes are announced with a clear populist slant, as the topics raised by these headlines refer to issues people can easily relate to, such as drinking, eating and travelling.

The fact that Europe and the EU are extensively discussed denotes that their meaning carries implications for our society as a whole. Yet, Europe's definition, and especially the way in which the EU uses it and contributes to it, remains essentially vague. This is particularly the case of cultural perspectives. As such, important questions still need to be asked about the relevance and significance of the contemporary idea of Europe.

The global appeal of contemporary European cinema

Likewise, European cinema not only occupies a central place in film history, it has also received increasing attention, notably with the expanding work on transnational cinema. Ever since the beginning of film studies, scholarly publications have examined the cinemas of Europe. However, the majority of these concerned specific auteurs or specific nations. Within the new and growing framework of analysis centred on cross-border and cross-cultural cinemas, European film has consolidated its position as an entity in its own right. The *Encyclopaedia of European Cinema* (Vincendeau 1995a), featuring entries on key films, stars, directors and movements, is a seminal example of the new understanding of European cinema as a unified object of study. Other publications appearing in the 1990s explored issues of representation in European cinema, especially through the prism of film and society (Sorlin 1991; Petrie 1992; Hill, McLoone and Hainsworth 1994). The acceptance of European cinema as a discrete subject matter was consolidated during the first decade of the 2000s, as testified by a growing body of scholarly work (Forbes and Street 2000; Holmes and Smith 2000; Ezra 2003; Galt 2006; Wood 2007). In addition to reference works, overviews and anthologies, scholarship on European cinema can be divided into three main areas: industrial aspects, from the first pan-European audiovisual policies (Dale 1992; Finney 1996) to the resurgence of co-productions (Wayne 2002; Rivi 2007) and the development of cultural policy in Europe (Bondebjerg, Novrup Redvall and Higson 2015); theoretical understandings, for instance, the relationship between film and European identity (Everett 2005), the positioning of European cinema in the world (Elsaesser 2005; Harrod, Liz and Timoshkina 2015) or European contributions to film theory (Aitken 2001; Trifonova 2008); and main themes and genres, from history and the past (Mazierska 2011; Vidal 2012) to migration, diaspora and borders (Berghahn and Sternberg 2010; Loshitzky 2010; Merivirta et al. 2013).

Contemporary European films demonstrate the emergence of a pan-European communication sphere. They circulate across borders, mirroring a European society. This is particularly true of art-house, auteur and festival films, even if they reach relatively small audiences. By contrast, as is well known, popular genres such as comedy are generally consumed by national audiences only. At the same time, European films at both ends of the art/mainstream spectrum are released beyond Europe, having, for instance, been a constant presence at the Academy Awards. Six European films received Best Foreign Language Film prizes at the Oscars between 2000 and 2010: *No Man's Land* (Danis Tanovic, 2001), *Nirgendwo in Afrika/Nowhere in Africa* (Caroline Link, 2001), *Mar Adentro/The Sea Inside* (Alejandro Amenábar, 2004), *Das Leben der Anderen/The Lives of Others* (Florian Henckel von Donnersmarck, 2006), *Die Fälscher/ The Counterfeiters* (Stefan Ruzowitzky, 2007) and *Hævnen/In a Better World* (Susanne Bier, 2010).

The industrial aspects that characterize European cinema at the turn of the twentieth century, at production, distribution and exhibition levels, raise questions about contemporary film practices more generally. The product of a film industry existing in a complex network of market forces and state subsidies, European cinema also proves a particularly relevant object of study for the understanding of institutional frameworks, policies and initiatives in support of the audiovisual sector. Despite this, the number of scholarly publications devoted to European cultural policy is relatively small. On the one hand, this is to do with the fact that this is a reasonably recent topic. On the other, political scientists see legislation for this sector as having a limited impact on society and therefore lacking in status. Chris Shore's (2000) study of the history of EU cultural policy, from the post-war period to the signing of the Maastricht Treaty, as well as Monica Sassatelli's (2009) research on initiatives such as the European Capital of Culture developed by the EU, thus constitute significant exceptions.

Publications about film policy are equally scarce. Studies tend to be focused on one country, such as Margaret Dickinson and Sarah Street's *Cinema and State* (1985), which offers a historical study of film policy in the United Kingdom. With a contemporary and transnational focus, Albert Moran's (1996) account of film policies around the globe at the end of the twentieth century is a valuable overview. But with the exception of Patrice Vivancos' *Cinéma et Europe* (2000), there are no books exclusively devoted to the help given by European institutions to the audiovisual sector. Studies specifically concerned with Europe normally address film as part of the broader institutional support given to areas such as television, digital media and the internet (see, for instance, Bondebjerg, Novrup Redvall and Higson 2015). Some publications examine the legislation supporting such initiatives (Goldberg Prosser and Verhulst 1998; Herold 2010), as well as the institutional frameworks in which they are developed (Collins 1994). Others are focused on the European film industries, looking at policy only tangentially, as in the case of Anne Jäckel's (2003) monograph on this subject. One particular issue raised by these studies concerns the relationship Europe establishes with internal and external partners. For instance, the impact of European policies has been analysed in national contexts (Strode 2000). Philip Schlesinger (1997), on the other hand, has looked at policy developments in the EU in relation to the construction of a European cultural identity and how this is opposed to that of the United States.

Significantly, the vast majority of these studies adopt a generally dismissive tone. We only need to consider the way in which scholars have been quick to enthusiastically embrace the expression 'Euro-pudding' and its negative connotations, despite the shortage of analyses of its actual meaning and consequences of its use (Liz 2015). Miguel Casado (2006), for instance, looks at the influence of EU initiatives in the audiovisual sector, concluding that there has been little investment and therefore few results, in the same way that Jäckel (2003) questions the success of EU film policy in emphasizing the cultural importance of film in Europe. Even if EU policies have had a limited economic and financial impact (which in any case is extremely difficult to assess, especially in smaller European film industries), they do have implications for the relevance of cinema and culture more generally in the construction of the idea of Europe. The role of politics and policies in the shaping of concepts and meaning cannot be ignored in a sector that is highly subsidized and that relies heavily on European institutions. As a key player in the European film industry, the EU makes a significant contribution to the understanding of European cinema, and although this may very well be challenged, it must, first and foremost, be examined.

Visions of Europe in European cinema

Euro-Visions asks what idea of Europe emerges, is represented and constructed by contemporary European cinema. Cinema is not just an industrial art form (a purposefully contradictory formulation which embodies the complex nature of film), but also a particularly useful means for the dissemination of cultural ideas. At stake is also our understanding of the role state and political institutions play in the promotion of the audiovisual industries and of cinema in particular. *Euro-Visions* questions the extent to which the work carried out by political organizations shapes our perception of the society we live in, examining the influence of the EU on the European film industry, as well as on cultural conceptions of contemporary Europe.

This is a particularly timely investigation. The year 2014 was crucial in the history of the EU. First, the European Parliament elections running in May that year bore testament to an increasingly polarized Europe. No doubt fundamental transformations would have to take place, following unavoidable consequences to what many commentators dubbed the 'political earthquake' caused by the election results, whereby the three main centrist blocs lost seats, mostly to Euro-sceptic parties – the big winners in a series of European countries, including France and the United Kingdom. The idea of Europe is intensely challenged by contemporary events. The refugee crisis resulting from the war that broke out in Syria in 2011, the Paris terrorist attacks of November 2015 and the subsequent reinstating of border controls in France and a number of other European nations part of the Schengen Agreement testify to a profoundly divided European society, not to mention EU. Such incidents have not only political, but also cultural implications: across and beyond the continent, in traditional press and social media, questions are being raised about whether the concept of Europe stands for freedom or restraint, tolerance or bigotry, universality or exclusion.

The year 2014 marked also the launch of Creative Europe, a seven-year €1.46 billion programme, which merges previous EU initiatives in support of music, literature, heritage and the audiovisual industry under a new, more general, umbrella. Of particular relevance for this book, Creative Europe signified the end of the MEDIA programme as a single and independent programme. In place since 1992, this was, until 2014, the EU's signature initiative in support of European cinema. To pinpoint the ways in which Europe and European cinema are understood by the EU, as well as what role European institutions play in the cultural conception of European cinema, is particularly crucial at a time when Europe is undergoing a series of structural changes. This research not only sheds light on a particular period of Europe's contemporary history, it also crucially frames forthcoming debates on institutional ideas of Europe, as well as visions of European cinema.

This book is structured into four chapters. Chapter 1 is centred on the meaning of the idea of Europe. Divided into two sections, the chapter offers first a historical and then an institutional account of the idea of Europe. As the EU was only officially formed and named as such with the signing of the Maastricht Treaty in 1992, the abbreviation EEC and the expression it refers to, the European Economic Community, are used to designate what we now know as the EU when referring to its history and work before then.

Chapter 2 opens with an overview of the key issues in contemporary European cinema, as well as the main features of the European film industry, setting the context for the analysis of the MEDIA programme. After describing the emergence, main goals and initiatives of MEDIA, the chapter ends with a discussion about the promotion of this EU programme. At stake here is the way in which the EU's vision of European cinema is projected to a wider public. This chapter also looks at how the idea of Europe frames institutional discussions of the audiovisual industries.

Euro-Visions examines fiction features released with the support of MEDIA. Through close textual analysis, it highlights ideas of Europe in these films' form and content. While over 200 films are considered, case studies include the films that are 'advertised' most frequently by the European Commission, for instance, in memos and press releases. Case studies originate from as many different European nations as possible, including 'big' and 'small' countries and audiovisual industries, and belong to different genres, comprising both big-budget and independent productions.

Chapter 3 begins an in-depth analysis of the portrayal of Europe on screen by examining historical films. It looks at the emergence of a European cultural memory, as well as at the extent to which this is defined by issues of quality and prestige, emotional attachment to or intellectual engagement with the continent's past. This chapter is divided into three main sections: from the celebration of European history to the cinematic representation of war in Europe and, finally, an analysis of films exploring Europe's recent political past.

By contrast, Chapter 4 examines screen portrayals of contemporary Europe. The first half of this chapter is especially concerned with spatial representations of the continent, examining touristic and cosmopolitan visions. Departing from an essentially positive representation of the continent, the chapter then looks at dystopian views of what has been labelled 'Fortress Europe'. The journeys of welcomed visitors (i.e. tourists) and those normally excluded (e.g. migrants) overlap, which highlights the multifaceted meaning of the continent today. A brief conclusion highlights the main tensions characterizing the idea of Europe in contemporary European cinema.

Throughout, the book combines an analysis of scholarly work and official EU documents. This research also draws on four interviews held with senior policymakers working at the European Commission in Brussels. Conducted in September 2009, these interviews took place at a time when EU institutions were undergoing a series of transformations. A new commission, led for the second time by José Manuel Durão Barroso, had just been elected, which meant new departments and posts would be created. To these forthcoming changes was added the prospect of the approval of the Lisbon Treaty, which would create new institutional figures (viz. the president of the European Council). This treaty was finally ratified in December of that year. In 2009, policymakers talked passionately and positively about the challenges faced by the EU and the aspects of its work that, in their view, had to be improved. This is in stark contrast with the tone I encountered during a more recent visit to Brussels in May 2012, when a sense of crisis and uncertainty was evident among the European institutions. By speaking to individuals with privileged access to and knowledge of EU cultural and audiovisual policies in 2009 this research benefitted from more up-to-date information than that available to the general public. The interviews were also useful as they provided me with the opportunity to hear views that differed from the official discourse of European institutions, thus offering a new perspective on the idea of Europe, MEDIA and contemporary European film. Participants asked for their responses to remain anonymous; the gap between official discourse and the interviewees' views is clearly a reason for this request for anonymity.

Euro-Visions charts the contemporary history of an idea, an institution and a cinema that have simultaneously shaped and been shaped by the most significant changes taking place at the end of the twentieth century and the start of the twenty-first century. As questions are increasingly asked about the meaning of Europe, the EU and the identity of contemporary European film, this book hopefully contributes to important debates about their future.

The Idea of Europe: When, What and Who

As the introduction to this book has shown, Europe is discussed by many different actors. Yet, what 'Europe' means varies significantly. Writing about European cinema, for instance, Dimitris Eleftheriotis (2001: 1) suggests that understanding Europe in geographical terms is the only way to avoid its problematic meaning. However, even the continent's borders are contentious. This has been the case throughout Europe's history, particularly in relation to its frontiers to the east. Not only is Russia's relationship with Europe still debatable today, Eastern Europe as a whole was until very recently perceived as an 'other' within the continent. From a geopolitical point of view, as alliances such as the Council of Europe and the North Atlantic Treaty Organization (NATO) are consolidated, the notion of Europe becomes enmeshed with a Western or Northern perception of the world. The European Union (EU) itself is a good example of Europe's blurry boundaries, as the members keep growing, a number of non-member countries participate in its programmes and not all members share the same legislation – as in the case of the opt-outs from the Schengen Agreement, as well as the Single Currency. What other approaches towards the definition of the idea of Europe should then be considered?

This chapter introduces the main issues in the study of the idea of Europe. First, it draws a brief history of the relevant scholarly literature. It examines the meanings attributed to Europe by cultural and political approaches, from the ongoing significance of the Hellenistic world and Christianity to the intimate link between Europe and democracy, law and human rights. Investigating the relationship between European, national and global forms of identification, as well as the ostensive contrasting notions of Euro-centrism and universality, this chapter also discusses Europe's 'others'. It thus follows a questioning of the 'when' and the 'what' with an analysis of the 'who' in terms of who defines and is defined by European identity.

The second half of the chapter turns to the examination of the ways in which the EU (named as the European Economic Community [EEC] before 1992) has contributed to this debate. It questions how the notion of European identity has featured in EU official documents and initiatives, as well as what idea of Europe emerges from the work of European institutions. The EU symbols, including the flag, the anthem and the motto 'united in diversity', are examined. In addition to looking at EU treaties and public communication, this section also draws on a series of interviews conducted in Brussels in 2009. Attitudes towards Europe have alternated between peaks of disparagement and enthusiasm; the advancement of the European integration process has had an impact on the body of work on the idea of Europe, in terms of volume and tone. Bringing together scholarly and institutional visions of Europe, this chapter provides historical and theoretical grounding to the subsequent study of EU audiovisual policy, as well as to the forthcoming analysis of contemporary European films. *Euro-Visions* is particularly concerned with the idea of Europe that is shaped by European integration. For a wider history of the meanings associated with Europe, see, for instance, Bell (2006).

The idea of Europe and European integration: A concise history

Although the concept of Europe and the identification with the European continent have existed for centuries – going back to ancient Greece – an institutional idea of Europe only emerged in the 1950s. Previous projects devoted to the maintenance of world peace and European integration include the League of Nations, founded in the aftermath of the First World War. But with the signing of the Treaty of Rome in 1957 (which would officially establish the EEC in January of the following year), what is today known as the EU appeared as the first federalist project capable of achieving concrete results. The year 1957 is thus a landmark in the history of the idea of Europe.

Hartmut Kaelble (cited in Sassatelli 2009: 20) signals two main phases in the study of European identity: first, from the post-war period, reaching a particular crescendo in the 1960s; and second, from the late 1980s to the present day. Directly influenced by the aftermath of the Second World War and the signing of the Treaty of Rome, the literature produced during this first phase can be divided into historical and political approaches, as it either discusses the idea of Europe as a continent with cultural significance or reflects the development of the EEC. From a historical perspective, Denys Hay's *Europe: The Emergence of an Idea* (1957) is of particular relevance. Focused on the later Middle Ages, it looks at the notion of Europe and its relationship with Christendom – a distinctive (albeit problematic) element of the term's cultural definition. Hay questions not only the interconnections between Europe and religion as a defining cultural trait, but also those between Europe and the Christian territory in physical and symbolic terms. Europe is both: a land and an idea. It is telling of the strong links between the idea of Europe and European integration that such concerns arose in the post-war era, as Europe was increasingly seen as a unified continent, in geographical and political terms.

Emerging in this period are also a number of pieces written by politicians, including the EEC's 'founding fathers' (Konrad Adenauer, Alcide de Gasperi and Robert Schuman, among others), who directly address the European integration process and put forward a positive view of its development. An important example is Altiero Spinelli's *The European Adventure* (1972) – a title that nevertheless denotes a sense of uncertainty and risk. Here, Spinelli argues for a federalist view of Europe, suggesting that, despite 'confusing' visions of Europe and national variations, there is a widespread pro-European attitude and strong popular enthusiasm for the EEC's project (6).

The literature of the late 1980s and early 1990s on Europe was influenced by discussions about the Maastricht Treaty and the growing importance of culture within the EEC – examined in greater detail later. Two key texts are emblematic of this second phase. In *Penser l'Europe* (1987), Edgar Morin defines Europe with regard to its dialogical essence, arguing it is founded on opposites, united but diverse. For Morin, Europe is a *communauté de destin*, a community made together by its common destiny, or in other words, a community that was destined to be (191). He roots the understanding of Europe in a distant past, that of Greek and Roman heritage, vehemently condemning the continent's colonial history. Similarly, Jacques Derrida (1992) argues that Europe needs to be reborn. He stresses the existence of another 'heading' ('heading' here meant in the sense of 'orientation'), reminding us, like Morin, that it is possible for Europe to go in a different direction (14), that is, to overcome Euro-centrism as a dominant perspective on the world. Looking forward to a future that cannot adopt the strategies that led to war and destruction, both writers aim for a new configuration of the continent. Morin and Derrida place Europe in a chronological, rather than geographical, framework. The past, present and future of Europe, as well as the way in which they are brought together in a common narrative, are, as this book argues, crucial elements in the definition of this idea.

While the Europe discussed by Morin and Derrida is not overtly political, a reflection on its meaning cannot be disentangled from contemporary developments. Table 1.1 lists some of the most significant dates in the European integration process, pinpointing key policy changes and identifying the expanding number of EEC and EU member-states. As the integration process moved forward, other writings emerged that dealt with Europe's institutional dimension.

Soledad García (1993), for instance, discusses the issue of legitimacy, which is at the core of contemporary criticisms of the EU and its institutions (Herrmann, Risse and Brewer 2004; Checkel and Katzenstein 2009; Sternberg 2013). García (1993: 3) stresses the distinction between European elites (those working in Brussels) and citizens, questioning the ability of the EEC to communicate with and represent those affected by its policies. Equally negative is Gerard Delanty (1995: 5), who alerts readers to the dangers of bringing cultural identities into the political realm, as they can become ideologies. These topics will re-emerge in the discussion about the soft power of European cinema vis-à-vis European integration and the development of the idea of Europe.

García's and Delanty's works illustrate a new body of literature that explicitly merges the thinking on Europe with that on the EU, although these are written not from an institutional (as in Spinelli's contribution) but from a scholarly point of view. Seen in conjunction with the work of Morin and Derrida, García's and Delanty's writing further points up a suspicion towards the idea of Europe, as what it asks stresses a radical questioning of the very existence of the EEC and then EU: can Europe rethink itself? Can it head in a different direction? Is it legitimate? Can we trust the EU's discourse as more than just political ideology? The idea of Europe is thus mostly seen through a

Table 1.1 Timeline of most important EU dates and facts, including member-states

	Key events	Member-states	
1957	The Treaty of Rome is signed, creating the European Economic Community (EEC)	BE, FR, IT, LU, NL, GFR (DE from 1990)	6
1973	*Enlargement*	DK, IE, UK	9
1979	First European Parliament elections		
1981	*Enlargement*	GR	10
1985	Schengen Agreements are signed		
1986	*Enlargement*	SP, PT	12
1986	The Single European Act, the first major revision of the Treaty of Rome, is signed		
1992	The Maastricht Treaty or Treaty on the European Union is signed, formally establishing the European Union (EU)		
1995	*Enlargement*	AT, FI, SE	15
1997	The Amsterdam Treaty is signed, incorporating the Schengen Agreements and creating a borderless Europe		
2002	Euro coins and notes are introduced		
2004	*Enlargement*	CY, CZ, EE, HU, LV, LT, MT, PL, SK, SI	25
2004	The Treaty establishing a Constitution for Europe is signed by 25 member-states		
2005	The ratification process of the Constitutional Treaty comes to an end, unsuccessfully		
2007	*Enlargement*	BG, RO	27
2007	The Lisbon Treaty is signed		
2013	*Enlargement*	HR	28

positive light between the 1950s and 1970s, but through a negative perspective from the 1980s to the early 2000s.

According to Michael Wintle (2009: 3), 'enthusiasm for "Europe" has waxed and waned over the last few centuries'. It fluctuated even more in the twentieth century – and, as we will see, in the first decade of the 2000s. Whereas in the 1950s European integration theories were primarily aligned with anti-nationalist feelings emerging from the devastating effects of the Second World War, in the 1990s there was a rise in nationalism following the break-up of the Soviet Bloc and the conflict in the Balkans, leading to a new and profound questioning of Europe. Wintle also suggests attitudes towards Europe are in tune with changes in the capitalist economy (407). Hence, when the continent faced an economic crisis, such as during the Great Depression of the 1930s, European societies experienced a sense of Euro-despair (much like in the years following the euro-zone crisis which began in 2009). And when there was an economic expansion, namely, after the implementation of the Marshall Plan in Western European nations, the mood was of Euro-euphoria.

Euphoria also describes the general attitude towards Europe in the early 2000s. This was a period of widespread enthusiasm for the European integration project as the European Monetary Union was launched and the EU's largest expansion (with the enlargement to ten new countries) started to be prepared. At the same time as the EU pushed for more integration, the issue of legitimacy was brought alive by the refusal of the Constitutional Treaty in 2004. Enthusiasm towards Europe reversed back to dismissal in the space of one decade only. European identity, not exclusively tied to, but propelled by the politics of integration, thus became a key issue for the twenty-first century.

Within the second phase of writings on Europe identified by Kaelble, and starting in the 1980s, it is therefore important to highlight a vast body of scholarship arising at the turn of the twentieth century. Literature on the idea of Europe has risen dramatically since the 2000s. While reprising some of the previous publications on European identity, more recent studies have expanded the discussion about the meaning of Europe to include lessons from postcolonial and postmodernist theories, as well as a consideration of globalization as an increasingly relevant phenomenon to the debate about the construction and definition of European identity.

The meaning of Europe: Political and cultural approaches

Among this vast scholarship, two main approaches emerge. First, there has been a growing body of literature on political and institutional conceptions of Europe. Berezin and Schain (2003) and Balibar (2003), for instance, have investigated the notions of borders, territory and citizenship and their bearing on the constitution of Europe. Scholars have also considered the implications EU policies have in contemporary society, establishing an explicit connection between European institutions and the emergence of a European identity (Herrmann, Risse and Brewer 2004; Mayer and Palmowski 2004). According to these studies, the EU does, at least in institutional terms, contribute to the formation of ties that bind European citizens together. This important conclusion validates, at the same time as it shows the need for, an investigation into the impact of the EU's work also in cultural terms.

In fact, at the same time, scholarship on the definition of Europe as a cultural rather than a political concept continues to expand. Luisa Passerini (2003) has examined the role of symbols and myths in the construction of European identity. Similarly, Michael Wintle (2009) has looked at the part played by maps, logos and buildings in the shaping of the idea of Europe. Political and cultural approaches shed light on the role of the EU in the formation of identities on the one hand, and on the meaning of Europe on the other. When combined, these two perspectives offer unique insight into the EU's contribution to the definition of a European cultural identity, as well as into the cultural idea of Europe as understood by the EU.

For instance, the idea of Europe has been prominently associated with notions of the past and oldness (Steiner 2006). This is also something the EU pursues in initiatives for the support of cultural heritage, as is discussed in Chapter 3. Being 'old' is, for Europe, more than a defining trait. The meaning of Europe has also been linked to particular moments in the history of the continent. Among those placing the roots of the idea of Europe in the past, García (1993: 5) invokes particular moments such as

Hellenism, Roman law and Christianity as the founding blocks of European identity. Anthony Pagden (2002) includes in this narrative the myth of Europa and the bull, and, after the Greek and the Roman Empire, the Enlightenment.

The myth of Europa, a Phoenician princess, narrates her abduction from the shores of modern Syria and Lebanon by Olympian chief god Zeus. Struck by Europa's beauty but wishing to hide his feelings from his wife Hera, Zeus metamorphoses into a beautiful and tame white bull. He surprises Europa as she gathers flowers at a seaside meadow, and encourages her to get onto his back. Zeus takes Europa away as her attendants are distracted and swims across the Mediterranean Sea, taking her to Crete. It is only when they reach the western island that Zeus reveals his identity. He then seduces Europa, who becomes the mother of Minos, the future king of Crete.

Although as Wintle (2009: 463) recognizes, the links between the story of Europa's abduction and the European project are vague, this myth is frequently cited in contemporary discussions of Europe. Wintle argues that, through the references made to this myth as a significant component of Europe's heritage, the continent has been attributed features such as 'nobility and queenliness, kinetic energy and the technology of travel' (151). The positive associations drawn here might account for the fact that statues and visual representations of Europa and the bull can be found outside the headquarters of and inside the buildings of several European institutions in Brussels, as well as on the Greek €2 coin. Quality and mobility are key aspects of the idea of Europe that are also visible in contemporary European cinema.

Equally significant, as argued by Stuart Hall (2003: 38), is the fact that the myth gives the continent a sense of *telos*, that is, a sense of purpose. Both Morin and Derrida stress the importance of eliminating a certain European heritage; they critique sections of Europe's history, namely, colonialism. Yet, they also link Europe – which is 'destined to be', and will develop if it chooses the right direction – to the notion of progress. As this book will show, the notion of progress has also been transferred to the realm of European culture via concepts such as high-art, quality and prestige. A key issue in the study of the idea of Europe is the tension between valuing Europe's self-perception of progress and restraining the continent's sense of superiority.

By being placed in the past, the idea of Europe gains status and authority; this myth, seen as a narrative that has endured the test of time, as a 'classical' and therefore respected story, provides the idea of Europe with a sense of prestige. This, however, is a 'challenged' prestige (Passerini 2003). The myth of Europa and the bull not only pinpoints Europe's specific origin, it also aims to position Europe in the centre of the world. The myth gives Europa a mission: to form a new world. At the same time, since Crete, which becomes the birthplace of this new, greater empire, is further west in relation to Phoenicia, the myth problematically highlights the historical association between Europe and the West – and, by consequence, as discussed later, a refusal of the East too.

From Greek Hellenism and the Roman Empire the idea of Europe has inherited the concepts of city and citizenship, politics and democracy, as well as, according to Pagden (2002: 42), a 'law for all humanity'. Similar concepts characterize the vision of Europe that emerges with the Enlightenment. But just as Morin and Derrida dismiss

Europe's colonialist strand and Passerini's reading of the myth of Europa challenges its imperialistic tone, there has been widespread criticism of the universal conceptions of Europe emerging from Classicism and the Enlightenment.

Before looking at the universal dimension of the idea of Europe in more detail, it is important to note that European identity is also defined in opposition to different 'others'. The 'other' is a crucial element in the definition of identities. Identities are by nature oppositional, relating to distinct meanings, groups and signifying practices. For Stuart Hall (2003: 38), 'nothing could be more true of Europe'. As he argues, ' "otherness" was from the beginning an invention of European ways of seeing and representing difference. [Europe] has been reinventing "the Rest" ever since' (43). The 'Rest' mentioned by Hall is also to be found within the continent; in the first instance, Europe is in (internal) opposition to the nation.

The idea of Europe emerged before the very concept of the nation-state, as demonstrated by Hay's (1957) study of the relationship between Europe and the Christian world. However, throughout the twentieth century and during the first decade of the twenty-first century, Europe has appeared in different moments either as more important than the nation (viz. in the post-war years, with the development of, for instance, town-twinning [Zelinsky 1991]), or as a problem for the nation (in the late 1980s, as noted earlier, as well as in the early 2000s in a number of Euro-sceptic nations such as the United Kingdom, which has seen the rise of UKIP, the UK Independence Party, and its lobbying for the country to leave the EU). García (1993) and Delanty (1995) insist that 'national nationalism' and 'European nationalism' are not only compatible, but they need each other. Studies about the connections between Europe and the nation-state adopt a multitude of approaches, ranging from questioning whether we are witnessing the formation of a European *nation*-state, that is, is Europe a political unity, as, for instance, the United Kingdom or France? (Shore 2000; D'Appollonia 2002); or to what extent Europe contributes to definitions of national identity, for instance, does one feel more British by feeling European? (Af Malmborg and Stråth 2002). The relationship between the nation and the idea of Europe is also the subject of a vigorous debate in film studies, as transnational cinema gains currency as a category of scholarly enquiry (see, for instance, Ezra and Rowden 2006) and the ability to locate the national is questioned by a number of contemporary European films.

Much of the thinking about Europe borrows terms inherited from the study of the nation-state. Almost all of the literature reviewed in this chapter takes Benedict Anderson's (2006 [1983]) seminal study as a starting point. In addition to characterizing the nation as an 'imagined community', Anderson describes the cultural systems that precede the nation-state's emergence, including a new temporality. As he suggests, '[T]he idea of a sociological organism moving calendrically through homogeneous, empty time is a precise analogue of the idea of the nation, which is also conceived as a solid community moving steadily down (or up) history' (26). By mirroring the political foundation of the nation-state, Europe is tied to the idea of progress. And as it becomes a continuum, Europe is able not only to make up for its past, but also to break with this same past. Europe's past is increasingly perceived as an 'other' in itself; European integration stems from wanting to avoid the repetition of earlier mistakes and devastating events, especially the Second World War and the Holocaust. As heritage becomes more and more about trauma (as argued in Chapter 3 in relation to contemporary films representing Europe's history through the perspective of its victims), Europeans try to distance themselves from a series of compromising past moments, thus reshaping Europe's narrative.

Beyond the nation, other key oppositions are highlighted by studies of the idea of Europe. Delanty (1995) pinpoints binary oppositions such as Christianity versus Islam, the Jews as the eternal enemy and the Orient as the other as archetypal European dichotomies – the latter vividly emerging in the myth of Europa's abduction. Internal and external opposites, such enemies and others are defined as non-European because of their religion, ethnicity and language (issues also addressed in Chapter 4).

Particularly controversial has been Europe's Judeo-Christian foundation. In the tradition of Hay's (1957) study of the emergence of the idea of Europe and Christendom, there has been extensive work on more recent links between Europe and religion, namely, on the faith of the EU's founding fathers, as well as the role played by Christian Democratic parties in Europe's political construction (Kaiser 2007). The connection between European identity and Christianity has also been attacked by many who claim it involves disregarding the major contributions to European culture made by other religious groups, specifically Jews and Muslims (Kumar 2003). Europe's perceived narrow-mindedness was the target of strong contestation during the writing of the Constitutional Treaty, which prompted the then president of the European Commission José Manuel Durão Barroso (2009: 21) to point out that Europe's Christian heritage should only be invoked if understood as signifying a tradition of ecumenism and universality.

Diversity and openness have become defining keywords in contemporary understandings of Europe and the EU. At the same time as Europe is perceived to be in opposition to the 'other', European identity has either been seen as compatible with other identities or, paradoxically, equated with universality. Derrida (1992: 83), for instance, feels European 'among other things'. Similarly, the EU has stressed the importance of creating an identity that is collective but remains a guardian of national, regional and local forms of identification. It is in this context that Anthony Smith's (1992: 70) seminal article on the unity of Europe describes a 'situational' identity that should represent a 'family of cultures made up of a syndrome of partially shared historical traditions and cultural heritages … a family of elements which overlap and figure in a number of (but not all) examples'. Smith highlights the importance of identifying common elements shared by European citizens, citing as examples Roman law, democracy, parliamentary institutions, romanticism and Classicism. However, he also hints at the inescapable divisions some of the traditions and heritages mentioned before have created.

After Smith, many have commented on the uncertainty of today's fragmented and global society, at the same time stressing that an individual will, at different moments, choose to defend his or her local, national or global identity, without ever having to deny any of these forms of allegiance (García 1993; Kohli 2000; D'Appollonia 2002; Sørensen 2004). Characterized by a universality that wishes to avoid clashes with other forms of identification, the contemporary idea of Europe runs the risk of becoming too vague – an issue the EU has also had to deal with, as discussed later.

Featuring prominently in contemporary discourses about Europe – as well as in contemporary European cinema, as is the case of *Joyeux Noël/Merry Christmas* (Christian Carion, 2005), analysed in Chapter 3 – the notion of universality can be traced back to the medieval era but was particularly developed at the time of the Enlightenment. Linked to this concept is also cosmopolitanism, a term inherited from the Stoics (third century BC) that gained currency in the eighteenth century. Broadly defined as the positive association with other countries and cultures, cosmopolitanism has also been recently rediscovered in literature across the humanities and social sciences (Delanty 2005; Appiah 2007; Beck and Grande 2008), as well as in film studies (Chapter 4).

Particularly important for the examination of the integration of the peoples of Europe, as well as of the unifying dimension of the European idea, is Kwame Anthony Appiah's understanding of European cosmopolitanism as closely linked to humanism. For Appiah (2007: 113), contemporary cosmopolitan citizens feel close to all other individuals in the world, not so much through a respect for difference as through a respect for human beings. The association of the idea of Europe not just with universality, but with this humanistic strand of cosmopolitanism in particular, echoes Georg Sørensen's (2004: 83) discussion of contemporary identities as underpinned by what he defines as a 'community of sentiment': a relationship between groups of citizens structured around a common culture and history, shared myths, symbols and art. The role of cinema with regard to the consolidation of the idea of Europe might precisely lie in the strengthening of the emotional ties between Europe and its citizens – a relationship not necessarily dependent on a rational, bureaucratic link to European institutions. The idea of Europe as understood and promoted by the EU necessarily has an institutional facet, but relies primarily on the cultural aspects of Europe – and hence the significance of cinema as a means to endorse and disseminate it.

On a political level, the concept of universality can be illustrated by the positioning of the EU as a global actor. Financially surpassed by emerging economies in other continents, Europe has struggled to maintain its significance, including at a political and cultural level. The 'de-centring' of Europe as a consequence of globalization is, for instance, discussed, in relation to cinema, by Thomas Elsaesser (2015). Since the signing of the Lisbon Treaty, the EU has increased its efforts to become not only a recognized but also a respectable protagonist on the world's political stage, from the negotiation of an international agreement on climate change in the 2010 Copenhagen Conference to its much-debated diplomatic involvement in the Ukraine's political crisis of 2014, framed globally as a West versus Russia struggle. Europe's position in the globe is, however, and as the Ukraine example also shows, extremely complex. Derrida (1992: 76) discusses the 'Duty of Europe' as what underpinned the formation of the global empires of the sixteenth century. However, the notion of mission has been severely questioned because of its ominous resonance with Europe's colonial history.

A need to be perceived as universal denotes an exclusive vision of Europe that construes itself as superior. Euro-centrism, which has its roots in the desire to force-fully impose a set of values on others, is a common criticism of the definition of the idea of Europe, as well as of the EU. Most texts cited in this chapter have been written in Europe – and this might account for Europe's alleged sense of superiority. However, much of the writing about Europe labels the official discourse of the EU as 'propaganda' (Shore 2000; Wintle 2009). Aiming to avoid the Euro-centric trap, many writers adopt instead a bias against the work of European institutions, systematically questioning their official discourse. This is, nevertheless, a discourse worth examining.

The EU necessarily inherits the meanings attributed to the idea of Europe even before its institutional foundation. The challenge for European institutions is to continue to be strong political actors, including in the cultural realm – for instance, by supporting the arts sector – while avoiding a superior stance on the individuals they represent, as well as a colonialist attitude towards the people beyond Europe's borders. The next section looks at how the EU has defined Europe, as well as itself, taking into account the oppositions highlighted so far, including between specificity and universality, the nation and the globe and Europe and the other.

The institutional definition of Europe: From the EEC to the EU

Jean Monnet, one of the most prominent of the EU's founding fathers, is believed to have said: 'If I were to begin again, I would start with culture'. This quote provides crucial information about the relationship between identity and culture in the European integration process, at the same time as it presents a number of contradictions. First, while it positions culture at the core of the EU's development, it also highlights the fact that this was not one of the EU's initial concerns. Second, it denotes the importance of European elites and the founding fathers in particular for the public perception of European integration, at the same time denouncing one of the main problems faced by the EU: miscommunication. In fact, this often-repeated statement that has now almost achieved the status of a myth is not an accurate quotation but a fabrication. Monnet did not say this; explanations either claim the quote was reported speech in the conditional form, that is, Monnet would have said this (Sassatelli 2009: 46), or that the quote had a different author (Gil 2009: 7). Regardless of whether Monnet did or did not suggest culture was missing from the European integration process, like all myths, the significance of this quotation lies in the fact that for years it has been reproduced in EU publications, being often cited by its officials.

While the importance attributed to culture by European institutions has been on the rise in recent years, it has not had a linear evolution. The EEC played a prominent role in promoting the idea of Europe during the 1970s. In 1973, the public opinion survey Eurobarometer was launched, followed by the signing of the Declaration on European Identity. Still published today, the Eurobarometer consists of 1,000 biannual face-to-face interviews conducted in different European countries. It has, in the words of a European Commission official, 'given the EU institutions ears' (Wallström 2008). It also inaugurated a quantitative approach to the understanding of European identity that is continually used (see, for instance, Duchesne and Froigner 1995; Bruter 2005).

Investigating the popularity of the EU institutions among European citizens, the Eurobarometer emerged as a response to claims about the EU's lack of legitimacy. For Shore (2000: 31), these surveys have been used to 'construct and mobilize a host of new "European" meta-concepts and categories, including "European opinion", "European public" [and] "European consumers"', among others, thus becoming a key tool of European integration. Eurobarometer questionnaires also set a European agenda through the questions posed. These often address topical issues, which have included the repercussions of inflation in 1974, the understanding of the Maastricht Treaty in 1992, reactions to the EU's enlargement in the early 2000s and the euro-zone debt crisis in 2011.

Although the results of the Eurobarometer surveys are also analysed in qualitative reports published by the EU, the Declaration on European Identity (1973), signed in the same year, is the 1970s document that offers the greatest insight into the idea of Europe from an institutional point of view. The first EU official publication directly addressing the topic of European identity, the Declaration is structured into three sections. First, it discusses the unity of 'the Nine', that is, the EEC's member-states at the time: West Germany, France, Italy, the Netherlands, Belgium, Luxembourg, Denmark, Ireland and the United Kingdom. Second, it mentions their positioning in relation to the world and the nation, addressing the issues of universality and the 'other'. Finally, it discusses the dynamic nature of European unification.

Referring to the latter, Peter Bugge (2003: 62) notes how the Declaration on European Identity 'articulated a crudely functionalist view of identity-building, which was seen not as a pre-requisite for, but rather as a by-product of, economic integration'. For the founding fathers, the more the European institutions developed, the more people would feel connected to them; the Single Market would, in their opinion, bring European countries together not only in political and economic terms, but also in cultural terms. Discussions about the meaning of Europe have indeed risen as European integration proceeds. Yet, while there has been some spillover in terms of political and financial integration transforming into cultural approximation, the institution of the Single Currency (which can be seen as a natural consequence of the Single Market), for instance, has actually highlighted, rather than erased, major gaps in European unity. This has particularly been the case in Greece, where Euro-scepticism has been growing since the country's first bailout in 2010, with consequences also for national cultural production (see Kourelou, Liz and Vidal 2014).

The Declaration on European Identity (1973) suggests that, in addition to the named member-states, the integration process is open to those European nations that share the same ideals and objectives. Speaking of changes for Europe in a new world, it positions Europe's 'other' in a global sphere, including Mediterranean and African countries, the Middle East, the United States of America, Japan and Canada, the USSR and East European countries, China, other Asian countries and Latin American countries. These are described as 'the other industrialized countries', 'major player[s] in international affairs', as partners and friends. For the Nine, the 'other' lay outside its borders; this 'other' was valued because of its historical, political and economic significance.

In turn, the European nation-states did not appear as 'others', but were seen as coexistent with Europe. The document issued by the Nine refers to these states' 'cherished values of their legal, political and moral order', as well as to the effort to 'preserve the rich variety of their national cultures'. At the same time, there is, in the Declaration, a seemingly paradoxical appraisal of variety and uniformity, which resonates with the motto of the EU, 'united in diversity' – examined in more detail later. As the Declaration reads:

> The diversity of cultures within the framework of a common European civilization, the attachment to common values and principles, the increasing convergence of attitudes to life, the awareness of having specific interests in common and the determination to take part in the construction of a United Europe, all give the European identity its originality and its own dynamism.

The 'rich variety' mentioned earlier is in contrast with the sense of uniformity emerging in this passage, as the Declaration lists 'common values and principles'. These include, as Passerini (2002: 194) notes, the fact that European identity 'should be based on a common heritage ... on the principles of representative democracy, the rule of the law, social justice and respect for human rights'. As such, the Declaration echoes those approaches that define the idea of Europe through its Hellenic and Roman past, as well as through concepts inherited from political science. Just as in the scholarly literature previously examined, Europe appears here as simultaneously different from an 'other' (very clearly placed beyond Europe) and as universal (since 'representative democracy' or 'respect for human rights' could hardly be seen as exclusively European values). The twin drive towards specificity and universality is thus a main feature of the EU's definition of Europe.

The Declaration of 1973 has remained the only document published by the EU to explicitly discuss the issue of European identity. However, a contribution to the understanding of the idea of Europe is also visible in the work of the EEC in the 1980s and early 1990s, as European institutions developed the first initiatives in support of culture and the arts. After the impetus of the 1970s, European policies were recentred on the topic of culture with the publication of the report on 'A People's Europe'. A first version of this report, written by Pietro Adonnino, was published in March 1985, followed by an extended version in June of the same year. The endeavour to think about the idea of Europe and the way in which it relates to the work of EEC institutions must be seen in the context of reforms set in motion by Jacques Delors (then president of the European Commission), namely, the Single European Act signed in 1986, the first major revision of the foundational treaties.

The People's Europe report (1985) spoke of 'tangible benefits' for Europeans. In an effort to make 'the Community more credible in the eyes of its citizens', it made way for the Treaty of the European Union signed in Maastricht in 1992, as it proposed, among other changes, the opening of borders and freedom of movement for citizens and goods, the creation of a European passport, the implementation of transnational rights of residency for the citizens of EEC member-states and new pan-European education initiatives such as the Erasmus programme. It also introduced the issue of culture, claiming it is through culture, as well as through communication, 'which are essential to European identity and the Community's image in the minds of its people, that support for the advancement of Europe can and must be sought'. With a clearly positive tone and presenting the development of European integration as inevitable, the report also proposed a number of new initiatives for the culture and communication sectors, including a Euro-lottery, transnational television directives and the naming of 1988 as the 'European Film and Television Year'. Finally, it argued that the creation of a People's Europe 'required new symbols for communicating the principles and values upon which the Community is founded' (Shore 2006: 14). The most important of these symbols were the European flag and the EU anthem.

Adopted by the Council of Europe in 1951 and by the EEC in 1986, the European flag (although not exclusive to the EU) has been the EU's most prominent emblem. According to a Eurobarometer survey of 1992, 86 per cent of European citizens recognize it. In 2004, after the EU's widest enlargement (to twenty-five countries, most of the new ones coming from Eastern Europe, joined by Romania and Bulgaria in 2007 and Croatia in 2013), 87 per cent of the people interviewed, including citizens from the new member-states, were able to confirm that the European flag was blue with yellow stars.[1] This wide recognition, however, is at odds with the understanding of its meaning. Of the people questioned in 2004, 67 per cent incorrectly believed the flag had a star for each country. Rather, there are twelve stars on the flag, arranged so that these appear in the position of the hours in a clock, because this number stands for perfection and wholeness.

Among scholars, too, contrasting explanations for the flag's visual composition have been presented. The colour blue, for instance, is a source of dispute. Wintle (2009: 439) claims that blue is the colour of the European continent. By contrast, Johan Fornäs (2012: 120) suggests this was the only colour not previously given a specific meaning ('red for socialism and communism, green for Islam, black for mourning, yellow for quarantine and white for capitulation') and therefore available to European institutions. Similarly, the choice of stars proves problematic. Five-pointed to avoid Jewish connotations, the stars on the European flag have been associated with Christian imagery, either as single objects, compared to the star of Bethlehem and thus linked to a notion of elevation as well as a sense of mission (122), or in relation to their disposition in a never-ending circle, which is similar to the Virgin Mary's halo (Shore 2000: 48). According to Wintle (2009: 439), however, this circle aims to represent the strong union of the peoples of Europe.

Open to different readings, this symbol's significance is not only complex, but also the target of vague and easily challenged interpretations. However, as is the case in national contexts, doubts about the meaning of the European flag do not undermine its impact as a tool for political communication. The significance of the European flag lies in the symbol's widespread use and recognition. Of those answering the Eurobarometer surveys in 2012, 95 per cent 'have seen it'. In cinema, the European flag might not be a prominent feature on screen, but it very clearly frames the support given by European institutions to the development and circulation of films. It is an obvious feature of the logo of the EU's MEDIA programme and of the pan-European initiative Europa Cinemas.

Although Eurobarometer surveys provide no statistical data on the public perception of the European anthem, the latter is not as well known as the flag. According to Esteban Buch (2003: 88), not many Europeans know that Europe has an anthem. It is possible that Marc-Antoine Charpentier's *Prelude to Te Deum*, a song played before the Eurovision Song Contest and a key European reference in popular culture – also parodied in a sequence about Erasmus and the bureaucracy of European integration in Cédric Klapisch's *L'auberge espagnole/Pot Luck* (2004) (Figure 1.1) – is more closely associated with Europe. Nevertheless, based on the Ode to Joy movement of Beethoven's Ninth Symphony, the European anthem is an important symbol of the EU, as it embodies significant features of European culture.

When the EEC was considering adopting the hymn, other melodies were put forward for consideration, but Buch (2003: 91) suggests these were dismissed in favour of a quest for excellence. Mabel Berezin (2003) has noted how historically, European culture was reserved for the educated elites who normally spoke three European languages. However, as she goes on to suggest, 'post-Maastricht European identity claims to be popular and inclusive' (16). Vividly exemplifying this tension, the European anthem is a paradoxically popular classical musical piece, which aims to bring together the peoples of Europe, but is tied to a sense of exclusivity. Writing about the representation of classical music in film, Janet K. Halfyard (2006: 76) argues that 'European identity and classical music are regularly elided in Hollywood films' and generally 'positioned in direct opposition to American popular culture'. The idea of exclusivity is also explored in coming chapters in relation to perceptions of European cinema as

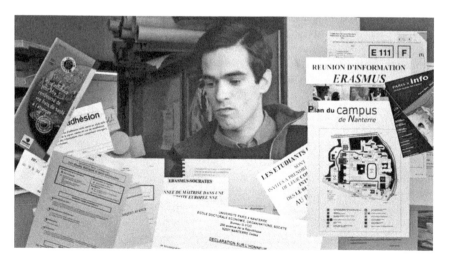

Figure 1.1 An 'unspeakable mess': Bureaucracy and the Erasmus programme in *Pot Luck*.

art cinema (often in contrast to mainstream American film), in the same way that an association of Europe with quality is voiced through the figure of the great auteur – and here, Beethoven, the great composer par excellence.

Fornäs (2012: 160) has stressed the fact that the EU has particularly highlighted Beethoven's status as a European composer and that 'much emphasis was put on his seriousness and the way he was engaged in the complex issues of his day: issues of progress and fate, emancipation and oppression, destruction and hope, war and peace'. Hence, Beethoven's work was chosen not just because of its association with quality, but also with universalism. In an attempt to surpass national references (viz., German, when one considers, in addition to Beethoven, Friedrich Schiller, the author of the poem *Ode to Joy*), the EEC decided to have an anthem with no words. However, its universality was undermined by the fact that, as Fornäs (2012: 180) has also noted, the *Ode to Joy* was the national hymn of the state of Rhodesia (renamed Zimbabwe in the 1980s) and, perhaps more significantly, that the official recording of the European anthem was conducted by Herbert von Karajan, an Austrian composer who had been a member of the Nazi Party.

Both the flag and the anthem highlight some of the concepts and contradictions that will be revisited in the upcoming discussion of contemporary cinema and the idea of Europe, namely, tradition, exclusivity, quality and universality. While the strength of the European symbols is jeopardized by the attempt to give them such general meanings, for Wintle (2009: 442), their vagueness is a sine qua non of their potential mass appeal and universality. Michael Bruter (2005: 166), for instance, claims they have been key in forging a collective European identity increasingly developed since the 1970s. Regardless of their sociological impact, as European symbols, the flag and the anthem testify to an active engagement of the EU in connecting with its citizens through visual representations and artistic forms of expression, on an abstract and emotional level. As such, they become a testimony to the EU's commitment to present and define a cultural idea of Europe.

From Maastricht to Lisbon via the failed constitution

With the signing of the Treaty on the European Union or Maastricht Treaty (the first document to empower the EU in the cultural sector) in 1992, cultural policies and initiatives addressing the idea of Europe were further developed and assigned ever-increasing budgets. Although the Treaty on the European Union was a significant step for the inclusion of culture in the European integration process the EEC was 'operating a *de facto* cultural policy long before the Maastricht Treaty gave it the legal right to do so' (Shore 2000: 46). This is testified by the use of European symbols analysed above. Launched in the aftermath of the Maastricht Treaty, programmes such as Kaleidoscope (1996–1999), aiming to encourage artistic and cultural creation and co-operation with a European dimension; Ariane (1997–1999), devoted to the pan-European circulation of books and promoting, for instance, the translation of key literary works; and Raphael (1997–1999), complementing national policies in the area of cultural heritage, constitute further examples of the significant increase in the EU's support of European culture throughout the 1990s – including of course the MEDIA programme, which is closely examined in Chapter 2.

In line with the expanding scholarship on the meaning of Europe in the 2000s, the EU's work also saw a recentring on culture at the turn of the twentieth century. The Maastricht Treaty was followed by the treaties of Amsterdam (signed in 1997) and Nice (signed in 2001). But it was the writing of the European constitution, formally labelled as the Constitutional Treaty (signed in 2004 but never ratified) that triggered a crucial debate about a political conception of European identity. The project to create a European constitution, later abandoned and replaced by the Lisbon Treaty (signed in 2007 and effective since December 2009), also signalled a particularly troubled period in the history of the EU, and one that raises important questions about the idea of Europe.

The constitution aimed to address the issue of legitimacy (a major critique of the EU emerging throughout its history) by bringing forward a series of institutional reforms. As peace among European nations had long been established and economic integration was well under way, the European constitution, it was thought, would bring the EU to a new phase, after having achieved the goals set in the post-war years (Habermas 2001). Hence, the constitution was also fundamentally concerned with the issue of European identity. Its preamble mentioned Europe's history, as well as the values shared by Europeans, namely, human dignity, freedom, democracy, equality, the rule of law and respect for human rights – many of which had already been listed in the Declaration of 1973. The constitution further updated the symbols of the EU, listing them explicitly as the flag with the twelve stars, the anthem based on the *Ode to Joy* by Beethoven, the currency of the euro, Europe Day on 9 May and the motto 'united in diversity'.

At the core of Europe's economic integration, the euro's significance extends beyond the financial realm. Its symbol, €, is based on the Greek letter epsilon. The association between Europe and Greek culture has however been severely questioned since 2009, after Greece suffered a particularly austere financial crisis and it was announced the nation might be leaving the currency. The meaning of Europe Day, another symbol listed in the project for the constitution, instead relates to the history of European integration. It commemorates the signing of the Schuman Declaration on 9 May 1950, a document that aimed to prevent, once and for all, the disastrous experience of the European wars. Just as discussions about the future of the Single Currency highlight existing tensions between European nations (especially the way in which Greece and Germany have since 2009 been portrayed as opponents in the media across Europe), so does Europe Day stress the regional divisions still at play in the continent. The anniversary of the Soviet Union's victory over Nazi Germany in 1945 also falls on 9 May, and as Nicole Scicluna (2012: 6) notes, 'For central and eastern Europe, the end of World War II brought not only victory and liberation, but further defeat, occupation and oppression'. Although these symbols signify a strong institutional will to construct a visual representation of political integration, when analysed in detail, they prove utterly divisive, questioning the unity of contemporary Europe.

This tension is clearly highlighted in the final European symbol listed in the constitution, the motto 'united in diversity', which has been used by European institutions as the motivation for further integration since the 1960s, although informally and with slight variations. 'Unity in difference', for instance, emerged as the winner of a competition organized by a French journalist in 1998, which asked school pupils to send in proposals for a European motto (Fornäs 2012: 105). Chosen by a jury chaired by Jacques Delors, the motto expresses the opposition between Europe and individual nations, as well as the existence of different cultures, religions and languages within the continent. Significantly, however, the motto begins with a reference to unity, thus strengthening the premise that it is possible to think of Europe as a cohesive concept.

The legal status of the symbols listed in the constitution, especially the increasingly dismissed euro and the historically tainted Europe Day, was harshly questioned after the document's rejection in public referenda in France and the Netherlands in 2005. After the votes, the project of a European constitution was dropped and a new EU treaty was signed in Lisbon in 2007. No European values or symbols are mentioned in the Lisbon Treaty. However, this has not prevented citizens and institutions from using such symbols. At the same time, the absence of references to the flag, anthem, currency, day and motto in the Lisbon Treaty's final text does not entirely constitute a step backwards in the EU's institutional commitment to cultural ideas of Europe.

Although abandoned, the constitution remains an important reference point to understand the role of culture in Europe's political history. Crucially, its rejection constitutes a milestone in the European integration process, as it marks significant changes to the way in which the idea of Europe is featured in official EU documentation. For instance, Barroso (2009: 19) has stressed the fact that the word identity was explicitly removed from revised versions of the Constitutional Treaty after strong criticism. Barroso's comments came at a time when, as argued by Rogers Brubaker and Frederick Cooper (2006: 36), the term 'identity' was losing currency. For them, identity either tends to mean too much or too little. And because of its 'multivalent, even contradictory theoretical burden', it becomes, as they suggest, a useless term.

Echoing the questioning of the term in the academic context, for Barroso (2009: 21), 'one recognizes identity, one does not define it. Europe can be recognized, but it is hardly defined'. Since the European institutions continue to financially support the arts and culture because of the sector's contribution to the shaping of European identity, this appears as a blatantly disingenuous affirmation. Yet, recent EU documents present the idea of Europe as a fluid and shifting concept – a vagueness that, as Wintle (2009) has argued in relation to the European symbols, is seen by many as necessary for a prospective widespread acceptance of European political integration. The EU's reaction to the rejection of the constitution has been to offer a less precise definition of Europe. To rephrase Barroso's claim, it is as if, for the EU, Europe can be defined, but only to some extent. The investment in culture has not ceased (on the contrary, as we will see in Chapter 2, budgets have continued to expand), but a new discourse, which refuses predefined ideas of Europe and places an emphasis on diversity (as testified by the European Commission's ratification of the UNESCO Convention on Cultural Diversity in 2006), has emerged.

At the same time, new areas of action have been developed. Reading the dismissal of the constitution not as a refusal of integration but as evidence that it was out of touch with its citizens, the European Commission made communication a priority of its work after 2005. The communication tasks carried out by the European Commission include the development of the website Europa, the 'largest public website in the world' in the words of the Commission.[2] This website testifies to the commitment of the EU to being closer to the citizens it represents, especially younger citizens, through the use of new technologies. The qualification offered by the European Commissions gives the website a sense of grandeur, at the same time as the designation 'Europa' hints at the idea of universality: it comes from the myth, thus also carrying a certain historical weight.

According to a high-ranking official at the European Commission, who I interviewed in 2009, since the signing of the Lisbon Treaty there has been a growing understanding by EU institutions that 'soft' policy areas such as education, citizenship and culture are key to building a sustainable political project. For this EU policymaker, 'citizenship' is a more solid term than any of the European values listed in the constitution, which he dismisses as only useful in political discourse. The EU thus seems to have shifted its emphasis from a theoretical to a more practical conception of European culture. In line with the neo-functionalist view of European identity shared by the EEC founding fathers, who believed people would naturally feel more European as economic integration proceeded and peace flourished in Europe, the EU's official stance after 2005 contends that the idea of Europe will naturally emerge from the work carried out by the European institutions, especially in a new context of further transparency and proximity to the people they represent, rather than from any institutional attempts to pinpoint the meaning of this concept. The void left by the European institutions' new stance in the construction of a European identity has, however, most likely contributed to the failure of the EU's communication effort. Communicating 'Europe' without defining what 'Europe' is might instead have exacerbated Europe's significance crisis.

Three key phases in EU cultural policy, framed by debates held within its institutions about the meaning of the idea of Europe, have emerged in this chapter. After the initial impetus of the 1970s, which placed Europe between the nation-state and the globe and established ties with its citizens through mass annual surveys, the EU adopted an active role in the promotion of European identity, launching a campaign to promote the European symbols, as well as a series of initiatives in support of culture in the late 1980s, reinforced by the ratification of the Maastricht Treaty. However, following the rejection of the European constitution in the early 2000s, there was a significant shift from a prescriptive to a practical (and ever more diffuse) view of the cultural idea of Europe, despite a continuous expansion of budgets for the arts sector.

This brief historical survey allows for a comparative analysis of notions of European identity as understood by European institutions and the idea of Europe emerging in academic writing since the 1950s. Visions of Europe have not developed in a linear fashion, with support and scepticism varying at different periods and Euro-phobia and Euro-euphoria often coexisting in time. Europe's meaning is entrenched in paradigm shifts and wider reflections taking place in European society, including the rise and fall of nationalism, as well as the state of the economy. Allegations of lack of legitimacy have undermined the EU's significance. Growing voices of dissent emerging against Euro-centrism have also led many to question the relevance of Europe in the world. Despite this, or precisely because of the passion generated by this concept, a significant number of attempts have been made to pinpoint Europe's meaning.

The variety of approaches identified here suggests even a geographical conception of Europe is problematic. Europe has, of course, also emerged as a political concept, with attempts to define it leading to institutional views (e.g. the work of the founding fathers), as well as critical perspectives from scholars. Since the 2000s, notions inherited from political science such as citizenship have been put forward as a tool to help define the idea of Europe, at the same time as scholars have suggested EU institutions and programmes provide a form of identification with the continent. Finally, cultural conceptions of the idea of Europe, which characterize Europe through references to its past, stress key moments in its development and pinpoint some of its main influences, defining Europe in terms of authority and universality.

The EU also uses some of these definitions. First, it adopts from scholarly writings the principle that European identity, as other forms of identification, is multilayered. It also positions the idea of Europe in relation to a signifying 'other', to be found both in the global and national sphere. On the one hand, Europe is positioned in the world through the pinpointing of universal allies and partners as in the Declaration of 1973; more recently, the EU has looked for further affirmation as a global actor through a series of new policies, in areas as diverse as climate change and environment or the audiovisual sector (Chapter 2). On the other, the EU's motto 'united in diversity' (which has, in recent years, stressed the significance of diversity) shapes the relationship between European countries. The past has both been seen as an 'other' – since Europe is perceived as belonging to a historical continuum where ideas of progress and improvement are key – and as a privileged element in the definition of Europe. EU official documents suggest history is at the core of the meaning of the idea of Europe. The most concrete characterizations of the continent emerge through the values listed in the Declaration on European Identity and the failed Constitutional Treaty (democracy, freedom and human rights, among others), as well as the symbols used since 1986, which put forward keywords such as Christianity, exclusivity, cosmopolitanism and universality.

These general values are in line with the elusive approach towards the idea of Europe the EU has adopted since the rejection of the Constitutional Treaty. The work of European institutions has been characterized by a permanent tension between wanting to actively promote and define the idea of Europe and choosing to remain an observer of its development, between assuming a prescriptive or descriptive role. For the EU, the idea of Europe has in recent years become more and more about the formation of a community and less and less about a clear definition of what propels its unity, which suggests a turn to an emotional rather than a rational engagement between European institutions and citizens. The European film industry plays a crucial role in the development of this community, and hence the EU's investment on its economic and cultural development.

The MEDIA Programme: Framing European Cinema

In the previous chapter we saw how the meaning of the concept of Europe has evolved in a complex history. We now need to turn to European Union (EU) cultural policy and see, especially, how it affects cinema. This chapter focuses on the MEDIA (*Mesures pour Encourager le Développement de l'Industrie Audiovisuelle*, French for Measures to Encourage the Development of the Audiovisual Industry) programme, the major EU initiative in support of the European audiovisual sector. Since the 2000s, the EU has expanded its budget in support of the arts. The decision not to renew MEDIA after 2013 thus came as a surprise. MEDIA is now a subprogramme of the Creative Europe initiative. What changes this will bring in terms of the EU's involvement in the audio-visual sector, as well as to the European film industry more generally, is not clear. This transformation nevertheless cues us to assess the programme's impact and achievements up until that point.

After the EU announced its decision regarding the future of MEDIA, over 300 film-makers from all over Europe, including Wim Wenders, Mike Leigh, Catherine Breillat, Cristian Mungiu and Fatih Akin, signed a letter to Durão Barroso, at the time the president of the European Commission, asking him to reconsider. If the list of signatories reads like a 'who's who' of contemporary European film-making, the content of the letter gives a sense of what perception of European cinema, as well as the role the EU should have on it, was held by these directors. The letter argued that abolishing or merging the MEDIA programme with another EU initiative was unacceptable. The film-makers demanded that funding options be reviewed, describing the programme as a 'lifesaver for the industry over the last twenty years'. The end of MEDIA, they claimed, would compromise the financial health of the European film industry and have immediate economic repercussions, including job losses. But the 'real losers', they continued, would be cinema audiences across the continent, not to mention the EU's cultural integration project, as 'without cultural diversity and circulation of European works, the EU will lose one of the foundations of its identity' (cited in Blaney 2011). An initiative often challenged by critics and scholars, as will be discussed in this chapter, MEDIA was defended in this petition because of its positive impact in economic and cultural terms.

The film-makers' letter was reproduced in trade publications devoted to the film industries. However, it had a small impact on public discourse. Moreover, although these European directors demanded to see Barroso, the European Commission did not meet them and went ahead with its intentions. The petition nevertheless raises important questions about the EU's institutional support for the audiovisual industry. Was MEDIA, until 2014, a 'lifesaver' of the European film industry? What role did the programme play in the construction of European identity? In order to understand the history of MEDIA, we must start by looking at the key issues in the definition of European cinema, as well as the main features of the European film industry. On the one hand, MEDIA was shaped by and helped to shape the idea of European cinema. On the other, it reacted to, and, arguably, had an influence on, changes taking place in the European film industry. The impact of the programme is analysed particularly in relation to the distribution sector. As we will see, MEDIA also contributed directly to the idea of Europe because of its own communication. Hence, this chapter concludes with an examination of a series of short films produced by the European Commission to promote the programme. As a key element in the EU's definition of 'Europe', cinema is also a crucial tool in the formation of a cultural European community.

The 'idea' of contemporary European cinema

Scholarly attention to transnational European cinema has been growing since the 1990s. In the last decade of the twentieth century, studies were motivated by the development of the European integration process, particularly the EU's new involvement in the cultural sector (with, for instance, the launching of the MEDIA programme in 1991), as well as by the negotiations around the General Agreement on Tariffs and Trade (GATT) that took place in Uruguay in 1993. Two main issues have since then defined the idea of contemporary European cinema: the contrast between Europe and Hollywood on the one hand, and the dichotomy 'art versus popular cinema' on the other.

The historical opposition between European cinema and Hollywood echoes the geopolitical perception of the idea of Europe, as well as the views that define it in relation to its 'others'. While there is a long history of the contrasting relationship between European cinema and American popular film (Higson and Maltby 1999), the 1990s were a crucial moment for its development. During the Uruguay round of GATT negotiations European countries, especially France, opposed the United States and fought to exclude cultural goods (including films) from the agreements, arguing these should not be subjected to a purely economic logic when travelling across borders. France then put forward the famous *exception culturelle*, a protectionist measure, which aimed to prevent Hollywood's dominance of the European audiovisual market, and instead boost the pan-European release of European films.

In 2013 film-makers voiced their concerns about the Transatlantic Trade and Investment Partnership (TTIP) – a free trade agreement between the United States and the EU – echoing the protests that had emerged twenty years earlier. In a petition led by Belgian directors Luc and Jean-Pierre Dardenne – and supported by names recognized across the world, including David Lynch, Jane Campion and Walter Salles – film-makers demanded audiovisual products be left out of the TTIP negotiations, claiming the cultural exception was, is and should always be non-negotiable.[1] The general perception both before and since the GATT negotiations of 1993 is that, against Hollywood's market-oriented nature, European cinema is an art form, rather than (exclusively) an industry. The main concern of these film-makers is not with profit but with artistic value. This 'special' labelling of European films is a significant means of distinction, and it echoes associations of the idea of Europe with notions of quality and prestige. However, this is a partial view of European cinema, which ignores popular and commercial European films.

Studies of European cinema also note the way in which it is characterized by a split between art and popular films. Like the idea of Europe described in Chapter 1, European cinema is simultaneously defined by its elitist quality and by a wish to be democratically inclusive. The majority of the literature on European cinema, including film criticism in specialized magazines, privileges a view of European cinema that frames it as the sole product of an auteur. Jean-Luc Godard, Michael Haneke and Pedro Costa, for instance, are key figures in European art cinema. Their films are focused on reflection rather than on action and generally have a slower pace than popular cinema. Although released internationally in specialized circuits, including film festivals and art-house cinemas, the films of European auteurs reach only limited audiences.

Meanwhile, despite being ignored by many critics, European cinema has produced incredibly successful and profitable popular films, which are watched by sizeable audiences – even though many of these are confined to national borders. European national hits in recent years include *Bienvenue chez les Ch'tis/Welcome to the Sticks* (Dany Boon, 2008) in France and *Ocho apellidos vascos/Spanish Affair* (Emilio Martínez-Lázaro, 2014) in Spain. *Slumdog Millionaire* (Danny Boyle, 2008), *The Artist* (Michel Hazanavicius, 2011) and *12 Years a Slave* (Steve McQueen, 2013), having won Best Film prizes at the Academy Awards, are examples of the transnational appeal of popular European cinema. Unlike art or auteur films, the popular cinemas of Europe are characterized by an attention to storytelling and entertainment; they cast well-known screen stars and typically follow generic conventions. Despite being the preference of audiences across (and beyond) the continent – and therefore arguably generating images of European society that will more clearly resonate with European citizens – popular European cinema is generally dismissed as lacking in value and seriousness.

Even though these two oppositions continue to frame scholarly investigations of European cinema, they have in recent years changed slightly. Just like the idea of Europe at the turn of the twenty-first century, so is European film faced with important questions about its contemporary significance. First, in an increasingly globalized world, Hollywood no longer appears as Europe's only 'other'. While Hollywood remains undeniably omnipresent, audiovisual industries beyond the Western world have been gaining market share, including within Europe. The rising circulation of cinemas from all corners of the globe has positively resulted in a growing attention to other cinemas, by critics and audiences alike. In turn, the internationalization of the global film market has challenged European cinema's central position as the beacon of art cinema. In international film festivals, for instance, European cinema competes with films from many other countries. For Thomas Elsaesser (2015), faced with this situation, European cinema is diluted into world cinema, becoming increasingly insignificant. The idea of European cinema is rethought in a context of increasing globalization and scholarly attention to world cinemas (Harrod, Liz and Timoshkina 2015).

Second, as the definitions of art and popular cinema are remapped, new terms for the characterization of contemporary cinema emerge, which attempt to combine aspects from both strands of European film. Helle Kannik Haastrup (2006), for instance, speaks of a new category, the 'popular European art film', whereas Mary Wood (2000) examines the rise of 'quality films' in Europe. The two expressions echo the notion of the 'middlebrow' film, which has also been gaining currency, and is seen as a middle ground between serious, critical art films and stylish, generally consensual mainstream productions (Bergfelder 2015). Such films have at the same time wide appeal and markers of quality, including 'difficult narratives' (Haastrup 2006), 'high production values, large budgets and wide distribution', as well as the fact that they are generally filmed by an auteur (Wood 2000). The perceived quality of European cinema is here tied to critical and commercial success. However, it should be said that 'quality films' and mainstream art films were also prominent in European cinema of the 1950s and 1960s (Betz 2009). More than pinpointing a new type of film, categories such as the ones listed here testify to the emergence of a new vision of European cinema that, as we will see, also informs the work of EU institutions in the audiovisual sector.

The two defining parameters of European cinema, as well as the ways in which these have been challenged, also emerge in the discourse of film professionals. British director Steve McQueen repeatedly described his film *12 Years a Slave* as 'a global tale' (see, for instance, BBC 2014). Tom Tykwer, the director of *Lola rennt/Run Lola Run* (1998), discussed setting up the production company X-Filme Creative Pool (of which he is a co-founder) to make 'arty mainstream movies' (cited in Jäckel 2003: 32). The oppositions that define the idea of European cinema are both critical constructions and industrial realities. The issues outlined here have implications not only for the idea of European cinema, but also for the European film industry. Hence, it is important to look at the main issues that characterize it, in relation to film production, distribution, exhibition and promotion.

The European film industry: Key issues

According to the European Audiovisual Observatory (EAO), a record number of 1,145 feature films (including documentaries) were produced in the EU in 2008. For the EAO, this follows a rising trend in film production in Europe, which, as the data published on the institution's website shows, has been growing by an annual average of 7 per cent since 2004.[2] A total of 1,159 films were produced in Europe in 2009, with the numbers rising to 1,216 in 2010, 1,246 in 2011 and 1,336 in 2012. Not only had the number of films produced in Europe been increasing, it was also, at this stage, significantly larger than those completed in the United States, one of the world's biggest film industries and European cinema's historical 'other'. According to the Motion Picture Association of America (MPAA) 818 feature films were produced in 2011.[3] On its own, the number of films produced in Europe is not a reliable indicator to assess the current state of the European film industry. This is, in any case, an extraordinary sign of vitality.

In those years European films were extremely successful worldwide. Examples include *The King's Speech* (Tom Hooper, 2010) and *The Artist*, Academy-Award winners released in Europe with the support of the EU's MEDIA programme. *Skyfall*, the 2012 instalment of the James Bond series, directed by Sam Mendes and starring Daniel Craig in his third performance as the British secret agent, was also a particularly suitable illustration of contemporary European cinema's dynamism. Watched by forty-four million people across Europe, according to the EAO, *Skyfall* was single-handedly responsible for a historical boost in the market share of European films within the EU, which rose to 33.6 per cent in the year of the film's release – the highest figure since the year 2000. Mostly a British enterprise, although backed by a US studio, *Skyfall* became a model case study for the success of European films in Europe, as well as beyond the continent's borders.

Despite the enthusiasm of the EAO, however, when it comes to film distribution and exhibition in Europe, *Skyfall* might very well be the exception that confirms the rule. While a restricted number of European films have achieved unprecedented accomplishments in the international market, a large proportion of the European films made every year are never screened, within or beyond the countries in which they are produced. This can be explained by the existence of an insufficient distribution network in Europe – discussed in greater detail later. It is also related to different conceptions of European cinema. For some, Europe produces too many films in relation to its exhibition capacity. Nik Powell (1996: ix), nominated chairman of the European Film Academy in 1996, has argued that a significant step for Europe to improve its competitiveness would be precisely 'to concentrate its resources and significantly reduce the number of films that it makes each year'. Powell is here privileging one particular type of film. Films that are successful with audiences – as precisely *The King's Speech*, or even larger budget productions such as *Skyfall* – are, in this logic, favoured to the detriment of those unable to appeal to audiences beyond national borders, as well as art films attracting only a restricted public. While potentially a viable economic strategy, this is against the sense of artistic quality traditionally associated with European cinema.

Whereas film production has been flourishing in Europe (in terms of numbers of films produced), the European distribution sector has faced greater challenges. As Table 2.1 shows, Hollywood films largely dominate cinema screens across the continent. European films, the majority of which originates from France, account only for a quarter of the films shown. There was a 4 per cent rise in the market share of European films across Europe between 2004 and 2008. But although the situation has improved slightly in recent years, there have been no significant changes since 2004, or before, as has been discussed in relation to the GATT negotiations of the early 1990s. Even if Hollywood has lost its place as Europe's significant other in theoretical and critical

Table 2.1 Origin of films distributed in the EU (all values in %)

Origin/year	2004	2005	2006	2007	2008 est
United States	67.3	60.2	63.4	63.2	63.2
European films	24.6	24.6	27.9	28.6	28.4
France	8.6	9.2	10.6	8.4	12.6
United Kingdom	4.5	3.9	2.8	6.1	2.2
Italy	2.2	2.9	3.0	3.8	3.6
Germany	4.3	3.2	4.8	3.8	3.5
Spain	2.4	2.3	2.8	2.1	1.4
Other European countries	2.7	3.1	3.9	4.6	5.0
European films including US co-productions	5.8	12.5	5.5	6.3	6.8
Other	2.3	2.7	3.2	1.8	1.6

Source: European Audiovisual Observatory, http://www.obs.coe.int/ (accessed 16 September 2014).

terms, it very much remains the main competitor of European films across Europe. This data might also account for the importance attributed to *Skyfall*'s outstanding results in 2012. While this table does not break down figures according to country of exhibition (the nations listed in the table refer to place of origin), there are, as we will see, national variations across Europe.

With political and economic integration, the European film market has been expanding. But as Viviane Reding (2003: 13), formerly in charge of supporting the audiovisual industries at the European Commission, noted in the early 2000s, 'there are some areas where cinemas never show a European film ... cinema goers do not see European films because we do not give them the opportunity to see them'. This situation was what propelled the EU's action, in the vein of pan-European distribution networks previously existing in Europe – namely, the Film Europe movement of the 1920s (Higson and Maltby 1999). For the European Commission, the best way to face the insularity of national European cinemas, and the difficulties films have in reaching screens within and beyond borders, was to join efforts at local, national and, significantly, transnational levels. EU initiatives supporting this area of the film industry are examined in more detail later.

The disparity between the market share of US and European films highlighted in Table 2.1 is also to do with the fragmentation of the distribution sector across Europe. There are several small distribution companies in Europe that tend to work with restricted budgets. For some critics, Europe's corporate culture, as well as conception of cinema, has also had an impact on the success (or lack thereof) of European cinema. Seeing films not as products but as works of art has meant that not much is done to advertise them. As argued by consultants Coopers and Lybrand (1993), European films are not able to compete with Hollywood because of the limited budgets generally allocated in Europe to film promotion and advertising.

The way in which European films are sold and marketed has been affected by the rise of film festivals, which have, in recent years, experienced an authentic boom in terms of number and visibility (De Valck 2007). Contributing to changes in the way

European films are sold to audiences within and beyond Europe, the international film festival circuit has become key for the promotion of film projects and initiatives. Festivals have both an economic and a cultural impact in the positioning of the films screened, as well the places where they are set. Cannes, Berlin and Venice have long been authentic brands that contribute to the positioning of films within and outside Europe, and they have been joined by a host of other smaller events, such as the Motovun Film Festival in Croatia, IndieLisboa in Portugal and the San Sebastián International Film Festival in Spain. In the best European tradition, festivals have become markers of quality, that is, also a positive means of distinction. Many of the films examined in this book, including *Buongiorno, Notte/Good Morning, Night* (Marco Bellocchio, 2003), *A fost sau n-a fost?/12:08 East of Bucharest* (Corneliu Porumboiu, 2006) and *Le Silence de Lorna/The Silence of Lorna* (Jean-Pierre and Luc Dardenne, 2008), can be seen as 'festival films', having taken advantage of the media exposure this label entails.

In addition to being international markets where films are sold for distribution, festivals constitute key promotional opportunities. One way in which they maximize the media exposure of the films presented is by inviting and welcoming international stars, placed at the centre of photo shoots and press conferences. Festivals are both the home of auteur films and an attractive environment for popular stars. As a European phenomenon, they testify to the extent to which, as the tensional idea of Europe, European cinema too is founded on a series of contradictions.

Stars play a crucial part in the promotion of cinema, including European cinema. The European Commission has encouraged the development of a European star system by supporting the work of the European Film Promotion (EFP) office and the Shooting Stars initiative in particular. Shooting Stars aims to boost the careers of young European actors by organizing a series of industry events, including press conferences and meetings with cast directors at the Berlin Film Festival. Its general aim is to raise the international profile of European film. Despite the limited budget of Shooting Stars, the director of this programme claimed in 2007 that 'we've now got a pan-European star system off the ground, and the networking is better than before' (cited in Kirschbaum 2007: A11). Daniel Brühl and Daniel Craig have participated in this project, but as a EU policymaker who I interviewed in 2009 noted, the programme's success has been measured by the presence of these actors in Hollywood rather than in European cinema. Craig in particular can be seen as a good example of the 'Bond factor' in promoting European stars, such as Sean Connery, Mads Mikkelsen and Javier Bardem, as can the French 'Bond girl' Eva Green (Figure 2.1). At the same time, female stars like Audrey Tautou and Marion Cotillard have made small inroads in Hollywood by becoming involved in the promotion of global European luxury brands (Chanel and Dior, respectively).

Initiatives such as the EU-sponsored Shooting Stars are evidence of the way in which institutions supporting European cinema end up fighting Hollywood in the latter's terms. They also show the extent to which European cinema seems to depend on Hollywood to achieve global success. This relationship has an impact on the identity of European cinema, which is often defined in negative terms, and therefore struggles to

Figure 2.1 The global appeal of European stars: Daniel Craig and Eva Green in *Casino Royale*.

positively assert its position as a supposedly (and as wished by European institutions) universal cinema.

A key feature of popular European cinema, stars are also a sign of quality and prestige. In many instances, the glamour and fame associated with film stars, as well as the press attention devoted to them, is, in Europe, transferred to film directors. Lars von Trier is a good example of the high-profile European film-makers generally welcomed at festivals. Von Trier was at the centre of a major polemical incident in the 2011 edition of the Cannes Film Festival after having declared to be a Nazi. Political issues related to Europe's present have been equally picked up on by the media. Fatih Akin, for instance, a German-Turkish film-maker, has emerged as a new type of cosmopolitan director after receiving the Golden Bear at the 2004 Berlin Film Festival for his film *Gegen die Wand/Head-On* (Erdoğan 2009). The focus on directors reflects a traditional perception of European cinema as an industry of auteurs, where the notion of quality plays a central role. The combination of the exclusivity of the auteur with the glamour of stars also becomes a further example of the blending of artistic and mainstream conceptions of film that characterize contemporary European cinema.

Supported by a sporadically successful film industry and simultaneously defined by 'artistic' tendencies, contemporary European cinema is tied to, at the same time as it tries to overcome, the division between art and popular film. Released in film festivals, relying to an increasingly greater extent on stars (including star-directors) and being part of a fiercely competitive global market, where Hollywood is no longer the only significant player, European cinema is both an industrial and a cultural reality. Conscious of the deep intertwinement between these two aspects of European film, the EU has turned to the audiovisual sector to boost Europe's financial situation in the world and its own cultural identity within the continent. The features of the European film industry highlighted so far have thus promoted and simultaneously informed the EU's action in this domain.

The history of MEDIA: Between industry and culture

The first EU audiovisual policies were established around 1990. It was not the EU, but the Council of Europe, the first European institution to develop a programme in support of the film industries. It is therefore important to clarify the distinction between the two. The EU is the closest European institution to a government, with a political involvement in the film industries. The Council of Europe, on the other hand, is a human rights organization, established in 1949, to promote democracy and the rule of law across Europe. Today, it has forty-seven European members, and it also includes the United States, Canada, Japan and Mexico as observers. The Council of Europe's official webpage insists on the difference between its institutions and those of the EU, urging visitors 'not to get confused'.[4]

The Council of Europe supports European cinema through its Eurimages programme set up in 1989 – an initiative often wrongly attributed to the European Commission and/or the EU. In 2014, Eurimages had thirty-six members. The programme's budget was of over €20 million in 2008; MEDIA's last budget was a lot bigger than Eurimages'. For example, since its establishment, Eurimages has supported 1,266 European co-productions for a total amount of approximately €375 million – a sum which represents half of the budget for MEDIA's last phase. Apart from the sums invested, the main difference between MEDIA and Eurimages is that only the latter gives direct support to film production. Whereas MEDIA's budget has been allocated to pre- and post-production initiatives, over 90 per cent of Eurimages' funding is attributed to co-productions. Conversely, in the last phase of MEDIA, 55 per cent of the budget was devoted to film distribution, whereas only 3 per cent of Eurimages' support was given to that area.

The period during which the EU's first audiovisual policies were being prepared was a time of major institutional reforms. As discussed in Chapter 1, the launch of MEDIA must be seen in the context of the Maastricht Treaty. Before 1992, although debates about cinema in the European Economic Community (EEC) covered the cultural aspects of film, legislation could only be prepared for the economic dimension of the audiovisual sector. Prompted by a desire for greater integration and a new legislative framework that enabled the work of the EU in the cultural sector, the MEDIA programme attempted to address the main problems of the European audiovisual sector. As stated earlier, these include difficulties in ensuring films reach screens across Europe, as well as in captivating audiences for European cinema.

Policies in support of the film industry within the EU not only have a complex history, but are also shaped by a series of tensions. The opposition between culture and economy, for instance, has been a key feature of MEDIA throughout its history. Such a duality was identified by the European Commission as early as 1988 in a document stating that the policies developed were 'designed either to make the audiovisual industry more competitive, or to give a specifically European character to the sector's cultural dimension' (Commission of the European Communities 1988: 46). EU film policy can be seen as shifting, or as functioning in a permanent tension, between these two poles: the financial on the one hand, the cultural on the other. European institutions have tried to promote a transnational film industry that is at the same time financially sustainable and culturally relevant. However, 'European cinema' stands, as highlighted by the examples listed earlier, for a series of very different realities, from blockbusters such as *Skyfall* to art-house films by directors including Pedro Costa. EU initiatives in support of the audiovisual sector therefore often lack relevance or impact, as this is a clearly fragmented and diverse area of European culture.

At the outset, policies for the support of European cinema had a clear financial impulse, partly because the EU, at the time EEC, did not have any power over cultural matters. Hence, in 1985, Jacques Delors highlighted the economic aspects of the film industry, such as the creation of jobs (Collins 1994: 26). By the time the first initiatives were developed, the European common market was already larger than that of the United States, which was also seen as an indisputable economic advantage (Commission of the European Communities 1986: 6). However, there is also evidence of an institutional cultural conception of film in 1988. The conclusions of a European Council meeting in Rhodes, for example, stated that the policies set in motion for the experimental phase of MEDIA launched the same year 'contribute to a substantial strengthening of a European cultural identity' (cited in Commission of the European Communities 1990: 7).

After the naming of 1988 as the 'European Film and Television Year', in 1989 an experimental phase of MEDIA was launched. The goals of MEDIA, as presented in the programme's official website, read as below:

> To strive for a stronger European audio-visual sector, reflecting and respecting Europe's cultural identity and heritage; to increase the circulation of European audio-visual works inside and outside the European Union; [and] to strengthen the competitiveness of the European audio-visual sector by facilitating access to financing and promoting use of digital technologies.[5]

These refer to the last phase of the programme, MEDIA 2007, which ran between 2007 and 2013. Such statement of intent highlights not only the main aims of the EU's work in the audiovisual sector, but also the rhetoric that frames initiatives by the European institutions in the realm of culture and cinema in particular. While the first statement hints at the generally challenging situation of the European film industry, at the same time highlighting the cultural side of MEDIA, the second and third goals mention concrete actions supported by the programme, namely, film distribution and access to financing. The European audiovisual sector is presented as in need of help (as denoted by the use of words such as 'strive'), as the EU claims the commercial aspects of European cinema need a boost (viz. through the word 'competitiveness'). Old and new problems are mentioned, such as the lack of funding and the development of digital cinema, respectively. The concern with the circulation of European films beyond EU borders is also, as we will see, a recent development of MEDIA. The use of words such as 'identity' and 'heritage' shows how, for the EU, films are important both as texts that represent European culture and as artefacts that need to be preserved.

Table 2.2 presents the different phases of the MEDIA programme since its official inception in 1992. Despite having gone through four different phases and the

Table 2.2 MEDIA at a glance

Phase	Initiatives/areas supported	Budget	Countries
MEDIA I 1992–1995	12 initiatives, 19 after 1993, including: • Training – MEDIA Business School (Madrid) • Production – European Script Fund (London) • Distribution – European Film Distribution Office (Hamburg) • Cinema exhibition – Europa Cinemas (Paris) • Film archives – Lumière (Lisbon)	ECU 200 million (€175 million)	EU member-states
MEDIA II 1995–2001	Media II – Development and Distribution Aims to foster the development and transnational circulation of European films by encouraging and consolidating cooperation between European distributors	€265 million	EU member-states
	MEDIA II – Training Promotes the provision of training schemes in order to improve the skills of audiovisual professionals	€45 million	
MEDIA Plus 2001–2005 **(extended until December 2006 to match the end of the EU's financial framework)**	Main branch: Development, Distribution, Promotion MEDIA Plus also supported pilot projects which would improve access to European works, taking advantage of new technologies	€350 million Raised to €453.6 million because of the extra year and the 2004 EU expansion	EU member-states, including 10 new countries after 2004
	MEDIA Training (continuing from MEDIA II) Main goals: • Improving knowledge of new technologies for producing and distributing audiovisual programmes • Teaching business, management and legal skills • Promoting script-writing and narration techniques	€50 million Increased to €59.4 million	
	i2i Audio-visual Stimulate access for funding	€1 million in 2002 and €2.2 million in 2003	

Phase	Initiatives/areas supported	Budget	Countries
MEDIA 2007 2007–2013	Pre- and post-production activities through a single programme: • Distribution – 55% • Development (single projects, catalogues, new talent, co-productions) – 20% • Promotion (market access, festivals, heritage) – 9% • Training (scriptwriting techniques, financial management, digital technologies) – 7%	€755 million *Increasing budget:* Year/€ million 2007/75 2008/93 2009/97 2010/100 2011/103 2012/105 2013/107	EU member-states plus Norway, Iceland, Liechtenstein, Switzerland and Croatia
MEDIA International 2008–2010	Designed to prepare proposals for possible future programme; 3 years maximum Main objective: strengthen cooperation between Europe and third countries Initiatives:	€2 million 2008/2009	The call is open to proposals from legal entities in the 27 EU member-states and any third country
Preparatory Action	• Training of professionals • Distribution of cinematographic works • Cinema networks	€5 million 2009/2010	
MEDIA Mundus 2011–2013	Stems from MEDIA International Main goal: as earlier	€15 million	As MEDIA International

annulment of some and creation of other initiatives, for the European Commission, MEDIA is an example of continuity in EU policies. However, a closer look at the history and evolution of the MEDIA programme reveals that there were significant changes. One key transformation was based on political concerns. Whereas the first fifteen years of the programme were dedicated to the development of the European film industry, the MEDIA International initiative launched in 2008 extended this support to non-EU members and candidate countries, at the same time promoting joint initiatives for European and American, Asian and African countries. The EU wishes to show European films beyond the continent and at the same time to attract, through partnerships, global investment for the European film industry. This reveals an effort by the EU to have an influence on the global film industries and to be perceived as a global actor (a trend highlighted in Chapter 1). A similar shift towards universality occurs in the identity of contemporary European cinema, as Chapters 3 and 4 will show.

Over the years, MEDIA's size and structure was also transformed. MEDIA's budget almost doubled at every new phase, which highlights the EU's growing commitment during this period to the development of Europe's cultural sector. The focus of the programme's initiatives, however, suffered a number of changes. MEDIA started by supporting nineteen projects, in areas as varied as training, film exhibition and the consolidation of film archives, with offices in different European cities. These were then joined under two different strands: development, distribution and promotion on the one hand, and training on the other, centrally run in Brussels. When setting up MEDIA 2007, the European Commission insisted on the need to have a single programme. Significantly, this was chiefly focused on film distribution. As argued earlier, this is one of the most challenging areas of the European film industry. The idea behind the European Commission's efforts to support European cinema is that the more people watch European films, the greater knowledge they will have of other countries in Europe and the more European they will feel. Supporting film distribution has implications not only for the financial aspects of the audiovisual sector, but also for the cultural value of contemporary European cinema.

In focus: MEDIA and the distribution of European cinema

MEDIA supported the distribution of European films through two main schemes: automatic and selective support. Table 2.3 presents the details of the application process, as well as the different stages and outcomes of each of these schemes. It is worth noting that the automatic support scheme encourages reinvestment in co-productions. However, although beyond distribution the programme also includes pre-production initiatives that fund project development, including the writing of scripts, a key point is that MEDIA does not directly sponsor film production and therefore the EU is not involved in the actual contents of European films.

Groups of at least five European distributors can apply for the selective support scheme for the release of a European film that is not from their own country. In view

Table 2.3 MEDIA support for distribution

	Objectives	Application procedure
Automatic support	To encourage European distributors to invest in the co-production and distribution of films from other European countries	• Phase 1 – 'generation stage': distributors declare box-office receipts from European films they distributed the year before • Phase 2 – 'reinvestment stage': after determining the amount available, support is given for reinvestment in new films from other European countries, either as co-production, minimum distribution guarantees or distribution costs
Selective support	To fund distribution costs, including the cost of promotion, copies (including digital), dubbing and subtitling of European films with a maximum budget of €15 million	• Directed at groups of at least five European companies distributing a European film outside its home country • Point system: award criteria include the number of eligible distributors, the production cost of the film, the origin of the film, its genre, the presence of the selling agent/producer as coordinator and his/her nationality • The projects are then listed in ascending order. A group of experts examines their budgets and determines the amount of support that will be given by MEDIA

of the limited funds available, the selective scheme is based on a handicap point system, which organizes films in ascending order. Films produced in France and in the United Kingdom will be given zero points; those from Germany, Spain and Italy one point; films from countries with low production capacity two points; and those from the latest countries to have joined the EU (Cyprus, Czech Republic, Estonia, Hungary, Latvia, Lithuania, Malta, Poland, Slovakia and Slovenia in 2004, followed by Bulgaria and Romania in 2007 and Croatia in 2013) three points. A director's first or second feature receives two extra points, also awarded to documentaries, animation films or films directed at children. This system highlights MEDIA's commitment to diversity, by adopting an attitude of positive discrimination towards countries and genres less well supported, thus also avoiding financing the biggest film industries in Europe only.

The results of the calls for MEDIA support through the selective scheme can be accessed online, where lists of successful applicants are published.[6] These lists quote the title of the film supported, its origin, the distributors involved, their nationality and the amount of support given. They also offer an overview of film distribution in Europe, highlighting some of the titles released across national boundaries. For instance, the analysis below focuses on the calls issued between 2005 and 2008. Until 2014, the selective scheme competition took place three times a year, with calls in April, July and December. In the twelve calls considered (three per year, in 2005, 2006, 2007 and 2008), a total of 212 films received support from the programme.

Table 2.4 lists the number and nationality of these films. It includes all of the thirty-two countries participating in MEDIA in 2008, although some of them were not initially EU members (Bulgaria and Romania in 2005 and 2006; Croatia up until 2013).

Table 2.4 Origin of films distributed with the support of the MEDIA
Selective Scheme, 2005–2008

Country	2005	2006	2007	2008	Total
Austria	3	3	3	1	10
Belgium	1	1	3	3	8
Bulgaria	–	–	–	–	0
Croatia	–	–	–	–	0
Cyprus	–	–	–	–	0
Czech Republic	3	–	3	–	6
Denmark	8	8	1	3	20
Estonia	–	1	–	1	2
Finland	1	1	1	2	5
France	16	8	11	9	44
Germany	5	5	4	4	18
Greece	1	–	–	1	2
Hungary	4	2	1	1	8
Iceland	–	1	–	–	1
Ireland	1	–	1	–	2
Italy	3	2	2	6	13
Latvia	–	–	–	–	0
Lichtenstein	–	–	–	–	0
Lithuania	–	–	–	–	0
Luxembourg	1	–	–	–	1
Malta	–	–	–	–	0
Netherlands	2	1	–	1	4
Norway	2	1	3	2	8
Poland	–	1	1	2	4
Portugal	–	–	1	–	1
Romania	–	2	1	2	5
Slovakia	–	–	–	1	1
Slovenia	–	1	1	–	2
Spain	10	5	4	1	20
Sweden	3	–	1	2	6
Switzerland	–	2	2	1	5
UK	5	5	3	3	16
Total	69	50	47	46	212

Others are countries external to the EU (Croatia in this specific period, Lichtenstein, Norway and Switzerland at the time of writing), some of them in negotiations for EU accession (e.g. Iceland – although the accession process was put on hold by the Icelandic government in May 2013). All EU members are listed in the chart, even if some do not provide any films. This is a significant absence, which reveals the disparities that characterize the European audiovisual sector.

Of the 212 films listed, 20 per cent are French. With a total of forty-four films distributed with the support of MEDIA in other European countries between 2005 and 2008, France's presence is much higher than that of any other national cinematography. It is followed by Denmark and Spain and only then by countries such as Germany, United Kingdom and Italy, considered solid European film industries. Conversely, smaller European industries seem to export only occasional films. On the one hand, MEDIA's objective of promoting the circulation of European films is accomplished, as films from various European countries, including France, travel to other European markets with the support of MEDIA. On the other hand, it seems only natural that France, as the country producing the largest number of films in Europe, stands out in this picture.

The impact of the programme should also be assessed in relation to the number of films from different European nations distributed in specific countries. The figures relative to how many films are distributed with the support of MEDIA only make sense when compared to the total number of films released in each country and to the reality of each country's film industry and film market. Portugal and the United Kingdom are two useful case studies of MEDIA's impact on the distribution of European cinema within the EU. Despite both being Western European countries, there are major differences between Portugal and the United Kingdom in terms of their film industries. As a small audiovisual market traditionally characterized by art and auteur films, Portugal offers a particularly engaging counterpoint to an examination of film in the United Kingdom – one of the biggest film producers in Europe, and one with privileged ties to the United States, as exemplified by *Skyfall*. Portugal produces an average of fifteen films every year. Only seldom do these films travel outside the country, and when they do, they are generally exhibited at film festivals, rather than in commercial cinema screens. Miguel Gomes's *Tabu* (2012), winner of the Alfred Bauer Award and the FIPRESCI prizes at the Berlin Film Festival, is a particularly well-known example. The majority of the films released in Portugal are US productions. The same is true of the United Kingdom, despite its much stronger production capacity: 342 feature films were produced in the United Kingdom in 2010. The number lowered to 331 in 2011; 249 in 2012 and 241 in 2013.[7] This downward trend might be partly explained by the abolishment of the UK Film Council in 2011 (see Doyle et al. 2015).

Graphs 2.1 and 2.2 present the number of US (excluding co-productions), national and non-national European (NNE) films released in Portugal and in the United Kingdom between 2005 and 2008.[8] There are no significant changes in time (with the exception perhaps of a slight rise in national films distributed in the United Kingdom after 2006). The United Kingdom not only produces a larger number of films than Portugal, it also has a larger film market, where more titles are released each year. Although the UK screens a lot more US films than Portugal, the percentage of US films released in Portugal and in the United Kingdom is similar, and in both cases significantly higher than the percentage of national films distributed. The major difference between Portugal and the United Kingdom in terms of the origin of the films released is to do with the NNE films. In absolute terms they are fairly the same in both countries, but they represent a much higher percentage in Portugal. In Portugal, the gap between the number of NNE and US films released is more nuanced. The acceptance of foreign language films in the United Kingdom is lower than in Portugal, where subtitled films are the norm, in theatres and television screens. This difference also highlights the major disparity between these two countries in terms of their production/distribution ratio. A lot more national films are released in the United Kingdom than in Portugal.

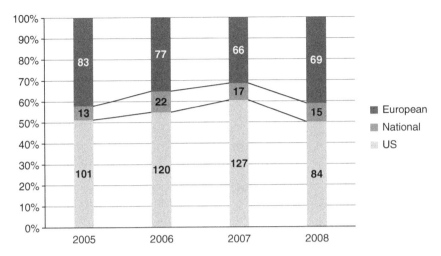

Graph 2.1 Film distribution in Portugal, 2005–2008.

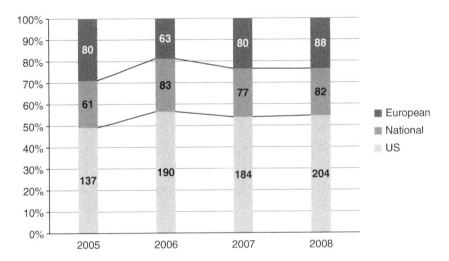

Graph 2.2 Film distribution in the United Kingdom, 2005–2008.

Whereas in Portugal the percentage of national films is much smaller than NNE films, in the United Kingdom, these have similar market share. British films occupy the UK national screens otherwise filled with NNE productions in Portugal, although this has no impact on the market domination of US productions. The historical opposition to Hollywood, as well as its ongoing significance, is confirmed here.

Table 2.5 compares the support Portugal and the United Kingdom received from MEDIA for the distribution of NNE films between 2005 and 2008. On average, MEDIA supports 30 per cent of the NNE films released in both countries. Hence, despite

Table 2.5 NNE films released in Portugal and in the United Kingdom with the support of MEDIA's Selective Scheme, 2005–2008

	NNE including co-productions	2005	%	2006	%	2007	%	2008	%
PT	Total	83	100	77	100	66	100	69	100
	MEDIA support	24	29	22	28	14	21	25	36
UK	Total	80	100	63	100	80	100	88	100
	MEDIA support	24	33	17	27	25	31	17	19

Source: ICA – Instituto do Cinema e Audiovisual and UK Film Council.

premiering more European films than the United Kingdom, Portugal gets the same support from MEDIA. While the positive discrimination adopted by the EU applies to the nationality of the films supported, it does not take the country in which they are released into consideration. MEDIA encourages the circulation of European films from all nationalities, but does not attempt to balance the production/distribution ratio in individual European countries. The programme aims to promote the development of the European film industry as a whole, without boosting specific national markets.

Focusing on two of the countries receiving support from the MEDIA programme is also useful to examine the films released in Europe with the support of the EU. For example, between 2005 and 2008, 127 films were released with MEDIA support in Portugal and in the United Kingdom. This includes a mixture of popular and art films, of mainstream and auteur productions. In the same inventory we find the big budget Hollywood style *Zwartboek/Blackbook* (Paul Verhoeven, 2006) alongside the auteur low budget *The Silence of Lorna*. Other auteur films listed include *Il divo* (Paolo Sorrentino, 2008), *Gomorra/Gomorrah* (Matteo Garrone, 2008) and *Entre les murs/ The Class* (Laurent Cantet, 2008), which have all received awards at the Cannes Film Festival. We can also identify European film-makers working in Hollywood, with the remake of *Funny Games*, directed by Michael Haneke (2007), as well as an American film-maker working in Europe, as in the case of Woody Allen in *Match Point* (2005). Non-European directors such as the Mexican Carlos Reygadas are also featured, with *Batalla en el Cielo/Battle in Heaven* (2005). This pinpoints the complexities of iden-tifying a film's national, as well as European, identity in contemporary cinema. Seen in this light, the selective scheme secures the objective of cultural diversity proposed by MEDIA, in terms of budget and, as hinted earlier, the nationality of the films sup-ported. It is also worth taking a closer look at these 127 films to consider the differ-ent genres that are distributed across Europe. Table 2.6 organizes the films released in Portugal and the United Kingdom between 2005 and 2008 into broad genres. While there are no significant differences between Portugal and the United Kingdom, the variety of titles listed is in line with the diversity of European cinema that MEDIA aims to promote.

Graph 2.3 visualizes the genre distribution of these MEDIA-backed films. Documentary and animation, two of the genres awarded extra points in MEDIA's selective scheme for distribution, are strongly represented. The majority of the films

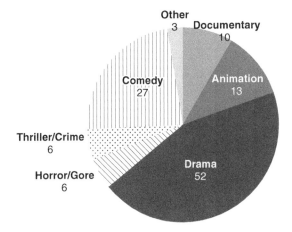

Graph 2.3 Genre of films released with MEDIA support in Portugal and in the United Kingdom, 2005–2008.

supported, however, are drama films, including historical and war films, as well as heritage films, one of the European genres par excellence (examined in more detail in Chapter 3). Thriller and crime films are also abundant, as well as, more surprisingly, comedies, a genre traditionally confined to national audiences. Table 2.6 lists a number of romantic comedies, a subgenre of comedy customarily more exportable and that has been through a significant boom in the past fifteen years or so. The prominence of drama and comedy seems to suggest European cinema is generally focused on emotions – an idea also at the core of MEDIA's own promotion, as discussed later. There are no films from genres relying on larger budgets, for instance, because of the use of special effects, such as fantasy and adventure – although we find here six horror and gore films. Among the 127 titles listed there are no action films, which has been seen to define European cinema in opposition to Hollywood (see, for instance, Elsaesser 2005: 487; Martin-Jones 2012). Key absences include the two Bond films released in this period: *Casino Royale* (Martin Campbell, 2006) and *Quantum of Solace* (Marc Foster, 2008).

Arguably, an explanation for the absence of both big budget productions (such as the films in the 'Bond' series), as well as more avant-garde work, might be that such genres were not put forward for funding. This survey nevertheless offers a picture of what could essentially be labelled as the cinema of the EU. Grouped in this way, these European films acquire a new significance. As 'MEDIA films' they mirror the diversity of contemporary European cinema – yet one that is framed by meaningful boundaries. While films from different nationalities, genres and with varied budgets are released with MEDIA support, the vast majority of these occupy the central, 'middlebrow' area of the 'art versus popular' spectrum. The cinema of the EU is fundamentally characterized by a distinctive, 'prestigious' quality. This is a vision of European cinema that also emerges in MEDIA's own communication.

Table 2.6 Genre of the films distributed in Portugal and in the United Kingdom, 2005–2008

Genre	Title	PT	UK
Documentary	*Back to Normandy*		✓
	Brasileirinho		✓
	Crossing the Bridge		✓
	Czech Dream		✓
	Elle s'appelle Sabine		✓
	Maradona by Kusturica	✓	
	No Body Is Perfect	✓	✓
	The White Planet		✓
	Viva Zapatero!		✓
Docu-fiction	*The Road to Guantanamo*	✓	
	Astérix and the Vikings	✓	
	Franklin and the Turtle Lake Treasure	✓	
Animation – children	*Kirikou & the Wild Beasts*	✓	✓
	Max & Co	✓	
	Midsummer Dream	✓	
	Niko & The Way to the Stars	✓	✓
	Renart the Fox	✓	✓
	Strings	✓	
	Terkel in Trouble	✓	
	The Ugly Duckling and Me	✓	
Animation – adults	*Persepolis*	✓	✓
	The District		✓
	Waltz with Bashir	✓	✓
Drama	*Atomised*	✓	
	Battle in Heaven	✓	✓
	Evil		✓
	Factotum		✓
	In Your Hands	✓	
	Involuntary		✓
	Irina Palm		✓
	Longing		✓
	Slumdog Millionaire	✓	✓
	The Edge of Heaven		✓
	The Secret Life of Words	✓	
	Time to Leave		✓
Drama/family	*Brothers*		✓
	Dalecarlians		✓
	Delta		✓
	Hell	✓	
	Home	✓	✓
	Paris	✓	✓
	Quiet Chaos	✓	
	The Cave of the Yellow Dog	✓	✓
	The First Day of the Rest of Your Life	✓	
	The Grocer's Son	✓	
	The World Is Big and Salvation Lurks around the Corner	✓	
Drama/social	*4 Months, 3 Weeks and 2 Days*	✓	✓
	Birdwatchers	✓	✓

Genre	Title	PT	UK
	Dear Wendy		✓
	Exiles		✓
	Heading South	✓	✓
	Import/Export		✓
	Princesses	✓	✓
	Shelter	✓	
	The Class	✓	✓
	The Silence of Lorna		✓
	The Son	✓	✓
	Transylvania	✓	✓
Drama/history	*Goodbye Bafana*	✓	
	My Brother Is an Only Child		✓
	Nuovomondo – The Golden Door	✓	✓
	Pan's Labyrinth	✓	
	Shooting Dogs	✓	
	The Dust of Time	✓	
History/war	*Blackbook*	✓	✓
	Merry Christmas	✓	
	The Counterfeiters	✓	✓
Biopics	*Becoming Jane*	✓	✓
	Molière	✓	✓
	Sophie Scholl	✓	✓
Literary Adaptations –historical	*Alatriste*	✓	
	Angel	✓	
	Fateless		✓
	I Served the King of England	✓	✓
	Lady Chatterley	✓	✓
Horror/gore	*Frontier(s)*	✓	✓
	Ils		✓
	REC	✓	
	Requiem		✓
	Taxidermia	✓	✓
	The Broken	✓	
Thriller/crime	*A Few Days in September*	✓	✓
	Funny Games (Remake)	✓	✓
	Gomorrah	✓	✓
	Hidden	✓	✓
	Just Another Love Story	✓	✓
	Lemming	✓	✓
	Lights in the Dusk		✓
	Manderlay	✓	✓
	Match Point	✓	
	My Summer of Love	✓	
	Red Road	✓	
	Revanche	✓	✓
	Savage Grace	✓	✓
	The Beat That My Heart Skipped		✓
	The Snake	✓	✓
	The Wave		✓

Genre	Title	PT	UK
Comedy/satire	12:08 East of Bucharest		✓
	A Christmas Tale	✓	✓
	A Soap	✓	
	Adam's Apples	✓	
	Cashback	✓	
	Dark Horse		✓
	Ex Drummer	✓	✓
	Garage	✓	✓
	Happy Go-Lucky	✓	
	Il divo	✓	
	It's All Gone Pete Tong	✓	✓
	Mid-August Lunch	✓	
	Mrs Henderson Presents	✓	✓
	O'Horten	✓	
	Rumba	✓	✓
	Summer Storm	✓	
	The Boss of It All	✓	✓
	The Bothersome Man		✓
	The Science of Sleep		✓
	The Wedding		✓
	Tricks		✓
	Volver	✓	✓
	You, the Living	✓	✓
Romantic comedies	2 Days in Paris		✓
	After Midnight		✓
	Emma's Bliss		✓
	Russian Dolls	✓	
Anthology	Paris je t'aime	✓	✓
Music	Johanna	✓	✓
	The Magic Flute	✓	

Promoting MEDIA: Joy, love and sadness

Cultural policies at EU level arise from soft competences, in other words, rules and guidelines that are not binding, as opposed to legislation. This means that the EU can support and encourage action across Europe, but cannot regulate or harmonize the laws of the different member-states. Guidelines issued by Brussels do not replace, but only complement, what is done at national level. As a result, European initiatives for the audiovisual sector have clashed with national policies, as well as with different conceptions of film and of the role of the state in supporting local film industries. In Portugal, for instance, film-makers have strongly criticized EU initiatives, which, in their view, see cinema merely as an industry and not as an art form (Vasconcelos 1994: 12). Conversely, in countries where there is less state support for cinema, contestation normally arises from film producers who stand against protectionist measures. This is the case of the United Kingdom, where David Puttnam argues Europe's attitude to 'film as art' (Europe here meaning European institutions) is 'ultimately self-destructive' (cited in Jäckel 2003: 14). Similarly, for Martin Dale (1992: 47), 'the MEDIA programme's principal achievement has been to circulate information and ideas within the European industry and to improve the development and distribution of smaller auteur films'. In reality, as we saw, the tables of films distributed with the support of MEDIA include both art and popular films. The programme is disparaged by being involved too much for some and too little for others.

In order to minimize the criticism of its actions, and of the MEDIA programme in particular, the EU recognizes the importance of communicating with different stakeholders. According to policymakers, the European Commission organizes groups of film industry experts, with whom regular discussions are held. These groups address, at the same time as they acknowledge, the lack of legitimacy that has characterized the public perception of the EU. The communication of the MEDIA programme, the direct responsibility of the European Commission, was also developed during the programme's last phase (2007–2013) – at a time when, as discussed in Chapter 1, the EU searched for new strategies to promote closer communication with the citizens it represents.

Promotional material for MEDIA has naturally been directed at film industry professionals across Europe, who, until 2014, were informed of the programme's initiatives by their national MEDIA Desks or regional MEDIA Antennas, located in all the countries participating in the programme. Under the new programme, these were replaced by national Creative Europe desks – arguably illustrating the lack of dedicated support for film, which the European film-makers cited at the start of this chapter predicted would become a reality once the programme was merged with other initiatives. MEDIA's efforts to reach cinema professionals also include stands at film festivals and publicity in trade publications. After 2007, the European Commission launched a series of initiatives for the general public, aiming to familiarize audiences with the political initiatives launched in support of the audiovisual sector. In this new phase in EU communication, cinema was seen as one of the most interesting, if not 'cool', intervention areas of the EU.

The most important of these initiatives was the production of five short films as promotional tools for MEDIA released in 2007. The European Commission identifies these films as 'clips'; I will also use this denomination. First presented at the Berlin Film Festival and later at Cannes, the 2007 MEDIA clips were also made available online, on the then recently created EUTube channel – the European Commission channel on YouTube. According to Margot Wallström, vice president of the European Commission responsible for its communication strategy at the time, the general aim of the MEDIA clips was to 'explain to European citizens the policies and programmes of the Commission … To do so in 2007, it is impossible not to use new technologies, especially those central to Internet users, such as the videos on YouTube' (cited in Castelli 2007). Just as was the case with the website Europa (Chapter 1), here the European Commission places the emphasis on 'new technologies'. This is clearly an area that was valued by European institutions at the turn of the century, in an effort to look modern and to be in touch with European citizens, as well as to reach out to young people. Significantly, these are not only key voters, but also audiences who normally prefer

Hollywood to European films. On the one hand, these clips were used as 'advertising' for the work of the European Commission; on the other, they contributed to divulging the success of contemporary European cinema. These short films both encouraged European citizens to watch European films and worked as a mise en abyme, mirroring the EU's idea of Europe in contemporary European cinema.

Composed of extracts of European films supported by MEDIA, these consist of one 'best-of' clip and four thematic short features: one clip each on joy and sadness and two clips on love. The analysis that follows is structured around each of these themes. By choosing to promote its major programme in support of film in these terms, the European Commission insists on the power of universal values. The selected themes also importantly testify to the creation of an emotional, rather than rational, connection between the public and the EU institutions. At the same time, the clips highlight the overconfidence of the EU in appropriating such general topics. Joy, love and sadness could hardly be seen as specifically European – just as is the case with human rights or pluralism, cited as European values in the Declaration on European Identity signed in 1973.

Twenty-four European films were used in the production of these 'clips': *8 Femmes/ 8 Women* (François Ozon, 2002), *Le Fabuleux Destin d'Amélie Poulain/Amelie* (Jean-Pierre Jeunet, 2001), *Todo sobre mi madre/All About My Mother* (Pedro Almodóvar, 1999), *Så som i himmelen/As It Is in Heaven* (Kay Pollak, 2004), *La Mala Educación/ Bad Education* (Pedro Almodóvar, 2004), *Billy Elliot* (Stephen Daldry, 2000), *Breaking the Waves* (Lars von Trier, 2006), *Girl with a Pearl Earring* (Peter Webber, 2003), *Good Bye Lenin!* (Wolfgang Becker, 2003), *Habana Blues* (Benito Zambrano, 2005), *Head-on*, *La vita è bella/Life Is Beautiful* (Roberto Benigni, 1997), *Merry Christmas*, *Nói albinói/ Noi the Albino* (Dagur Kári, 2003), *Pot Luck, Secrets and Lies* (Mike Leigh, 1996), *Sophie Scholl* (Marc Rothemund, 2005), *La meglio gioventù/The Best of Youth* (Marco Tullio Giordana, 2003), *Les Choristes/The Chorus* (Christophe Barratier, 2004), *The Dreamers* (Bernardo Bertolucci, 2003), *Mies vailla menneisyyttä/The Man without a Past* (Aki Kaurismäki, 2002), *The Pianist* (Roman Polanski, 2002), *The Sea Inside* and *Le Fils/ The Son* (Jean-Pierre and Luc Dardenne, 2002). The music of *Les triplettes de Belleville/ Belleville Rendez Vous* (Sylvain Chomet, 2003) and *Volver* (Pedro Almodóvar, 2006) is also featured.

As this list shows, clearly a decision has been made not to privilege any particular genre or nationality. There are mainstream (*Amelie*) and auteur (*The Man without a Past*) films; films from major European producers such as Spain (*Bad Education, All About My Mother* and *Habana Blues*) and low production countries such as Iceland (*Noi the Albino*); independent auteur films (*Breaking the Waves*) and major box-office successes, including Oscar winners (*Life Is Beautiful, The Sea Inside* and *The Pianist*). The choice of films for the clips seems to be dictated equally by their box-office success and their status as award winners, highlighting both European's cinema ability to produce popular films and its association with quality and prestige – in line with the EU's idea of 'MEDIA films' presented earlier.

Each of the thematic clips highlights one emotion, as well as a key aspect of European cinema, the idea of Europe and/or the EU and its institutional communication. For instance, the clip about joy, entitled *European films, what a joy!*, features a number of European stars in some of their most famous roles.[9] A close-up of Romain Duris in *Pot Luck* shows him running; Jamie Bell dances in *Billy Elliot*; a quick cut to close-ups of Ludivine Sagnier and Catherine Deneuve in *8 Women* presents the French actresses moving their heads (seemingly) to the sound of the cheerful soundtrack of *Belleville Rendez Vous*. Audrey Tautou in *Amelie*, Daniel Brühl in *Good Bye Lenin!* and Roberto Benigni in *Life Is Beautiful* scream, jump and celebrate. Discussing the preparation of the clips, a policymaker at the European Commission declared in an interview in 2009 that one of the major difficulties in putting these films together was to finalize the decision regarding what actors to include. The European Commission tried to choose recognizable faces, but this had a different meaning for each of the nationalities present at the discussion. A well-known Spanish actor would not be recognized by the German representative, who in turn wanted to include a German actress unknown to the Danish people. This highlights the problems inherent in defining a European star system (Hedling 2009) and pan-European stardom (Vincendeau 2015), as well as the fragmentation of the film industry in Europe. Nevertheless, even if audiences are unable to name a number of European actors, they would, according to the EU, hopefully recognize the film extracts used. Literacy of European cinema is an important aim of the MEDIA clips – and, as discussed later, also an important way to bring citizens closer to the European institutions.

The final scene of the short film about joy is a long shot of cinema audiences, in a dark cinema room, supposedly during a film projection. This is superimposed with the slogan 'with pleasure'. The joyful character of the edited images dissolves into the first concrete statement about MEDIA's action: '50% of all European films in cinemas every year. Europe supports European films'. The slogans added to the final images of cinema audiences (present in all 'clips') do not mention the EU or the European Commission (although they include the blue twelve-starred flag), but insist that it is 'Europe' who supports European cinema. Such a designation might reflect the arrogant attitude of the European Commission in making EU and Europe equivalent terms. On the other hand, it hints at a key communication problem. 'Europe' has become a synonym for the EU, especially in Euro-sceptic countries such as the United Kingdom. By choosing to use 'Europe' rather than 'EU', the European Commission stresses a spatial and cultural identification with the term, removing the political dimension. At a time when populations across Europe seem to lose interest in politics, the best strategy for the European Commission might precisely be to remain incognito, under the designation of 'Europe'.

While all the short films produced by the European Commission have a similar structure and final scene (showing audiences inside a theatre screen, followed by the slogan 'Europe supports European films' against a black background), the selection of extracts from the twenty-four films named earlier varies. Different soundtracks too illustrate the diverse moods intended by the Commission, and so the first clip about love, *Romanticism still alive in Europe's films*, is accompanied by a 1966 classic French pop song, 'Love me, please love me', by Michel Polnareff.[10] Starting with a succession of close-ups of European stars – from Belén Rueda to Daniel Brühl – the

Figure 2.2 Audrey Tautou and Mathieu Kassovitz in *Amelie*.

clip moves from scenes of people hugging, to others gazing romantically, to some couples kissing and then other couples in bed. Once more, these are extracted from recognizable films such as *The Sea Inside, Good Bye Lenin!* and *Amelie*, finishing with a shot of Audrey Tautou and Mathieu Kassovitz in the latter (Figure 2.2). The slogan superimposed on the final shot this time is: 'It started with a proposal'. This particular slogan – a pun on the word 'proposal' – leads to two very different readings of the film. While the romantic message connoted in 'proposal' wishes to appeal to a wide, mainstream audience, its other meaning betrays the EU's bureaucratic nature, so often alluded to by Euro-sceptic critics. What follows is pure statistical information, contrasting with the romantic, dream-like tone of the clip, as well as of the Polnareff song.

The decision to produce a film about the topic of love is also meaningful as love relates to certain cultural conceptions of Europe. Luisa Passerini, Jo Labanyi and Karen Diehl argue Europeans have historically been seen as 'superior' because of their capacity to feel and express romantic love. Although this was challenged in the 1960s in line with critiques of Euro-centrism, as they claim, Europeans have made the concept of love 'a fundamental part of their self-image and traces of this habit still linger today' (Passerini, Labanyi and Diehl 2012: 10). Similarly, romantic love is presented in the MEDIA clips as a characteristically European emotion. For the European Commission, love is also an emotion audiences are invited to develop in relation to Europe's own culture and film. *Romanticism still alive in Europe's films* edits images of romance on screen with images that invite viewers to feel attached to European cinema. The latter is here defined by its romantic character both in terms of film contents and in terms of viewership: it becomes in itself the target of this love, the object of this emotion. The aim of these clips with regards to general literacy of European cinema seems to be not just to 'inform' audiences of the existence of diverse films, but also to incite the development of a positive reaction towards them. The clips are not so much about getting to know European cinema, but more about beginning (or continuing) to like European cinema.

Before saying more about how this connection between citizens and cinema would, in the eyes of the EU, be formed, it is worth highlighting the extent to which the message put forward by these clips, as the majority of the messages released by the European Commission often are, was misconstrued. Much of the EU communication, including in the audiovisual sphere, is first and foremost challenged because it is perceived as 'propaganda' – echoing claims by Shore (2000) and others, as discussed in Chapter 1. This was particularly the case with the second MEDIA clip on love. In contrast to the romantic and nostalgic version of love presented in *Romanticism still alive in Europe's films*, the second clip on the same topic, entitled *Film lovers will love this*, starts with clothes being taken off.[11] The music this time is 'Las Vecinas', composed and interpreted by Alberto Iglesias for the soundtrack of *Volver*. The first sequence of people getting undressed is followed by sex scenes crosscut with shots from *Amelie*, which insinuate the sexual relationship between two of the characters in the film. Shots of glasses trembling on shelves, lights going off and shadows of the couple are followed by screams and orgasm scenes. The slogan, another pun, reads 'Let's come together … Millions of cinema lovers enjoy European films'.

European cinema has often been seen as more sexually explicit than, for instance, Hollywood; this particular clip also caused furore within the continent. Whereas *European films, what a joy!* has had four hundred thousand hits on EUTube and *Romanticism is still alive in European films* has been seen by one million people, at the time of writing, over nine million people have watched *Film lovers will love this*. The press coverage on this short film also led to a series of catchy headlines (here translated into English), including: 'The Quickies of the European Commission' (*Diário de Notícias*, Portugal); 'Free Sex for European Cinema' (*La Stampa*, Italy); 'It's red faces all round over EU's dirty movie' (*Daily Mail*, UK); and the openly critical 'On EU Tube (LOL!), Sex Sells (Duh!)' (*The New York Times*, USA). The media coverage shows the extent to which the work of the EU is under scrutiny. By highlighting the gap between the EU's intentions and the way in which these were misunderstood, these newspaper articles also illustrate the perceptions the EU and others have on the meaning of the idea of Europe, the significance of European values and the worth of European cinema.

Many raised their voices against the content of the clips, especially that of *Film lovers will love this*. The strongest critique emerged from traditionally Euro-sceptic countries and parties. Antonio Tajani, leader of Forza Italia in Strasbourg, dismissed the initiative as 'superficial and reductive of the Europe of great values in which we believe' (cited in Zatterin 2007). Similarly, according to the BBC, 'a Polish MEP from the conservative League of Polish Families has accused the Commission of using "immoral methods" to promote itself' (Mulvey 2007). The Polish reaction was the harshest in the EU, although British Members of the European Parliament (MEPs) were also among those criticizing the European Commission's action. For the Conservative MEP Chris Heaton-Harris, this was a clear waste of taxpayers' money. Godfrey Bloom, a UKIP MEP, on the other hand, told the BBC the clip was 'tawdry and tacky', adding: 'it is like watching an elderly relative trying to be cool, very embarrassing' (cited in Mulvey

2007). Quoted by the *Daily Mail*, the UKIP representative went further, stating: 'I suppose this film is appropriate. The EU has been screwing Britain for the past 30 years' (in Anon 2007).

The language used testifies to the strength of the reactions provoked by this clip, an index of reactions to the EU itself. The European Commission was not indifferent to this. Reijo Kemppinen, the European Commission's representative in London, told *The New York Times* that

> [t]he compilations were meant to convey emotion and they certainly seem to have got a reaction. In spite of attempts to whip up a scandal because of the sexy nature of one of the clips, hundreds of thousands of British people are learning more about the EU's MEDIA programme and almost all are reacting maturely and positively. (Cited in Riding 2007)

Kemppinen stresses the fact that the clips provide knowledge, highlighting the idea that European citizens should be educated about the work developed by the EU. Referring instead to the importance of values and emotions for European culture and cinema, Viviane Reding's view is that

> [t]he real scandal is the polemic around a piece of work that was extremely well received at the Berlin Film Festival. Our films respect the values on which a multicultural Europe in built: joy, sadness, love and diversity are the feelings that express the strongest and most recognized identity of our cinema. (Cited in Zatterin 2007)

According to the former commissioner, the fact that the films were screened at Berlin gives them a 'prestigious' quality. For Reding, the 2007 MEDIA clips are crucial, as they mirror European values, supposedly joy, love and sadness. Yet, how these mirror 'multicultural Europe' is unclear.

Another contentious, and typically European, issue to develop in the reception of the MEDIA clips was language. Although the copies distributed in Berlin were subtitled in the (at the time) twenty-three official languages of the EU, the clips posted on EUTube are exclusively in English. Versions in English, French and German were uploaded on the MEDIA programme's official website. The European Commission speaks the language of the 'EU' only, which is reduced to the three key working languages. As such, the European Commission centralizes, and by consequence brings a sense of uniformity, to the otherwise praised diversity of the continent's culture. Beyond form (i.e. language) and content, questions were also raised about the general significance of this initiative – which accentuates the distance between European institutions and citizens. A *Guardian* journalist, for instance, was unable to pinpoint the meaning of the clips. He followed the clip's link to the official MEDIA website to find long descriptions of various European Commission agencies. Ironically, he concluded: 'I'm not sure quite what all this means, but it doesn't sound obviously sexy' (Brooks 2007).

To return to the content and themes of the MEDIA clips, the incomprehension towards the EU finds a parallel in sadness, the topic of the final thematic short film, *Singing the blues on the silver screen*.[12] With music from Yann Tiersen, 'Comptine d'un autre été: L'après midi', from the soundtrack of *Amelie*, the film includes a series of shots of people crying, including Adrien Brody in *The Pianist* and Julia Jentsch in *Sophie Scholl*, as well as the protagonist of *Amelie* as a child. *Singing the blues on the silver screen* becomes another example of the use the EU makes of specific views of European cinema (in this case, the widespread notion that European films have no happy endings, as opposed to Hollywood cinema) while packaging them as universal (everyone cries: audiences across the world can identify with the images on screen). The emotions on which the clips focus are at the same time European and global. Claims of Euro-centrism thus undermine the EU's message, as the institution seems to prolong Europe's historical appropriation of universal emotions.

The 2007 short films produced by the Commission are a simultaneous attempt by the EU to reach out to the citizens it represents and a testimony to the communication failure that has characterized much of the European Commission's work in this area. The fact that the clips deal with joy, love and sadness reinforces the well-known, if not cliché, message that European cinema is about emotions. Hence, the underlying rhetoric is that these clips, like European cinema as a whole, are different from Hollywood's accent on action – we have seen how few action films are released through MEDIA's funding schemes. The 'intellectual' image of European cinema is absent too, giving way to new defining elements. The quality of these clips is not guaranteed by action and explosions, nor is it certified through beautiful photography, long shots, or reflection, particular auteurs, their names or their signatures. Instead, they rely on the presence of (relatively young) film stars with developing careers in Europe and in some cases beyond, as well as lively and engaging soundtracks from European box-office successes – testifying to a drive for more mainstream, global success for European films. At the same time as they insist on the diversity that characterizes European cinema, as they integrate images from different nationalities and genres, the clips prepared by the European Commission give a cohesive idea of Europe united through universal topics: we all laugh, cry and love. The clips work as a clear illustration of the way in which the EU aims to put forward a more contemporary application of the motto 'united in diversity'. This initiative is therefore a key component of the EU's efforts to create a European cultural community through cinema.

A European cinematic community

The final shot of *Singing the blues on the silver screen*, instead of the shot of audiences in a cinema used in the previous clips, is a close-up of the Argentinean actress Cecilia Roth in *All About My Mother* (Figure 2.3). Although Roth is, in the diegetic world of *All About My Mother*, watching a play, rather than a film, the inclusion of this scene is crucial for another key message conveyed by these clips. MEDIA's idea of watching a

Figure 2.3 Cecilia Roth in *All About My Mother*.

film still seems to take place in an actual theatre, not on other types of screens. Echoing the long shots of audiences used at the end of the previous clips, this image allows for an easier identification of those watching the clips with what is on screen. It also becomes a vivid representation of MEDIA's aim to promote the creation of a cinema going culture in Europe. Through this clip, the European Commission underlines the sense of community created by a united European film industry. The idea of community is reinforced by the inclusion of extracts from films many viewers would recognize and especially by the final shot of audiences sitting in a cinema. As viewers are brought together in the same space, the EU contributes to the formation of a cinephile community. Cinema is not just a way to give European citizens access to other (European) cultures; it also becomes a common interest.

After 2007, the European Commission produced two new clips, not made of excerpts, but shot as short films. In 2010, a film ending with the slogan 'European Cinema, Made for You' shows a woman accepting an award in the name of the European film public for best cinema audience.[13] The idea of glamour is very prominent; the setting of the clip is a dazzling old theatre with red velvet seats and golden décor, as the situation depicted (a major public event, perhaps a festival) adds to a sense of prestige and quality. However, the character at the centre of this narrative is not a celebrity but a worker who during the last rehearsal of the ceremony, seizing an opportunity to get on stage, removes her cleaning overall and drops her shoes, running to steal, from the hands of the presenter, an award statue. Aggressively looking at those trying to move her away from the microphone, she begins her speech, met with cheers and applauses (supposedly imagined in her head as the theatre is actually empty). 'I've been watching European films since I was ten years old', she says, and the main message of the clip seems to be that such a faithful audience should be rewarded. This short film strengthens the appeal to cinema audiences across Europe, who become not just the target of MEDIA's promotion (as in 2007), but also the protagonists. Audiences are given a central role in the growth of European cinema, side by side with the initiatives the EU sets in motion for its development.

The following year, a new clip was posted on MEDIA's website to celebrate the twen-tieth anniversary of the programme.[14] Here, a parallel is drawn between a romantic relationship and the evolution of MEDIA. As we see a couple getting ready to go out, a male voice-over says: 'It's our twentieth anniversary, I didn't notice time passing by; next to you, I've started seeing the world with different eyes'. The analogy suggests watching films is also a way of gaining knowledge, addressing one of the main goals of MEDIA, that of education: bringing European films to people across continent so they can learn about other countries in the EU. The couple drive to a restaurant, where they enjoy a romantic dinner by candlelight. The husband then hands his wife an envelope that contains an old cinema ticket. In a brief flashback, the clip dissolves into a screen-ing of *Il Postino/The Postman* (Michael Radford, 1994) twenty years before, possibly their first date.

Back in the contemporary era and in the same theatre (tellingly called 'Twelve Stars', in an allusion to the European flag), the couple spot their teenage son and the father walks up to him, handing him a flame. The clip thereby stresses ideas of continuity and tradition, conveying a sense of legacy that gives European films status at the same time as it binds people together. By depicting young audiences on screen, the clip further appeals to these particular demographics. A consolidation and potential growth of the public for European films is clearly important in economic terms. But the flame also represents a passion of watching films; the slogan of the commemorations of MEDIA, featured at the end of the short film, is: 'Twenty years of passion'. When the young couple go inside the cinema, everyone is holding a flame, which symbolizes the pas-sion for film that brings European audiences together. Once more, Europe, as well as European cinema, is associated with love.

Although, until 2014, the main focus of MEDIA was film distribution, in the last phase of the programme, the European Commission seemed to realize that the prob-lems in this sector went hand in hand with another major issue: the difficulty in attract-ing audiences to watch the European films being screened with EU support. A concern to be dealt with within the new Creative Europe framework, this might prove to be a particularly thorny challenge for an institution that has, in recent years, struggled precisely with attracting the attention of those it represents. The literacy of European cinema the 2007 MEDIA clips proposed gave way, in these more recent initiatives, to a clearer sense of cinephilia. The clips frame the knowledge of European cinema in a positive, 'loving' rhetoric. Titles such as *Romanticism still alive* and narratives such as the one told in the film celebrating the twenty years of the programme suggest there is also an important sense of tradition defining European cinema. The idea of Europe, as we saw in the previous chapter, gains authority and prestige because of its 'old-ness'. Similarly, so does the EU rely on European cinema's past glories to present to European citizens a more prestigious vision of the cinema of the continent. Like the idea of Europe, the idea of European cinema is also attached to notions such as history and legacy. As the following chapter will show, the commemoration of the past is also a key theme in contemporary European cinema.

Taking into account the number of films produced within the EU in recent years, the European film industry could be seen to be thriving. However, not only are a majority of these low-budget or independent productions, limited distribution across borders also means there have been limited audiences for the European film market. If distribution has been pinpointed as the main problem in contemporary European cinema, the growth of film festivals has created an alternative circuit and offered new promotion opportunities, as well as markers of quality. Festivals mirror the complex combination of notions of prestige and mainstream appeal, which defines the contemporary idea of European cinema. Like the EU's motto 'united in diversity', European cinema emerges from a series of tensions. Like the idea of Europe, it is defined by a dichotomy between art and commerce. The global status of European cinema is also changing – something that has not escaped the EU, whose work in the audiovisual sector has tried to address new universal challenges.

MEDIA was not the first pan-European policy in support of film to ever be introduced. However, it was the first with a true political agenda. Such an agenda is not denied by the European Commission, as the latter adds clear cultural goals to the economic benefits of the programme. MEDIA's positive discrimination in favour of low production capacity European countries might not be enough to increase the distribution of their films. Between 1992 and 2014, the programme nevertheless helped the circulation of European films within Europe more generally, offering support for up to 30 per cent of distribution costs, thereby sponsoring a wide variety of titles from different nationalities, from different genres and with different budgets. Significantly, these were framed by a sense of quality; the EU adopts an essentially middlebrow vision of contemporary European cinema.

Increasingly, the EU identifies as the primary role of cinema its contribution towards to the creation of a community, whose existence is underpinned by a sense of belonging. Interviewed in 2009, policy officers at the European Commission justified the focus of the programme on distribution precisely by the necessity of the European peoples to know each other better, having access to a diversity of visions. MEDIA's connection with the idea of Europe has less to do with objective parameters of how it can be defined and more with an emotion-based sense of binding people who share common values. Through the promotion of MEDIA the EU stressed the importance of emotions, from joy, love and sadness to passion. Such values highlight both the will of the EU to remain attached to stereotypical views of European cinema (romantic, generally more sexually explicit and characterized by sad endings) and a simultaneous wish to frame these in a universalist slant (anyone could potentially connect to these clips through the association of love, joy and sadness). The idea of Europe, as the identity of contemporary European cinema, must then be found in a tension between specificity and openness.

As the reaction to the MEDIA clips hinted at, and the 2014 European Parliament (EP) elections confirmed, Euro-scepticism has been on the rise within the continent. As the EU deals with extensive institutional reforms set in motion by the Lisbon Treaty and a political crisis aggravated by the debt catastrophe within the euro-zone and the internal divisions this is creating, communication with its citizens appears as a major challenge. In this context, the promotion of MEDIA has been increasingly directed at the larger public. The clips posted on EUTube and on the European Commission's website reflect the EU's view of European cinema, as well as what Europe stands for. Here, the adjective European stands for 'quality', for emotions, as well as for a need to connect with audiences. The following chapters examine in detail some of the EU films mentioned here, questioning the extent to which these represent, question and communicate a certain idea of Europe.

European History, European Memory: Trauma and Celebration between the Nation and the Globe

The idea of Europe has been defined in relation to key moments in the history of the continent, from the Hellenistic period to the Enlightenment. Europe's history has simultaneously been vehemently contested – from the enduring legacy of Christianity to war, colonialism and occupation (Chapter 1). The love–hate relationship the European continent has established with its past is also extensively explored in cinematic terms: history is an important theme and setting for films from different European countries. This chapter maps the different ways in which contemporary European cinema puts forward an idea of Europe tied to history and the past. Beginning with an examination of heritage films and biopics, and focusing on these films' festive tone and celebration of Europe's glorious past, it then looks at war films. This chapter considers the First World War as a European civil war and reflects on the permanence of the Second World War as a key topic in European cinema, examining the role of war heroes in a European memory of armed conflicts. Finally, turning to the analysis of films that represent recent moments in Europe's history, particularly those that self-consciously rewrite it, it looks at the extent to which concepts such as memory and nostalgia are relevant for an examination of contemporary European cinema. Before moving to the discussion about film and history, a word about how the European Union (EU) engages with Europe's past is necessary, as this will help to make clear the connections between an institutional vision of the idea of Europe and the films released through MEDIA schemes across the continent.

History, heritage and the EU

In 2005, George Steiner (2006) spoke at a conference at the Nexus Institute in the Netherlands where he presented 'a certain idea of Europe'. Among its features, he highlighted a strong reverence to the past (37). For Steiner, Europe's interest in history is best exemplified by the names of late artists, intellectuals and politicians given to streets and piazzas across Europe, in contrast with the functional denominations given to American urban locations (for instance, Fifth Avenue). Although Steiner highlights the Europeanness of this interest in and commemoration of the past by opposing it to American culture, the celebration of cultural heritage is not specifically European – nor is it, of course, entirely dismissed in the United States. Nevertheless, the degree to which European institutions, especially the EU, promote it places history at the heart of discussions of the idea of Europe.

One key term that emerges in discussions about Europe's history is the increasingly omnipresent concept of 'heritage', roughly defined as what is inherited from the past. Situating the discussion about the meaning of Europe within debates about heritage means placing European history in dialogue with the present. Through the heritage framework, the past is not just something to be remembered. It is also something to be instrumentalized. The question becomes what can, in the present, be done with such inheritance – with the potentially diverse usages of history being politically shaped and culturally challenged.

The protection of Europe's heritage is explicitly one of the main goals of the EU's cultural programmes. In the audiovisual sector, incentives for collecting, cataloguing, preserving and restoring films, in order to protect Europe's cinematic patrimony, have been a component of MEDIA from the programme's outset. The Culture Programme 2007–2013 (the main European Commission arts policy before the introduction of Creative Europe in 2014) actively promoted cultural activities across Europe, with a particular focus on heritage. A long list of monuments and historical sites, museums and memorials have been created, restored or restructured with the support of EU funding schemes. Through the 'European Heritage Days' initiative, which has been running since 1985 and is co-sponsored by the Council of Europe, many of these have also been opened to the public, either for the first time, on special dates only or under certain, exclusive conditions.

The launch in 2010 of the 'European Heritage Label', created to single out heritage sites that represent and celebrate European integration, provides further evidence of the increasing attention devoted to this sector. According to Androulla Vassiliou, at the time the commissioner for Education, Culture, Multilingualism and Youth, this label 'contribute[s] to strengthening European citizens' sense of belonging to the EU and promote mutual understanding in Europe' (cited in Anon, *EurActiv*, 10 March 2010). The development of programmes for the protection of heritage reflects an institutional need to safeguard and maintain markers of European history, and at the same time to create a transnational cultural memory. The first European Heritage Label award ceremony took place in 2014 and celebrated four sites: the Archaeological Park of Carnuntum between Vienna and Bratislava, Austria and Slovakia; the medieval Great Guild Hall in Estonia; the Nazi transit camp of Westerbork; and the Peace Palace in the Hague, which hosts the International Court of Justice – the last two located in the Netherlands. These awards clearly mark some of the most significant moments in European history, both positive and negative: from the ostensible humanism and universality of Roman culture to the dark memories of the Second World War, as well as Europe's commitment to be known as the global guarantor of peace and justice.

The definition of what constitutes European heritage is remarkably contentious, not least because in Europe the past is very often tied to national culture. Significantly, Europe's nations were once at war, but now engage in a political endeavour to form a transnational sphere of remembrance based on peace and mutual understanding. Condemnations of this new international memory dismiss it as fabricated, and therefore fake. As noted by Raphael Samuel (1994: 243), heritage is seen by critics 'as a "project", if not a conspiracy or plot then at the very least a strategy ... It is a "bid for hegemony", a way of using knowledge in the service of power'. Suspicion towards historical accounts has been growing in contemporary Europe – with implications also for cinematic narratives, as discussed towards the end of this chapter. Many in Europe perceive the work of the EU in this sector as 'propaganda', part of a political strategy that is not grounded in cultural terms (see, for instance, Vasconcelos 2011). On the one hand, the protection of history is praised, as the past is attributed an inherent value, especially in the shape of material manifestations of history (e.g. ancient ruins, houses of key historical figures and battlefields). On the other, memory, and the decisions concerning what sections of Europe's past are to be sponsored, as well as how these are to be included in the narrative of European integration, is highly disputed.

Criticism emerges not only in relation to the presumed construction or inauthenticity of European heritage, but also because of the latter's commercial exploitation. EU initiatives such as the European Heritage Label are therefore dismissed as 'a waste of taxpayers' money' (Vasconcelos 2011). As Samuel (1994: 242) argues, 'in a consumer-led society, in which everything has its price and market values are unchallenged, [heritage] "traffics" in history and "commodifies" the past'. Hence, as noted by Robert S. Peckham (2003: 3), museums become a 'commercial enterprise, which sells the past to the visitor as entertainment'. What is described here is the rise of a 'heritage industry', which has simultaneously been explored (commercially) and contested (in political terms). This tension between a will to reclaim to the public sphere forgotten or newly framed sources of heritage in Europe and a 'theme park', commercially profitable representation of the transnational past is also visible in contemporary European cinema.

Rose-tinted spectacles: Heritage cinema in Europe

Ginette Vincendeau (1995a: xv) identifies the two world wars as well as European historical and mythical heroes (and anti-heroes) as the most common topics in European cinema. Likewise, Wendy Everett (2005: 107) sees these as particularly important for an analysis of the idea of Europe since, as she argues, there is in European cinema 'an almost obsessive need to explore and interrogate memory and the process of remembering, apparently convinced that therein may be found the key to present identity'. The predominance of historical themes highlights the extent to which European cinema puts forward an idea of Europe tied to the continent's past. Many of the films retelling moments in European history have not only been praised by critics, but have also done exceptionally well with audiences across Europe, which suggests a resonance of such stories with its primary public.

A large number of contemporary European films set in the past have been read not only as historical, but also, and more specifically, as 'heritage films'. Encompassing costume dramas, literary adaptations and historical biopics, heritage cinema has, since the 1980s, been the subject of important critical debates about film, nostalgia and celebration (cf. Vidal 2012). Key features of the genre include, apart from a historical setting, high budgets, high production values, A-list directors, the presence of stars, polished lighting and camerawork, many changes of décor and extras, well-researched interior designs and classical or classical-inspired music (Vincendeau 2001: xviii). As Richard Dyer (1995: 204) notes, heritage films are 'often hugely popular in their country of origin, [but] sold as art cinema outside it'. As such, they are positioned between entertainment and quality – a key opposition in the understanding of contemporary European cinema (Chapter 2).

Perceived as 'mainstream', the 'problem' with the heritage genre is that it has been seen as celebrating the past without investigating it – or to put it in Andrew Higson's (1993: 113) terms, as offering no 'critical historical perspective'. Conflating heritage cinema with the costume drama, Robert Rosenstone (2006) contrasts the former with what he calls the 'history film'. For Rosenstone,

> [t]he costume drama ... uses the exotic locale of the past as no more than a setting for romance and adventure. A 'history film', by contrast, engages that discourse by posing and attempting to answer the kinds of questions that for a long time have surrounded a given topic. (45)

Romance and adventure are opposed to engaged discourse and reflection, in a formulation that mirrors the discussion about the (apparently thin or inexistent) value of popular cinema (Chapter 2). Unlike historical films more generally, which might be centred on the brutality or injustice of bygone eras, in heritage films the past is supposedly framed through a longing feeling. At the centre of a heritage film's narrative we find a mood best defined as a sense of 'something that no longer is', a past that exists to be cherished. It is this particular, supposedly rose-tinted tone that forms the core of the criticism of the heritage genre, as if these films' appreciation of the past prevents them from engaging with it in a rational way.

Original debates about heritage cinema emerging in the British context contrasted films such as *A Room with a View* (James Ivory, 1985) with a more realistic strand of filmmaking, perceived as committed and politically engaged. Best exemplified by Stephen Frears's *My Beautiful Laundrette* (1985) the 'other' British cinema of the 1980s faced head-on an increasingly multiracial and multicultural society, which at the time dealt with high unemployment and a general social malaise against the backdrop of an international capital recession (Higson 1993). Throughout the 1990s and 2000s debates about the validity of heritage cinema moved from a national to a transnational context. Yet, many of the issues remained the same. Writing twenty years later, Belén Vidal (2012: 61) notes how 'the critique of the heritage film in Europe has largely concentrated on the conservative retreat into national iconographies'. Heritage films are dismissed by critics not only because of the way in which they engage with the past, but also because they choose conformist historical themes. In doing so, they arguably ignore more pressing contemporary issues: social unrest in 1980s Britain, Europeanization and globalization (in Europe) at the turn of the twenty-first century.

Although they are often seen as glossy and superficial, and disparaged for not questioning the implications of history for contemporary society, European heritage films say as much about the past that they represent on screen as about the period in which they are made. As such, they offer fundamental insight into the European sense of collective memory and identity. While critics of the heritage genre have disparaged its conservative aesthetics and ideology, my analysis takes it as a serious vehicle for complex historical representation, as well as the articulation of cultural ideas about Europe's past and present. Higson (1993: 118) goes on to note that 'a more generous reading of these films might suggest that ... the heritage film creates an important space for playing out contemporary anxieties and fantasies of national identity, sexuality, class and power'. Likewise, for Dyer (1995: 205), 'the genre has provided a space for marginalized social groups, a sense of putting such people back into history, for instance, women'. The ambiguity of heritage cinema makes it particularly interesting for debates about European cinema, especially as this is defined through the prism of the 'quality film'. Like the popular European art film described in Chapter 2, historical films emerge as both entertainment sites (and therefore entertaining) and 'smart', allowing for reflection; they are carefully filmed and produced, and yet simultaneously appeal to a wide audience.

One particularly fruitful example among the films released with the support of the EU in recent years is *Girl with a Pearl Earring*, which features prominently in the 2007 promotion of MEDIA. The film was watched by over four million people in cinema screens across Europe. Adapted from Tracy Chevalier's 1999 novel, it tells the story of Griet (Scarlett Johansson). Forced to work as a servant in Master Vermeer's (Colin Firth) house, Griet becomes gradually interested in the work of the painter. At the same time, master and servant develop an ambiguous relationship, which has an impact on their personal and professional lives. *Girl with a Pearl Earring* (a UK, Luxembourg and US co-production) is set in Delft, Holland, 1665 – as viewers are informed at the beginning of the film through an intertitle. The film's main topic – seventeenth-century Dutch painting – is presented in contrast with domestic and urban life. Water, soap and boats in the canal are examples of items that clearly define the historical period represented, at the same time as, adding to the images of pig heads and other animals in the market, they construct an unpleasant and almost grotesque vision of life in the seventeenth century. However, while representations of the common spaces in the house and shots of the city add to a gloomy representation of this particular period, Vermeer's atelier, as well as his private world, which Griet later enters, are beautiful and serene. Thus, key indoor scenes focus on the camera obscura, the colours and the paints, highlighted through carefully composed photography by Eduardo Serra, who won a European Film Award in 2004 for Best Cinematographer for this film.

The sobriety of Johansson's performance was praised by critics; she is the subject of the painting the narrative focuses on and therefore for the most part of the film a still model. However, the problematic role of women in society seems to be left aside, used as a mere plot line imported from the novel (notably, a recent book, not a 'classic', as in many other heritage films). Vermeer's wife (Essie Davis) recognizes Griet is just 'a fly in his web – we all are!', but the matter is not further explored by the narrative. The main topic pursued here is not so much Griet and Vermeer's relationship as it is the painter's work. Other recent European films released with MEDIA support focus on painters and painting, including *The Mill and the Cross* (Lech Majewski, 2011), which is inspired by Peter Bruegel's work; and the avant-garde *Shirley: Visions of Reality* (Gustav Deutsch, 2013), which brings to life pictures by US painter Edward Hopper – with the world of high art emerging as a significant theme in European culture as well as film.

Similarly, although the historical period represented in *Girl with a Pearl Earring* is portrayed as bleak and bizarre, this film proposes a celebration of art, which it commemorates through style and cinematography. By being marketed not 'just' as a romantic costume drama, but also as a film about painting, *Girl with a Pearl Earring* achieves an artistic status. Johansson's presence (as an American star) positions the film as international, while the painting guarantees the Europeanness of the story. Vermeer's art is here the item to be celebrated as part of Europe's past. *Girl with a Pearl Earring* thus highlights a key contradiction in the association of Europe with the artistic world which takes place on screen: it has a commercial, poignant and wide scope, and yet a simultaneously restricted, exclusive and intellectual status. As a romance casting a universally acclaimed star and as a film about painting, *Girl with a Pearl Earring* has a dual appeal: it is associated with entertainment on the one hand and with knowledge on the other.

Girl with a Pearl Earring is a prime example of how contemporary European cinema is in line with the development of heritage tourism in Europe and in the Netherlands in particular. A 'Vermeer Tour' is available to those visiting Amsterdam, including a trip to The Hague to see the famous paintings 'A Girl with a Pearl Earring' and 'View of Delft'. Moreover, a 'Vermeer Centre' opened in Delft in 2007, inviting visitors to step into the seventeenth century and explore the stories behind the painter's life and work. Through such initiatives, Delft becomes explicitly a historical town. Culture is seen as a commercial opportunity for its development, as the Vermeer Centre includes a shop selling Vermeer gifts.

Peckham (2003: 4) argues the heritage industry is characterized by 'the marketing of history for external consumption by foreign tourists or by a native population encouraged to consider its "own" past as a foreign country that is at once reassuringly familiar and entertainingly exotic'. European tourists on trips to Delft and similar destinations, as European audiences watching *Girl with a Pearl Earring*, are likely to experience a simultaneous familiarity and distance to what is being portrayed. While the painting and this particular view of art would be known to a local, national and European public, the techniques used by Vermeer, his working practices and personal life are new to many. Moreover, the grotesque past visible in the film (for instance, the pigs' heads at the market) contributes to the sense of exoticism described by Peckham.

The appeal of *Girl with a Pearl Earring* lies in its representation of a period that no longer is and therefore must be cherished, in the same way that preserving the past becomes a political obligation for institutions such as the EU. Despite the film's apparent sombre setting, this is a story, a historical period and a figure (Vermeer, rather than the 'Girl') to be celebrated.

The engagement of heritage sites (and by extension, films) with the past is described by Peckham as 'entertaining', but *Girl with a Pearl Earring* establishes another, intellectual and 'more serious', connection with Europe's history. Given the detail of its visual composition, *Girl with a Pearl Earring* can also be seen as exemplifying Samuel's (1994: 177) notion of 'living history', a practice developed in the 1960s and since then increasingly used for pedagogical purposes. The film constructs a narrative about Vermeer's life, as well as, more crucially, his work. The tone of the film is in this sense didactic, and therefore attached to the idea of knowledge. *Girl with a Pearl Earring* creates an active spectator who learns, or is given the opportunity to learn, about Europe's history. By being focused on Vermeer's methods and his paintings, the film is similar to the Vermeer Centre mentioned earlier, as it allows the spectator to be immersed in the painter's atmosphere, to learn about the history of the specific painting at the heart of the narrative and, ultimately, to admire it. *Girl with a Pearl Earring* stresses the value of painting as one of Europe's cultural attractions. The film mediates the (European) past, making it comprehensible.

Extraordinary Europeans: Artist biopics

Whereas the cinematic attraction of European heritage seems natural in a film in which the topic is also visual, other themes in heritage cinema establish a positive relationship between viewers and the European past. This is especially the case of those concerned with the lives of European artists, from writers to performers. Literature in particular is a central element of Europe's cultural heritage. Visits to writers' homes have become common in today's European cities. At the same time, literature has been given special attention in the EU's latest cultural programme, for instance, through the 'Euroman' initiative, which aims to promote the circulation of Europe's lesser-known literary traditions. Literature is not only the source of many heritage films released with MEDIA support – *Alatriste* (Agustín Díaz Yanes, 2006), *Lady Chatterley* (Pascale Ferran, 2006) and *Jane Eyre* (Cary Fukunaga, 2011) emerging as key examples – but also a common theme in European historical cinema. This is the case of *Shakespeare in Love* (John Madden, 1998), *Sylvia* (Christine Jeffs, 2003), *Molière* (Laurent Tirard, 2007) and *Becoming Jane* (Julian Jarrold, 2007), films that narrate the lives of key European writers and that constitute recent examples of the literary strand of the boom in European biopics.

Scholarly interest in biographical films has also increased in recent years (see, for instance, Bingham 2010; Brown and Vidal 2014). Biopics constitute a particular subsection of the historical film, raising issues of authenticity, narrative and stardom. Most biopics adopt a classical narrative structure, which contributes to the presentation of

Figure 3.1 Anne Hathaway as Jane Austen in *Becoming Jane*.

their protagonists as 'normal' people. However, the events they portray focus on these characters' outstanding capacities and/or achievements. Thus, replicating discourses on stardom, biopics are often based on a dichotomy between the 'ordinary' and the 'extraordinary'.

Becoming Jane, for instance, is centred on the romance between young Jane Austen (Anne Hathaway) and Tom Lefroy (James McAvoy) (Figure 3.1). After a series of encounters where the two tease and provoke each other, they fall in love. But Jane and Tom's lack of money and a marriage proposal by the rich Mr. Wisley (Laurence Fox) forces them to reconsider the value of their feelings. The film uses well-known passages and episodes from the author's work to construct a fictional narrative about Jane Austen's rise and confirmation as a key literary figure – much like had happened with *Shakespeare in Love* and *Molière*; the cover of the UK DVD edition of the latter, for instance, reads: 'Shakespeare in Love … French style'.[1]

The presence of an American star (Hathaway) in this British production no doubt contributed to the success of *Becoming Jane* in the United States, where it grossed over $18 million. Seen as a popular film within the European market, *Becoming Jane* was curiously awarded a People's Choice Award in 2008 as the Favourite Independent Movie of that year. As expressed on the cover of the DVD edited by BBC Films, the film's plot line, 'between sense and sensibility and pride and prejudice was a life worth writing about', clearly highlights its topic – with the absence of capitals reinforcing the intended pun. As one critic has noted, 'for the first hour you might be watching an Austen adaptation rather than a biopic' (Beardsworth 2007: 56). 'The heart' and the defence of 'irony' are central topics in *Becoming Jane* – topics that are also present in the character's work and in her life, in the film and in Austen's novels (which the spectator is assumed to know). By placing romance at the centre of its narrative, *Becoming Jane* is

Figure 3.2 *Becoming Jane*: The 'feisty' writer plays cricket.

self-reflexive. The film is also intertextual in its relation to contemporary cinema. Jane Austen has had an exceptionally remarkable presence in European cinema, as a significant number of her novels have been adapted – including in the past twenty years or so – with commercial and critical success (see, for instance, Voigts-Virchow 2004). Examples include *Sense and Sensibility* (Ang Lee, 1995), *Emma* (Douglas McGrath, 1996) and the freer adaptation *Bride and Prejudice* (Gurinder Chadha, 2004).

In *Becoming Jane*, the presentation of the main character is based on a notion of extraordinariness, as the writer distinguishes herself from the society in which she lives. The protagonist of *Becoming Jane* is someone who is different: she is up (writing and playing the piano) while everyone is asleep; she walks behind the other members of the family as they go to church; she is feisty, volunteering to play cricket with the men (Figure 3.2). In the cricket scene, while everyone dresses in white, beige and similar light colours, Jane emerges out of the group of people watching the game (mainly women) in a red dress. This not only sets her apart from the crowd, but also from the landscape: the red colour of Jane's dress contrasts vividly with the green of the setting – with the Irish countryside, where the film was shot, standing for the green pastures of Hampshire, where Austen actually lived. The editing privileges the reactions of viewers and players to her bold gesture, bringing together a series of looks, from her mother's shock to Tom's amused curiosity, to which Jane 'replies' (visually) with defiance.

The film also shows the (internal and external) difficulties the writer overcomes. As in *Girl with a Pearl Earring*, we see in *Becoming Jane* the main character in the process of artistic production, being able to learn about what is extraordinary about key European historical figures. As such, the film functions as a living history memorial, in the vein of the houses of artists that can today be visited across Europe. More than *Girl with a Pearl Earring*, the title of which seems to denounce the relative centrality of Vermeer, *Becoming Jane*, as other historical films celebrating artists, can be seen as a filmic equivalent of statues and monuments, since it publicly celebrates Jane Austen's name and commemorates her achievements. Throughout the film, we see Jane writing. She begins writing *First Impressions* (the working title of *Pride and Prejudice*) as a commentary on what is happening to her and Tom, and reads passages from the novel at the end of a film, set twenty years later, when Jane Austen is already a reputed writer.

The extraordinariness of the protagonists of films such as *Becoming Jane* turns these characters into distinguished Europeans that serve as future references for younger generations. In *Becoming Jane* viewers are cued to identify with a talented and independent-minded young woman, who is devoted to her work and challenges social conventions, fighting for her freedom to live life as she wants. As such, the films mentioned here are about returning to the past to find inspiration for the present, about celebrating history so its glories are prolonged. Films that commemorate European heritage, and those concerned with the lives of European artists more explicitly, construct a narrative that highlights specific values that should be followed – and that therefore come to constitute Europe's cultural inheritance. These include determination and creativity, as well as the capacity to innovate and overcome prejudices about the role of artists – women artists in particular in the case of *Becoming Jane*, in which Austen's place in history is claimed to come at a cost. In the film's final scene, Austen's professional success as a writer is balanced by her personal 'failure' in not getting married – a common trope in the representation of women with careers.

A similar tale of rise and fall is evident in *La Môme/La Vie en rose* (Olivier Dahan, 2007), a biopic far from the intellectual concern of literature (or painting, as in *Girl with a Pearl Earring*). Like *Becoming Jane* and the more recent *Camille Claudel 1915* (Bruno Dumont, 2013) starring 'the perfect European star' Juliette Binoche (Vincendeau 2015), *La Vie en rose* is centred on a female artist – here the creator, rather than the 'muse', as had been the case with *Girl with a Pearl Earring*. Due to its focus on spectacle, as well as on popular culture, *La Vie en rose* is however closer to another strand of biopics released with the support of MEDIA in recent years, and which includes *Gainsbourg* (Joann Sfar, 2010), *Coco avant Chanel/Coco before Chanel* (Anne Fontaine, 2009) and *Coco Chanel & Igor Stravinsky* (Jan Kounen, 2009).

A French, British and Czech co-production, *La Vie en rose* tells the life of Edith Piaf (Marion Cotillard), from her poverty-stricken childhood to her first breakthrough as a singer and then huge fame, and finally to her death. More than five million viewers watched the film in France. *La Vie en rose* was a major box-office hit, grossing over $10 million in the United States, where it was shown theatrically for almost a year. While it won several prizes in Europe (six Césars – the national film award of France – though none of the four European Film Awards it was nominated for), the film's popularity in the United States can be partly explained by the number of awards received by the leading actress, including a Golden Globe and an Oscar – as well as, arguably, its overtly American-oriented narrative content.

Cotillard's performance and her mimesis of Piaf were the main aspects noted in the critical reception of the film, but its narrative structure was also scrutinized. *La Vie en rose* has been criticized for omitting crucial incidents in Piaf's life, in particular her ambiguous behaviour in occupied France during the Second World War (Bradshaw 2007: 9). With a non-linear episodic structure, the film makes abundant use of montage. It also follows many of the conventions of the biopic. Hence, it starts *in media res*, with a performance by Piaf in February 1959 in New York.

The stage is a central element of *La Vie en rose*, allowing for a particular kind of double framing. In the scene of Marcel's death, for instance, Edith goes directly from her bedroom to the stage, from crying to singing, from private to public. Reflecting the dichotomy between fiction and reality, this scene also highlights the film's focus on spectacle, which is particularly achieved through visual rather than audio devices. A long take of over four minutes, shot using a Steadicam, follows Edith as she wakes up in her bedroom, goes to the kitchen to make coffee, and frantically searches every room for a present she had bought for Marcel. The absence of music contributes to the sequence's eerie feeling. The focus here is on the performances, by Cotillard and other secondary characters, as well as on mise en scène, which carefully reconstructs period locations and uses spots of intense lighting to contrast the sunny weather outside with the dark emotions of the sequence indoors.

Music (diegetic or not) is always present during the childhood sequence, as it is obviously a crucial part of Piaf's life. However, in its entirety *La Vie en rose* uses mostly excerpts, rather than complete songs, which not only stress the film's accent on visual spectacle (as discussed earlier), but also suggests the film caters for a particular audience. In *La Vie en rose*, 'Frenchness' is negotiated for international viewers. The film has been accused of being made 'for tourists' (the dismissal of 'tourists' or foreign audiences as inauthentic is an issue I come back to in Chapter 4). This supposed consensual tone might also explain the absence of references to Piaf's cooperation with the Resistance in Nazi-occupied France. Moreover, the film's transnationality can be identified at different levels. The presence of Gérard Depardieu, for instance, a truly European, even global star (Vincendeau 2000: 215), suggests a move towards universality. Its international title, *La Vie en rose*, relies on the popularity of Piaf's songs rather than on the knowledge of her persona – since one of her nicknames, *La Môme*, is instead used in the original French title. Likewise, *La Vie en rose* is notably connected to the American market: the first words Piaf sings are in English and we see her travelling to different destinations around the world, including New York (where the film begins) and California (Figure 3.3). For Vanessa Schwartz, the film's popularity in the United States is also related to Piaf's similarities to Judy Garland (2009). [2]

The stress on American culture (both in terms of the film's plot and in terms of its style) might explain the film's success in the United States. However, it does not detract from its European character (in terms of its main story, its origin and the language spoken). Edith Piaf remains a European singer, and her life story is still a French narrative. The film's structure might use American codes, but it tells a French and European tale. In fact, to some extent, Frenchness stands for Europeanness in *La Vie en rose*. Just as Depardieu, who has featured in numerous large costume productions such as *1492: Conquest of Paradise* (Ridley Scott, 1992), has become a global European star, after starring in *La Vie en rose*, Cotillard was chosen as the face of the luxury brand Dior. The first promotional film she starred in for Dior, also directed by Dahan, was

Figure 3.3 *La Vie en rose*: Edith Piaf (Marion Cotillard) in California.

tellingly a short film noir (entitled *Lady Noire*). The film, which can be watched on YouTube, is part of a marketing campaign that draws on the association of France and Europe more generally (especially from an American point of view) with glamour, elegance and sophistication.

An analysis of *La Vie en rose* and its distribution and reception context offers a vivid example of the classical process by which European culture is defined in contrast to Hollywood, as well as of the way in which, at the same time, the European and US film markets are simultaneously interconnected. *La Vie en rose* is a film supported by MEDIA where the idea of Europe is mostly negotiated for an external audience, and emerges associated with a sense of excess (drinking, as well as passion) and with the bohemian feel and space of European cities. Moreover, and perhaps more originally, *La vie en rose* associates Europe with glamorous popular culture, representing the continent's artistic production as one ultimately based on exceptional talent.

The central protagonists of *Becoming Jane* and *La Vie en rose* relate to notions of extraordinariness and are thus presented as heroes in their community. Whereas Austen proves a woman can live 'by her pen' and encourages female independence, Piaf is placed in a fairy tale about overcoming a traumatic childhood and reaching fame, even if the film privileges the darker side of public recognition. The celebrity narrative in *La Vie en rose*, unsurprisingly for the biopic of an entertainer, is more focused on spectacle than on individual ideals. Compared to *Becoming Jane*, *La Vie en rose* also offers a more explicit discourse on stardom, partly because, in comparison to Jane Austen, Edith Piaf is a more recent famous figure, about whom there is a public and visual memory. Performance (especially in terms of the images created, and not so much the songs played, as argued earlier) is a central element of *La Vie en rose*, which justifies the number of awards received by the film's protagonist.

In relation to *Girl with a Pearl Earring*, *La Vie en rose* is less about knowledge and more about feelings. *La Vie en rose* seems to be constructed on impressions, as it includes very short scenes and fast-paced editing, as well as a series of montage sequences that bring together different settings, spaces and characters, often only seen once in the duration of the film. Whereas the genius and the dedication of European artists are celebrated in *Girl with a Pearl Earring* and *Becoming Jane*, in *La Vie en rose*, talent also becomes something to be celebrated as European. Hence, this particular film constitutes an example of how mainstream culture, generally associated with feelings rather than ideas, is also considered to be an important element of Europe's artistic heritage.

Girl with a Pearl Earring, Becoming Jane and *La Vie en rose* show that painting, literature and music are all equally important sources for the celebration of Europe's past. Just as history is in itself prestige, as argued in Chapter 1 in relation to the persistence of the myth of Europa in the discourse of European institutions, giving Europe a sense of tradition through high production values and 'cultural' topics, the popular films examined so far achieve an artistic status, being positioned as quality films. At the same time, by bringing the figures represented closer to audiences, these films transform the artistic practices they celebrate into tourist attractions. Their commercial character is highlighted, as these films position Europe as a visitor destination and appeal to audiences across and beyond the continent. This is a practice endorsed by the European Commission, which wishes to see an increasing number of visitors reaching, among other places, the recently nominated 'European Heritage Label' sites. *Girl with a Pearl Earring, Becoming Jane* and *La Vie en rose* operate similar functions to the statues, monuments and memorials actively supported by the EU. Equally, they illustrate the paradox that is the heritage industry by being simultaneously about quality and yet demanding a large number of viewers/visitors. The extent to which mass tourism is seen to challenge quality, as well as the connection of this idea to film is further explored in Chapter 4.

Heritage cinema packages Europe's historical prestige in a mainstream, popular art form, highlighting the promotion of Europe as an attractive tourist destination, based on culture as its unique selling point. In films such as *Girl with a Pearl Earring, Becoming Jane* and *La Vie en rose*, Europe is seen as a cultural hub, as a continent of the arts, spanning from Vermeer to French *chanson*. Through their commemorative tone, these films denote a Europe that despite being in crisis – as a political and economic reality, not to mention as a cultural concept – was once arguably as powerful, as admired and as influential as the artists and the practices depicted. Europe's cultural aura is appealing both for internal and external audiences, for local and international visitors, thus showing the desire of the EU not only to bring the peoples of Europe together, but also to be seen as a global actor – and more importantly one with a distinctive (cultural) trait. Culture is not just one of the key features of contemporary Europe. It is also a 'soft' political weapon, one that might contribute to a new, reconquered and reinforced position on the international scene.

The EU has supported the circulation of many other biopics within and beyond the continent, from *The King's Speech* to *The Iron Lady* (Phyllida Lloyd, 2011) and *Hannah Arendt* (Margarethe von Trotta, 2012). Because of their focus on art, the three artist films I have been discussing offer particularly vivid examples of the interconnections between cinema and the development of the heritage industry in Europe. These films progressively chart the history of European culture, from the seventeenth to the nineteenth and finally the twentieth century. *Girl with a Pearl Earring, Becoming Jane* and

La Vie en rose offer a sense of knowledge, of information, and at the same time appeal to audiences primarily on an emotional level. What brings these films together is also an overwhelmingly positive tone: this Europe, that should be studied, is especially to be celebrated.

The glory of such films and the figures they represent is however compromised by more dramatic memories. Side by side with the celebratory tone of the films examined so far, all over Europe other memorials have been built, representing a much darker past. Europe's 'other' history, defined by violence and suffering, emerges with particular strength in films that represent the First and the Second World Wars. These films are in stark contrast with the examples examined before – even if, as will be suggested, war films may still contribute to a positive reading of European heritage, as they celebrate a common history.

War and peace: Europe and armed conflicts

The two colossal military conflicts that took place in the twentieth century were denominated 'world' wars, but affected Europe in particular, in geographical, political and cultural terms. This is especially the case of the First World War. Having conducted a historiography of what has also been labelled 'the Great War', Jay Winter and Antoine Prost (2005: 204) note how, since the early 1990s after the fall of the Berlin Wall and the signing of the Maastricht Treaty, 'the link between war and nation … was severed, and henceforth the Great War appeared as a European civil war'. The First World War was not only triggered in Europe, but also fought between European countries and on European soil. Such an outlook on this conflict – which also makes it appear as 'less global' than the Second World War – is crucial for a historical understanding of Europe and for what is at stake in its contemporary definition. Seeing the First World War as a European civil war means acknowledging both the falling apart (during the war) and the coming together (after the conflict) of European nations.

The commemorations of the centenary of the start of the war in 2014 clearly highlighted the dual understanding of the conflict: national and divisive on the one hand, European and aggregating on the other. Approaches to this 'commemoration' differed significantly in degrees of enthusiasm. The celebratory tone adopted in France, Belgium and the United Kingdom (where government-funded school trips were organized to battlefields in Flanders, among many other initiatives), for instance, was in stark contrast with the muted engagement of Germany. Moreover, while an unprecedented number of exhibitions and public ceremonies were put in place across Europe, a large number of citizens, of all nationalities, dismissed the idea that such conflict might be celebrated. With over thirty-seven million casualties, many more people disappeared and devastating consequences for economies and societies across the continent, the First World War is in its brutal significance a crucial landmark in the history of European integration.

The importance of this war has also been reproduced in the official discourse of the EU. The theme of war – and by contrast peace – has particularly resurfaced after the attribution of the Nobel Peace Prize to the EU in 2012. In his acceptance speech, Herman Van Rompuy (2012), president of the European Council, argued that the EU's greatest achievement up until that point had been to form a permanent peace congress, so that 'where there was war, there is now peace'. The last session of the European Parliament in Strasbourg before the elections of May 2014, which took place on 16 April 2014, was also partly devoted to debating the legacy of the First World War. Opening the session, and echoing Van Rompuy's remarks two years earlier, Barroso (2014) argued the point of remembering this anniversary was to stress the fact that Europe had maintained peace for over sixty years. A dark period in Europe's history is used in the EU's official discourse to highlight the overwhelming gap between past and present – with the present (i.e. the European integration process) being valued because of its contrast with Europe's negative historical moments. Because, at least by negation, war is so important for the EU, it must, perhaps paradoxically, be continually remembered.

Contemporary European cinema plays a crucial role in this recollection process. Films depicting the First World War and released with MEDIA support include the French superproduction *Un long dimanche de fiançailles/A Very Long Engagement* (Jean-Pierre Jeunet, 2004) with an estimated budget of over €40 million. The film tells the story of Mathilde (Audrey Tautou), a young woman who refuses to accept her fiancé Manech has been killed in the war. While trying to discover what exactly happened to Manech, Mathilde finds out about many of the hidden practices adopted by the French government at the time in dealing with those trying to escape the front. *A Very Long Engagement* was successful with critics and audiences alike, having been nominated for a series of important awards at home and abroad. Michael Haneke's *Das weiße Band/The White Ribbon* (2009), although set just before the war, is another example of a European film offering a primarily national outlook on the conflict – or in this case, of a growing sense of evil that seems to precede it. The protagonists of the film are a group of children in rural Germany, seen by many as future representations of National Socialism (cf. Brooks 2009). *The White Ribbon*, an auteur film praised by critics across the continent, also achieved international popular acclaim, being nominated for an Oscar as Best Foreign Film in 2010 – a prize awarded to *El secreto de tus ojos/The Secret in Their Eyes* (Juan José Campanella, 2009) from Argentina.

With an undeniable transnational perspective, Christian Carion's *Merry Christmas*, also featured in the 2007 MEDIA 'clips', emerges, in relation to *A Very Long Engagement* and *The White Ribbon*, as an original First World War film supported by the EU. This is due not only to its multicultural and multilingual narrative, but also to its positive representation of the conflict. The film narrates a relatively unknown episode in the history of the First World War, when French, German and Scottish troops called a short ceasefire on Christmas Eve in 1914, leaving their trenches to sing, eat and drink, and celebrate Mass with their enemies. A European co-production (between France, Germany, the United Kingdom, Belgium and Romania) spoken in French, German and English, and labelled by critics as a Euro-pudding (see Liz 2015), *Merry Christmas* is a film project with a very strong European accent from its production set-up. Here war is not just highlighted as what has ceased to exist with European integration; *Merry*

Christmas finds an opportunity for peace even during the conflict, putting forward an overwhelmingly positive perspective of European unification.

Following the actions of key characters in the French, German and Scottish quadrants, *Merry Christmas* adopts a three-fold approach to the representation of the First World War. All nations are given equal footing. The film starts by working as a triptych, as there are always three languages, three camera angles and three points of view. In the first half of the film, there is a predominance of medium shots and close-ups. This structure is maintained up until the toast between the Scottish, German and French general, on Christmas Eve, to a Merry Christmas, *Frohe Weihnachten*, and *Joyeux Noël*, and then recovered towards the end of the film. The film's positive illustration of the solidarity between soldiers of different nations not only fits perfectly within the EU's 'united in diversity' motto, but also echoes Winter and Prost's reading of this conflict as a European civil war.

Before the three nations are merged and captured in one (wider) shot only, the fluidity of the editing already hints at the developing links the film will establish between different countries. During the opening sequence, for instance, children recite poems inciting war and encouraging soldiers. The sweet tone of the children's voices contrasts with the harshness of the words they utter: 'exterminate', 'hatred' and 'graves', to name a few. The vocabulary used is divisive, but similarities are drawn through film form. In addition to the analogous lines of spoken dialogue, framing is also continuous. A dolly in on each of the children frames the characters in different nations. This camera movement forward, which continues, through editing, even after cuts link France to the United Kingdom and then finally to Germany, brings the children's faces closer and closer to the viewer. In the process, the film strengthens the continuity between the different countries, presenting them almost as one.

The scene with the children, which precedes the film's credits, is a prelude to *Merry Christmas*. Fluidity also characterizes the first shots of the film's actual narrative. The action of *Merry Christmas* begins in Scotland, where church bells announce the war has been declared. Two young men, complaining nothing ever happens in their lives, leave church excited, slamming the door behind them. The wind turns out the flames of the candles that had been illuminating the space of the church, and the camera lingers on the smoke that comes out of them, framing also, just behind the candles, the concerned look of an older priest (Figure 3.4). In the next scene, set in an opera house in Berlin, concern after the announcement of the conflict is also mirrored in the characters' faces. Candles also feature prominently in the scene at the opera, this time as a German singer performs, standing just behind the candles (Figure 3.5). The scene set in Germany ends with a couple hugging, apprehensively reacting to the news about the war. Introducing a new character and moving forward in time, the next scene also begins with an image of a couple embracing – except this time on a picture, as a French captain nostalgically looks at it, in the trenches in France. In addition to presenting the three nations and the protagonists from each of these countries, as well as establishing, through mise en scène and camera work, links between the different story lines, this sequence also mirrors quickly transforming perceptions of the war. In the first few minutes of *Merry Christmas* we move from the enthusiasm of 'something exciting happening' to the horrors of the

Figure 3.4 Transitions in *Merry Christmas*: Candles in Scotland.

Figure 3.5 Transitions in *Merry Christmas*: Candles in Germany.

actual fighting during the war. This is reinforced by the soundtrack, which shifts from cheerful church bells in Scotland and beautiful lyrical singing in Germany to explosions, shouted orders and screams of pain on the battlefield.

Also important for a discussion about the idea of Europe is the fact that *Merry Christmas* is focused on three nations and sets of protagonists, rather than on the two fighting sides. This emphasizes the main theme of the film, that is, the coming together of Europe as a whole. When the ceasefire is called, on Christmas Eve, the three nations are fused through food, music and sport – activities that transcend linguistic and cultural barriers. First, the sound of the bagpipes reaches the German trenches, where a German tenor begins to sing – initially for his comrades, then, emerging from his camp, to the entire frontline. Joining the Scottish and German captains as these negotiate a possible truce, the French officials bring champagne. Hesitantly, groups of troops from all nationalities start to leave the trenches – a movement shown in the first extreme long shot of the film. On the second day of the truce, burying bodies and

Figure 3.6 Burying the dead: Extreme wide shot in *Merry Christmas*.

playing football become common actions (Figure 3.6). In these sequences, there is a predominance of wide shots, which include French, German and Scottish characters working together.

For Winter and Prost (2005: 29), a new history of the First World War has, since the 1990s, shifted from a military focus to social and cultural perspectives, becoming increasingly concerned with 'representations, feelings [and] emotions of men and women'. It has become a history of the intimate, the most moving experiences within a community, where 'memory and identity are inseparable' (27). Remembering the Great War as a European conflict is key to a continent aiming to forge a new, free-from-conflict identity. Equally important is the fact that this relies on the strong presence of individuals, rather than just large abstract groups or masses. With a clearly defined group of main characters at its centre, the film also explores the tension between individual and universal identification. In *Merry Christmas* there is no single protagonist. While the film invests a significant amount of time in personal stories (the German Captain who is married to a French woman; the French Captain who has a newborn son; the Scottish soldier who tries to conceal the death of his brother), it is largely concerned with a much more general humanitarian message.

Merry Christmas establishes new patterns for the heroism of those involved, as it speaks of humanism and compassion rather than egoism and nationalism. Despite this, the film also accentuates the differences between the high ranking officials and the soldiers. *Merry Christmas* aims to rectify history by glorifying the latter (to whom the film is dedicated) rather than the captains, who, conversely, are depicted as cold and brutal figures.[3] However, while the unity of these three nations might take place through a universal language and universal actions, it does not last forever. After two days of common activities, the soldiers return to their trenches and the officers are punished for high treason. The narrative and visual shift reverses: the shots become tighter and smaller in scale, the links between each camp are diffuse.

Carion's film was received by many as a metaphor for the contemporary political situation in Europe (cf. Nesselson 2005: 32). Links can be drawn between the message of *Merry Christmas* and the political attempt to bring the continent closer together, especially during the writing of the Constitutional Treaty. The film's ending, in turn, has resonated with the document's very public failure after referenda in various European nations. This is a typical case of a historical film being received as a film about the time in which it was made – and one with a particular significance for the cinematic vision of Europe. If, as Eric Hobsbawm (1994: 14) has suggested, the First World War marks the beginning of the end of Euro-centrism, the situation depicted in *Merry Christmas* is rightly placed at the historical root of Europe's crisis. However, at the same time as it highlights Europe's historical and contemporary fractures, Carion's film aims to contribute to the healing of such scars. The Great War is understood as a part of European heritage. *Merry Christmas* proposes a new use for this particular heritage: focusing, somewhat counter-intuitively, on the war as a metaphor for peace, the film celebrates it only through episodes that illustrate the interruption of the conflict.

Although *Merry Christmas* tries to recover a positive aspect of the First World War, it is undeniable this was a major period of crisis for Europe and European culture. The questioning of the idea of Europe became only more severe in subsequent years. Europe's decline was probably never as accentuated as during the international conflict that followed, and certain scenes in *Merry Christmas* hint also at the transhistorical message of the film. After the Scottish priest is told he will be sent back to his parish as a punishment for his involvement in the Christmas truce, the sermon for the new soldiers coming to the front is based on a clear order: 'you must kill the Germans, so that it won't have to be done again'. This comment clearly alludes to the Second World War, as does the final sequence, when the *Kronprinz* reprimands the German army, as they sit in a dark train carriage that is ominously reminiscent of Holocaust films.

At the same time as the First World War maintains its place within European history and culture, the trauma of the Second World War and the Holocaust continue to be represented in European film. The majority of films concerned with this topic are set in actual war settings, such as battlefields, destroyed cities and concentration camps. These include *Life Is Beautiful, The Pianist, The Counterfeiters* and *Sorstalansag/Fateless* (Lajos Koltai, 2005), films which narrate stories of Second World War survivors. But another strand of contemporary European films explicitly rethinks the involvement of nations and individuals in the war. In the first decade of the 2000s, a series of films emerged that explored issues such as collaboration and resistance. In doing so, many of these films challenge the notions of history and memory, as well as the official narrative of an integrated European past.

Heroes and anti-heroes: From traitors to saviours

Sophie Scholl is a key cinematic example of the rewriting of the history of the Second World War taking place in contemporary European culture. While the story told by the film had been widely depicted before, seen in conjunction with *Merry Christmas* and *Black Book* – discussed later – *Sophie Scholl* is an important piece of the new European narrative about this conflict emerging on cinema screens. The film depicts the last days of the eponymous heroine, a young female member of the White Rose Resistance group in Nazi Germany. Arrested for distributing flyers with messages against Hitler and the war, Sophie Scholl (here played by Julia Jentsch) was given a death sentence in a rushed trial. The film follows some of the conventions of the biopics analysed earlier. However, it is here examined as a particular kind of biopic: a hero film – or more precisely, heroine. Hence its main character is someone who not only dares to challenge the conventions of society, but who is also willing to risk her life in the name of a better future. While a significant part of *Sophie Scholl* delineates the main character as someone beyond the norm, her actions and the values she represents are not merely, as in *Becoming Jane* and *La Vie en rose*, extraordinary in the sense of being gifted, but are also tied to the notion of heroic sacrifice. The character of Sophie thus follows a tradition in the representation of great historical figures, normally 'Great Men', as embodied, for instance, by Colin Firth in his portrait of George VI in *The King's Speech*.

The first scene of the film shows us a close-up of Sophie and her friend shaking their heads and laughing to a song playing on the radio. Suddenly, the music stops; as they leave the building, the warm colours and lighting of their house is replaced by the grey, under-illuminated and deserted streets of Munich in the Winter of 1943. In the soundtrack, the jazz tune is replaced with more suspenseful music. By opposing the first minutes of the joyful song with the rushed and quiet exit from the house, this first sequence helps to establish one of the main themes of the film: the dual side of Sophie as 'just' a young woman and as someone 'different', a strong and decisive individual. Throughout the film this opposition is frequently explored. When printing flyers with anti-war messages, Sophie is especially brave, quickly offering to help. In the subsequent sequence, however, back at the house, she returns to a more traditionally 'feminine' role, making tea for her brother. Similarly, Sophie's confidence when answering questions during the first interrogation is contrasted with a close-up of her nervous hands under the table. During the second questioning, she asks to go to the bathroom and cries in front of the mirror; but just before leaving, she removes her hairclip and adopts a strong posture. The film's protagonist is initially presented as 'a normal young woman', which makes her sacrifice all the more valuable. The figure of the 'Great Man' is here complicated because of Sophie's gender, but her exceptional bravery sustains her presentation as a 'Great Woman'.

Sophie's extraordinariness is particularly highlighted through a comparison with the strength of her allies and her enemies. Her religious faith (a feature common to many of the members of the White Rose movement) is a fundamental element of her characterization as a hero, and she often prays to God for help. In these scenes, the décor is neutral and the lighting white and diffuse, with the film's mise en scène stressing an ambience of calmness and interior peace. The prison minister comes to see Sophie after she is condemned to the death penalty. They sit as equals on each side of a table inside her cell; they pray together and the minister blesses Sophie in a soft-spoken, soothing voice.

Conversely, the Nazi apparatus appears at its strongest in the court scenes. George F. Custen (1992: 186) has argued that in biopics,

[a] trial often states the issues in balder terms than they could be in another setting; it creates the drama of clearly opposed sides; it allows heroes to address the community with impassioned pleas for whatever it is they hold dear to their hearts.

In this film, Sophie is tried by a brutal judge from Berlin. The judge, taller than everyone else, wears a bright red gown and a matching hat. Never smiling, the judge shouts most of the time, and interrupts every line of dialogue spoken by Sophie or her comrades, in a markedly aggressive, totalitarian tone. Along with his entourage, the judge has been dismissed by a critic in the *Cahiers du Cinéma* as 'Carnival Nazis' (Neyrat 2006: 61). This comment, which suggests Sophie's opponents feel 'fake', echoes a traditional argument that disparages popular cinema because of its lack of realistic pretensions. But this oral and visual excess (even if not entirely 'realistic') is crucial for the reading of the film. It is also a key element in viewer identification, as a shot-reverse-shot sequence of close-ups of Sophie and the judge highlights the courage of *Sophie Scholl*'s protagonist.

The script of *Sophie Scholl* was written after detailed notes of the questioning of the prisoner were found in archives in East Germany. As Paul Cooke (2012: 175) has noted, '[T]he film is not constructed from the actual words spoken by Scholl but rather from the notes taken by the Gestapo during the interrogation'. Yet, the film's positioning is anchored on the 'realist' approach to the story it tells. The film begins with an inter-title, which informs the viewer that it 'is based on historical facts, as yet unpublished transcripts and new interviews with witnesses'. Jacques Le Goff (1992: xvii) has noted how scholarship throughout the twentieth century has criticized both 'the notion of historical fact (which is not a given object, because it is constructed by the historian)' and 'the notion of a document'. The 'factual' origin of *Sophie Scholl* is all the more interesting as the authenticity of historical accounts and the validity of historical facts and documents are increasingly challenged in a postmodern society dismissive of grand narratives. Even though these aren't actual transcripts, notes are seen to suffice; the film's positioning as a historical film 'based on real facts' gives it credibility with critics and simultaneously contributes to popular interest. *Sophie Scholl* was screened at the Berlin Film Festival, where it won a Silver Bear for Best Director and Best Actress, as well as the Prize of the Ecumenical Jury – an award created by Christian film professionals. Watched by one million viewers in Germany, the film was nominated for an Oscar as Best Foreign Language Film in 2005. Its popular character can be inferred from multiple Audience Awards for Best Director and Best Actress, for instance, at the European Film Awards and at the 2005 German Film Awards Ceremony, where it was also named, by the public, German Film of the Year.

As in *Merry Christmas*, elements of transhistoricity can be identified in *Sophie Scholl* – for instance, in the court scene, when Sophie claims that in future it will be the Nazi officials who will be judged (a future that was, as the spectator knows, to happen). This is a historical film concerned with the inheritance national heroes might leave to contemporary European culture. In a statement in the interior leaflet of the ICA DVD edition of the film in the United Kingdom, Marc Rothemund, director of *Sophie Scholl*, stated he wanted to confront young people with Sophie's bravery, exploring the notion of injustice. The German director has argued vehemently that, despite representing a historical event, he was interested in the contemporary understanding of such concepts, that is, bravery and injustice. After its premiere, the film was screened in a large number of schools in Germany and the director went on a national tour, participating in Q&A sessions that underline *Sophie Scholl's* pedagogic slant. As in the heritage films examined earlier, knowledge is an important part of the appeal of historical representations. The found documents the film is based on add to its educational credentials. But this factual 'knowledge', as in the films analysed earlier, is framed in a poignant tone, which allows viewers to engage with what is being said not just in intellectual terms.

In its attention to an individual and emotional memory of Nazi Germany, *Sophie Scholl* can also be seen to work within dominant trends in the historiography of the Second World War. Peckham's (2003: 206) study of heritage notes 'attitudes to history and memory are changing within the context of a new "moral politics", where the emphasis is on testimony, trauma and restitution'. As he goes on to suggest, 'the unknown soldier dies so the nation can live on. Here, loss is reinscribed with a positive meaning as "sacrifice"' (207). The idea of personal sacrifice is central to *Sophie Scholl*, as the main character suffers for her elder parents, and, in an attempt to spare the lives of her friends, tries at all costs to take the blame for the accusations thrown at her. Sophie sacrifices her life in the name of higher values that are not limited to the nation, but it is important to first consider the film's German identity.

German wartime suffering is a ubiquitous topic in contemporary Germany (see, for instance, Taberner and Cooke 2006). Such interest is confirmed by a rising number of films on this theme, including the hugely successful *Der Untergang/Downfall* (Oliver Hirschbiegel, 2004) and the critically acclaimed *Phoenix* (Christian Petzold, 2014). Occupying a central place in Germany's culture, this is a very specific aspect of the memory of the Nazi period. Helmut Schmitz (2007), for instance, describes an opposition between an institutionalized public memory centred on Nazi crimes and a private and personal memory that has been underpinned by notions of suffering, hardship and heroism. For him, not only is there a return to the memory of Nazi Germany, but also private memory seems to substitute or complement the memory of the perpetration of Nazi crimes, that is, the more public, as well as political, memory. As Schmitz notes, in addition to a more general discourse of pro-Germany rehabilitation, 'this renewed interest in family legacies coincides with a significant shift both in historiographical and popular discourse from a history of "hard" facts to "story", human interest and emotionalization' (5). *Sophie Scholl* is a prime example of this shift, considering especially its factual background – and the fact that this link to historical documents is very clearly stated at the start of the film. Nevertheless, the film creates a fictional narrative that is certainly centred on human emotion. In doing so, *Sophie Scholl* also gains wider international appeal.

Taking *Sophie Scholl*, as the director intended, as a film not specifically about the Second World War, but about the wider notion of injustice, means also placing it in a universal sphere – an idea very much in tune with the European filmic sensibility the EU supports. In fact, there is, in addition to its German character, an important European dimension to *Sophie Scholl*. The Second World War and the Holocaust in particular is one of the most significant traumas that constitute the self-understanding narrative of Europe and European cinema (Elsaesser 2015).

Thus, despite being told in German and set in a German context, *Sophie Scholl* belongs to a wider set of chronicles that narrate the struggle against fascist regimes. These can be found in films from many other European nations, including the Portuguese *Capitães de Abril/Captains of April* (Maria de Medeiros, 2000), the Spanish *El laberinto del fauno/Pan's Labyrinth* (Guillermo del Toro, 2006) and *Las 13 Rosas/13 Roses* (Emilio Martínez Lázaro, 2007), as well as the French *L'Armée du crime/Army of Crime* (Robert Guédiguian, 2009). All of these films present single or groups of heroes, with their protagonists being depicted as 'extraordinary' because they first emerge as someone 'just like us', but then embark on a journey of exceptional strength. Their narratives enact the classical dilemma faced by those fighting oppression, that is, whether to privilege personal safety or integrity, or indeed to sacrifice oneself.

In *Sophie Scholl*, Sophie speaks in court of a 'new international Europe' and bases her argument against the judge on universal beliefs such as human rights and freedom. White Rose leaflets, as referenced in the film, often referred to Anti-Nazi group *Europäische Union* (literally, European Union), which stood for a democratic and united Europe. By focusing on these values, we can identify in *Sophie Scholl* a move from a national to a universal focus, as also happens in *Merry Christmas*. The film tells a national story and is centred on a national figure but speaks of timeless values that underline its international, and in particular, European, scope. Through this film – also present in the 2007 MEDIA 'clips' – Sophie Scholl becomes an important figure in the European history of the Second World War.

Conflict emerges, in *Sophie Scholl* and in *Merry Christmas*, as the ideal backdrop against which to analyse the humane character of heroes and historical figures. In these films, as in the MEDIA 'clips' examined in Chapter 2, emotions guarantee the simultaneous Europeanness and universality of the stories portrayed. Significantly, the transnational appeal of these films is also justified by a focus on positive emotions – the ones that more easily allow for viewer identification. However, other perspectives on human behaviour during war, and more specifically on the European past, have emerged in contemporary European cinema. Of the films released with MEDIA support in recent years, *Black Book* is another crucial example of how the history of the Second World War is being transformed, albeit in a very different way to *Merry Christmas* and *Sophie Scholl*. Against hopeful messages about peace, humanism and the praise of heroes, *Black Book* brings to the fore the darkest emotions that link the idea of Europe with the continent's past.

Black Book tells the story of Rachel Stein/Ellis de Vries (Carice van Houten), a Jewish singer who joins the Resistance after seeing her family killed by SS officials when trying to escape Nazi-occupied Holland. The script, co-written by Gerard Soeteman and Paul

Verhoeven (who also directed the film), was developed for over two decades. It stems from historical sources, as well as from both men's memories of the war. Although key episodes in the film tell us about the brutality of the Nazi regime and the bravery of those fighting it, the key issue here is neither sacrifice nor extraordinary individuality. Throughout the film, a series of protest actions organized by the Resistance turn out to be traps; *Black Book* is a film about betrayal, where all characters are seen as heroes and then traitors at some point in the narrative. The constant failed missions, as well as the recurring episodes of suspicion within the group of fighters, also move the narrative forward, as the Resistance struggles to continue their work in increasingly more challenging conditions. *Black Book* is a thriller that uses the Second World War almost exclusively as a background, rather than an important element of its story. Yet, because of its original take on the conflict, this is a particularly useful case study to examine cinematic rewritings of Europe and war, as well as the connection between history, memory and European film.

Although, unlike many Second World War films, not set in the battlefield, but mostly shot in a city, *Black Book* uses a remarkable number of action sequences. This focus on action (with the first big explosion taking place within the first seven minutes of the film) has been associated with Paul Verhoeven's career in the United States, where he directed the action blockbusters *RoboCop* (1987), *Total Recall* (1990) and *Starship Troopers* (1997), among other box-office hits. The most expensive Dutch film at the time of its release (with an estimated budget of €18 million), *Black Book* was nominated for a number of awards in Europe but none in the United States, where it nevertheless grossed $4 million.

Black Book places a strong emphasis on spectacle, and not only in action sequences. The film follows the conventions of the heritage genre, using lavish visual and musical period details, which are particularly evident in the scenes taking place inside the SS headquarters. The Führer's birthday is a key example of the highly constructed scenes present in *Black Book* – in terms of its timing, which perfectly matches the music, of the complex camera movements, including long overhead shots, as well as the large number of extras present (Figure 3.7). This is, visually and musically, a very ebullient scene, which thus appears in contrast with the historical period the film revives.

Black Book has not only been read as a heritage film; it has also been disparaged as a heritage film. The period costumes and décor, as well as the captivating music, seem to mask the suspicious overtone of the film, not to mention ignore its dark historical setting. Critics have argued the film's attention to mise en scène leaves only space for the viewer to admire its pictorial construction. For James Naremore (2008: 58), for instance, the director's use of music and his handling of action are 'so entertaining that some viewers might not notice the film's underlying seriousness'. Naremore's point echoes the traditional opposition between spectacle and gravitas that characterizes debates about European heritage cinema, as if the presence of one invalidates the exploration of the other. However, as I have been arguing in relation to other European heritage films, *Black Book*'s entertaining or even 'pretty' status does not make it less important for a discussion about heroes and anti-heroes during the Second World War.

Figure 3.7 The Führer's birthday party: Ellis sings in *Black Book*.

The idea that *Black Book* might, for better or worse, work as a historical document has been addressed by Verhoeven himself. As he claimed in an interview:

> I feel it's a great story – and terrible too. On the other hand, I did feel some obligation to bring in young audiences and that it was necessary to use some device – a thriller or detective element – to keep them there with the 'lesson' and all the period stuff. (Cited in Williams 2007: 19)

Whereas *Sophie Scholl*, which catered particularly for younger audiences, speaks of the timeless notion of injustice, *Black Book* is chiefly concerned with the possibilities afforded by the historical period it represents in terms of visual and narrative spectacle.

Although the message of the film has also been read as up to date – connections to the Iraq War and to terrorism were also made by the director (cited in Naremore 2008: 58) – *Black Book*'s most striking and commented upon plot line is related to the film's view of Anti-Nazi Resistance. For one critic *Black Book* is about a 'dizzyingly complex world [in which] Nazis can be handsome and decent, and the Resistance's drab warriors corrupt' (Nathan 2007: 46). Such a contentious argument underpins the film's plot. As the director has claimed: 'I don't believe in this separation – the Nazis are all villains and the Dutch all heroes. The whole story is revisionism. So I had to revise the revisionism and tell people what the reality was' (cited in Williams 2007: 20). While Verhoeven's attitude was seen as challenging and part of his provocative enfant terrible persona, this must not be taken as the only reason for *Black Book*'s revisionism.

Historians have also examined the evolution of the collective memory of the Resistance in Europe. In the post-war years, the general assumption was that everyone had been part of it, and that whereas resisters were 'right and romantic', collaborators were 'wrong and repulsive'. In order to go beyond a blind glorification of Anti-Nazi Resistance and shed some clarity on this issue, Rab Bennett (1999: 32), for instance, suggests it is important 'to distinguish much more clearly between the principle of Resistance and the practice of Resistance'. *Black Book* is in line with the cultural challenging of memories of the Second World War, but it is precisely this distinction that the film seems to overlook. Doubts and dilemmas define the heroes of many other Resistance films (including *Sophie Scholl*), but this is taken further in *Black Book*. Here, one of the characters questions what takes place, confessing: 'I killed someone ... I'm just as bad as the Nazis'. The ongoing suspicion that surrounds the film's main characters means there are no opponents against which they can be defined as heroes – everyone is potentially good, everyone is potentially bad. The multiple twists in Verhoeven's film (which show the transformation of 'good guys' into 'bad guys') belittle the Resistance, but the fact that some of its members help the central female character Ellis get revenge towards the end of the film (some 'good guys' were actually fighting for the 'right' side all along) might just save the movement.

By questioning the value and morality of the Resistance, *Black Book* potentially undermines the chances of Europe to leave behind the Second World War and the Holocaust as dark passages of its shared history. The film seems to destroy any positive view of the Resistance without voicing a counter-message of hope or possible political change. In this respect it belongs to a growing band of European films adopting negative or at least ambiguous views of the Resistance, including Jacques Audiard's *Un héros très discret/A Self-Made Hero* (1996). But regardless of its dubious politics, *Black Book* raises important questions about what should be included in and left out of the official history of European nations, as well as, significantly, of Europe as a whole. At the same time as the film offers an unconventional reading of the past, *Black Book* raises questions about how this past is told – a trend that, as we will see, emerges also in films narrating episodes in the more recent history of the continent. The issue here is not only what versions of Europe's history can and should be told in the public sphere, but also how memory in general and histories from the war in particular are used in the increasingly widening narrative of European heritage.

Merry Christmas, Sophie Scholl and *Black Book* simultaneously adopt classical narrative structures, ending on moralistic tones, and revisit on behalf of public memory events that history has disregarded or tried to hide, offering new readings of the past. Whereas *Girl with a Pearl Earring, Becoming Jane* and *La Vie en rose* work towards a promotion of Europe, celebrating (and, to a certain extent, commodifying, for touristic consumption) its artistic glories, *Merry Christmas, Sophie Scholl* and *Black Book* are concerned with deconstructing dominant versions of Europe's history. These films are evidence of a renewed interest in the past and its connection to European culture, but illustrate the need Europe has felt in recent years to deny or define itself against parts of its history. As such, they are also examples of instances in which the past becomes an 'other' (Chapter 1).

These three war films can be seen as key contributions to the new European history of the First and the Second World Wars. *Merry Christmas*'s focus on cultural representations of the war, *Sophie Scholl*'s exploration of trauma and sacrifice and *Black Book*'s rereading of the Resistance are in line with recent historiographies of these conflicts. Centred on ordinary soldiers, on personal stories and at the same time on emotions and universal values, the message of *Merry Christmas*, especially when one considers the First World War as a European civil war, is utterly positive. A similar move can be identified in *Sophie Scholl*, where the shift from nation to humanism is evident, as Sophie sacrifices herself not only for Germany but also for universal beliefs. Such beliefs can furthermore be seen to contribute to the pedagogic tone of the film, in a similar vein to *Becoming Jane* (not least because it is also a biopic), given that the protagonist is seen as a role model for future generations. But whereas *Sophie Scholl* presents the thesis of the heroic paradigm so in vogue in contemporary culture, *Black Book* offers its antithesis, alerting us to the fact that even heroes can be questionable.

Knowledge and emotion coexist in *Merry Christmas, Sophie Scholl* and *Black Book*. These are films that tell viewers about Europe's history, at the same time as they engage audiences in visually appealing representations of the past. A focus on individual stories is the sine qua non for these films' appeal, as well as universality: it is because the extraordinary (in positive and negative terms) historical figures depicted on screen start by being presented as people 'just like us' that the films analysed here potentially resonate with audiences across Europe and the globe. The depiction of war as a human conflict (not so much a diplomatic, or even a military one) highlights a Europe of extremes, as well as the best (young Sophie as a heroin) and the worst (collaborators in Nazi-occupied Holland) of its history. Seeing the First World War as a European civil war has implications for a reading of the twentieth century. This becomes a period of conflict, characterized by a European crisis that spreads to the military, the political and the cultural domains – a crisis the EU founding fathers attempted to address.

Merry Christmas, Sophie Scholl and *Black Book* show also that commemoration and questioning are not necessarily opposites. Seen together, these films highlight the difficulties Europe had to surmount to become an entity (especially *Black Book*), but also the integrationist impetus that has characterized key episodes in its past (the truce in *Merry Christmas*, Sophie's sacrifice in *Sophie Scholl*). By stressing the traumas (as well as the values necessary to overcome them) that have triggered European reunification, they tell important tales for the narrative of Europe's integration process.

Across the continent, film-makers have also looked at more recent moments in European history. Contemporary European films set in the final decades of the twentieth century take the notion of deconstruction best illustrated until now by *Black Book* one step further. Bringing doubt and self-reflexivity to the fore, films such as *Good Morning, Night*, *Good Bye Lenin!* and *12:08 East of Bucharest* propose innovative histories of European nations, embedding new memories in their fictional plots. This questioning of history also takes place through an investigation of the role of the media, especially television, in the representation, as well as construction, of Europe's past.

Alternative histories: Fantasy in post-war Europe

In films depicting the more recent history of the continent, Europe is also framed as a political construct. In addition to a new wave of committed and politically engaged filmmaking that has resurfaced in recent years – gaining new momentum after the euro-zone crisis of 2009 and the harsh austerity measures that were implemented as a consequence in a number of southern European countries – many films thematically explore the political turbulence the continent has experienced since the post-war era. Released through MEDIA distribution schemes, films such as *The Dreamers*, which describes the events of May 1968 in Paris through the eyes of a young American, and *4 luni, 3 saptamâni si 2 zile/4 Months, 3 Weeks, 2 Days* (Cristian Mungiu, 2007), which looks at Romania under the Ceauşescu regime, are part of this trend. The distinction between Left and Right, the threat of terrorism and concerns about state security, as well as the legacy of totalitarian regimes, are key issues, albeit not exclusively, in contemporary Europe. By making these issues visible, and questioning their belonging to a shared European heritage or inheritance, the films examined here offer yet another perspective about the link between past and present, as well as this connection's relevance for the meaning of the idea of Europe.

Italian cinema constitutes a particularly fruitful case study of European film's engagement with politics. While in Italy this engagement dates back to at least the neorealist movement, politics has been a central theme for many films produced in the country in the twenty-first century. Examples include *The Best of Youth, Mio fratello è figlio unico/My Brother Is an Only Child* (Daniele Luchetti, 2007) and *Il Divo* – films featured, for instance, in the May 2010 issue of *Sight and Sound*, which was especially dedicated to the new Italian political cinema.

Good Morning, Night, also an Italian film and featuring in the MEDIA 'clips', is another key example of the cinematic treatment this topic has received. The film is also particularly useful for my discussion as it continues the questioning of history introduced by *Black Book* and pushes it further by representing an alternative version of history on screen. At the same time, it offers fundamental insight into the tension between Europe and the nation, as well as the definition of European cinema. As an auteurist, self-reflexive film, *Good Morning, Night* calls attention to the way in which the film's narrative is constructed. For example, the title is matched, within the film, by the title of a screenplay written by one of the characters. Crucial here is the distinction between fiction and reality, as well as the attention given to the different layers that compose the film's narrative.

Good Morning, Night narrates the kidnapping of Aldo Moro (Roberto Herlitzka) by the Marxist-Leninist revolutionary group *Brigate Rosse* (the Red Brigades) in 1978. Other recent European films have approached the issue of terrorism, including *Tiro en la Cabeza/Bullet in the Head* (Jaime Rosales, 2008) and *GAL* (Miguel Courtois, 2006), about the Basque separatist group ETA, in Spain; *Hunger* (Steve McQueen 2008), about the IRA, in Ireland; and *The Baader Meinhof Complex* (Uli Edel, 2008), about the left-wing German terrorist group of the 1970s. Such a wide number of titles testify to the rising trend in contemporary European cinema of depicting and exploring not only the recent past and terrorism in particular, but also the role and limitations of the state in many nations across the continent.

Aldo Moro was an Italian politician who served as Italy's prime minister between 1963 and 1968 and between 1974 and 1976. At the time of his kidnapping, he was the leader of Democrazia Cristiana (the Christian Democratic Party), and he was conducting negotiations with the Communist Party for democratic and parliamentary stability in the country. Directed by Marco Bellocchio, *Good Morning, Night* originates from a commission by RAI (the national Italian television). It commemorates the twenty-fifth anniversary of the 'Moro affair', a defining event in Italy's recent history and the subject of many films. Loosely based on the book *Il prigioniero* (1988), the memoir of Anna Laura Braghetti, one of the *brigadisti*, the film is centred on the figure of Chiara (Maya Sansa), the only woman in the group of four people responsible for the kidnapping and assassination of Moro.

Premiered at the Venice Film Festival, *Good Morning, Night* was well received by Italian and international critics. The press coverage, in Italy and abroad, noted the long-standing ovation Marco Bellocchio received at the festival and the excitement around the film (see, for instance, Retico 2003 and Guider 2003). However, *Good Morning, Night* failed to win the Golden Lion – awarded instead to the Russian *Vozvrashchenie/ The Return* (Andrei Zvyagintsev, 2003). As such, it became, as Marijke De Valck (2007) suggests, the official 'loser' of the festival. De Valck attributes this loss to the film's political content and to the influence of the Berlusconi government at the time (148). But *Good Morning, Night* was equally criticized by the Left (for presenting the Red Brigades as a naïve movement, detached from reality) and the Right (for whom it adopts a humane position on 'terrorists'). The polemics generated at the Venice festival were not so much about the film's politics; rather, they focused on its national character, with cast and crew regretting the opportunity to receive an award for an Italian film in Italy's most important film festival (Anon, *La Stampa*, 7 September 2003).

Released on 163 screens across Italy, *Good Morning, Night* was seen by six hundred thousand viewers, becoming the third most watched film in the country in the week of its premiere. Conversely, although exhibited in more than twenty countries around the world (but mostly in film festivals), the film was not particularly successful with international audiences. *Good Morning, Night* received the FIPRESCI prize in the 2003 edition of the European Film Awards, but remained mostly a national hit. The film's limited international success may be partly due to a lack of contextual information. In *Good Morning, Night*, politics are not explicit, and the narration is subverted by art cinema conventions; the film might appeal to international audiences on a stylistic level – which accounts for its presence in such a large number of film festivals – but it remains ultimately abstract for viewers unfamiliar with the political events depicted. Examining this as a European film thus means considering not only *Good Morning, Night*'s views on the Moro affair, but also the way in which these views are communicated.

Good Morning, Night begins with a tracking shot in a dark space. The empty property we see is where most of the action of the film takes place: the flat rented by members of the Red Brigades to hide Aldo Moro. Throughout the film, sound is crucial to guide the narrative. On the day of Moro's kidnapping, Chiara keeps busy with domestic tasks. Alone at home, she hears a helicopter and immediately turns on the television zapping through channels until she finds a special news bulletin. The Red Brigades operation was successful: Aldo Moro has been kidnapped. From this moment onwards, the television is permanently on. The presence of television becomes a sign of the 'realistic' historical construction the film adopts, since, as Alan O'Leary (2008: 37) notes, the Moro affair was 'the first example of round-the-clock news reporting in the Italian context'.

The centrality of television in the representation of historical events is an international phenomenon that has been spreading across Europe and the world since the 1960s, with implications for the way collective memory is built. As Elsaesser (1996: 146) has noted:

> 'Do you remember the day Kennedy was shot?' really means 'Do you remember the day you watched Kennedy being shot all day on television?' No longer is storytelling the culture's meaning-making response; an activity closer to therapeutic practice has taken over, with acts of re-telling, re-membering, and repeating all pointing in the direction of obsession, fantasy, trauma.

The Moro affair became a national trauma, but despite the whole affair having become a screen memory, the kidnapping itself was, of course, not broadcast. The absence of these images (with the exception of footage of the bodies of Moro's bodyguards, assassinated during the kidnapping) was compensated in the television coverage by maps, reconstitutions, reactions and comments. The obsessive and traumatic quality (to refer to Elsaesser's terms) of this event was thus paradoxically built not so much visually, but through narration and imagination.

Adopting a similar strategy to that of the national television coverage, Bellocchio's film mixes archive images of the days that followed Moro's kidnapping with fictional representations. The film also makes an original use of music, editing together popular tunes such as Pink Floyd's 'Shine on You Crazy Diamond' and classical pieces, from an excerpt of Verdi's 'Aida' to Schubert's 'Momento Musicale Op. 94 no.3'. The images produced by Bellocchio recreate what was absent from the news, at the same time as the presence of music adds new meaning to both the fictional and the archival images. For instance, high-pitched, eerie music is used in scenes of heightened drama to intensify emotion, as when Chiara watches the news and learns Moro has been kidnapped, or when she sees him in the flat for the first time.

As a film that dramatizes a well-known historical event, combining new and archival footage, *Good Morning, Night* is defined by the conjunction of fantasy and realism. Imagination is also a key narrative device. Inside the flat, Chiara is constantly looking through the hole in the door to Moro's hiding compartment, claiming: 'I must see him to reassure myself it's not just a dream'. Images from her 'actual' dreams are also part of the film, and these include footage of Stalin's Russia and a scene from Rossellini's *Paisà* (1946). As the narrative progresses, fantasy takes prominence. Hence, to the sound of the same ominous tune, used before to underline emotion, we see Moro walking around the flat at night – most likely an image formed only in Chiara's mind.

Equally, Chiara's hesitations towards being part of a plan to murder a man become gradually more central. Conscious of the nature of televised historical events, Moro pleads with the *brigadisti* to save his life, arguing: 'When television shows my dead body, people won't be able to understand [your actions]; they'll hate you!' Acting

Figure 3.8 Fantasy in *Good Morning, Night*: Aldo Moro walking free in the streets of Rome.

accordingly, as her *compagni* decide the assassination must take place that evening, Chiara pours sleeping pills into the dinner plates and warns the prisoner not to eat. Her imagination takes over the 'realistic' depiction of the events, and we see how, before starting to eat, the *brigadisti* make the sign of the cross. This brief shot is presented in slow motion and Pink Floyd's music underlines its dream-like essence. After this, Chiara unlocks the door of Moro's hiding place, allowing him to leave the house while everyone else is asleep (Figure 3.8).

By filming Moro's (imaginary) release, *Good Morning, Night* launches a debate about a new historical possibility, asking: where would Italy be today if Moro had not been killed? The film does not suggest what would have happened if the 'Moro affair' had had a dissimilar outcome. Yet, things would of course have been different. Running parallel to the 'true' narrative, the world of fiction thus creates new possibilities for Italian history. *Good Morning, Night* raises important questions about this crucial event in Italy's history also by reminding us that Chiara's 'dream' was not what really happened. After showing Moro walking on the streets of Rome, the film cuts to the three *brigadisti* who take him out of the flat, blindfolded (Figure 3.9).

The sequence of Moro walking free in Rome and that of the prisoner being moved from the flat are shot in a similar way. Nothing in the film style alerts the viewer to the distinction between (historical) fiction and reality, which is especially important for audiences unfamiliar with the 'story', that is, the Moro affair. The fact that the two narrative lines are edited side by side suggests fantasy and reality are equally important for film history. And if that is the case, all historical accounts can potentially be questioned. Have key moments, for instance, been left out? How much of the story told here, and of history more generally, is actually fantasy? Such questioning, which had

Figure 3.9 Reality in *Good Morning, Night*: Aldo Moro blindfolded by the Red Brigades.

already emerged in *Black Book*, appears with particular strength in films representing Europe's contemporary history, especially because this history, as indicated earlier, is almost always depicted not so much on film, but on television.

Good Morning, Night often integrates television footage into the film's narrative. At the start of the film, when, after hearing an helicopter above her building, Chiara goes in the backyard, she looks up and the film cuts to footage of a helicopter in the sky (as if this was a subjective shot from her point of view). Later, a 'reconstruction' of Pope Paul VI reading a letter from Moro is followed in *Good Morning, Night* by television archival footage of the Pope reading a statement in St. Peter's Square pleading for the prisoner's release. Similarly, after showing Moro, blindfolded and with the *brigadisti*, the film cuts to archive footage of the real Aldo Moro's state funeral, over which is read: 'Aldo Moro was assassinated 9 May 1978'. The text explains to the viewer that the entire Italian political class was at the ceremony, despite the absence of Moro's body, as the family chose to have a private funeral. The 'true' story is told through Bellocchio's words, but the images are not his, while those by the director tell a different tale.

Television images differ from the film's composition, especially because of the difference in tone and grain. Whereas Bellocchio's two versions of the film's ending (one 'real', one 'fictional') are stylistically very similar, briefly suspending the narrative (they prompt the viewer to question if Moro was, or was not, released), archival images of Moro's funeral, although visually very different, move the narrative forward. *Good Morning, Night* thus seems to highlight cinema's inability to compete with the realistic images produced and screened by television: fantasy emerges only in the narrative strand depicted by film. By underlining the extent to which historical events are mediated, the film nevertheless raises questions about the true character of television – Moro's funeral was partly in itself a fantasy, as the politician's body, not to mention his family, were absent.

Form and content are deeply intertwined in *Good Morning, Night*. On the one hand, the film highlights the importance of Europe's recent past for the construction of a shared, collective history. Significantly, this is a political past: Europe is, especially as understood here in relation to the EU, also an institutional idea; it is defined through rules, tensions and lengthy negotiation processes. On the other, *Good Morning, Night* questions the potential use of this political inheritance, by asking whether a difficult past can be validly integrated into Europe's historical narrative. This is especially significant since this recent history is inherently mediated; Europe's history seems to only exist when 'used' by television – and this use is political in itself too, as it inevitably makes a choice about what is shown and what is left out. From a celebration of European glories, artistic and otherwise, to the important remembering of the war (if only by negation, as the antonym of peace), we are faced with a European history apparently nationally specific in content, but significant across the continent at least in form.

A similar tension can be found in *Good Bye Lenin!* Not an art film but a popular comedy, the film offers a different vision to the one put forward by *Good Morning, Night* about the role played by television in historical (re)constructions. This German film is another crucial example of the way in which contemporary European cinema operates a rewriting of history, asking questions about the nature, legitimacy and authenticity of heritage, as well as the role of individual and (tele)visual memory in the process of remembering. Taking place just before and after the fall of the Berlin Wall in 1989, the story of *Good Bye Lenin!* concerns a young man, Alex (Daniel Brühl), who tries to conceal from his sick mother Christiane (Katrin Sass) that the frontiers of the German Democratic Republic (GDR) are open and that the communist government has fallen. A large number of films have since the 1990s addressed related issues, including, among the films released with MEDIA support, *The Lives of Others*, about a Stasi officer monitoring East Berlin, and *Barbara* (Christian Petzold, 2012), about a doctor who, after requesting to leave East Germany, is put under surveillance by the GDR secret police. Both *Good Bye Lenin!* and *The Lives of Others* have been extensively discussed by German film scholars (see, for instance, Cooke 2012). But despite being a comedy told against a national background, *Good Bye Lenin!* is also relevant for the discussion about Europe and cinema. The film's main event, the fall of the Berlin Wall, can be read in the general context of perestroika, and its consequences observed throughout Central and Eastern Europe. It is also particularly significant in the history of European integration: the European Commission made the celebration of the twenty-fifth anniversary of the Fall of the Berlin Wall a priority of the 'Europe for citizens' programme in 2014. Finally, *Good Bye Lenin!* is an interesting case study for the discussion of Europe in European cinema as a 'quality' popular film that rethinks the status and validity of history.

Good Bye Lenin! is one of the films policy officers at the European Commission cited as an example of a successful MEDIA film during the interviews I conducted in Brussels in 2009. The film also has a prominent presence in the 2007 MEDIA 'clips'. While its topic is central to the formation of Europe, *Good Bye Lenin!* is in line with the official discourse of the EU not only in terms of its plot, but also its production

context: it is a primary example of the 'quality film', combining elements of both popular and artistic cinematic traditions. *Good Bye Lenin!* was produced by the German
company X-Filme Creative Pool – a company that was formed to make popular 'smart'
films, characterized both by their quality and their mainstream appeal (Chapter 2).
The fact that the film was co-produced by the Franco-German cultural television channel Arte brings it closer to art cinema conventions, but with the presence of Eastern
German star Katrin Sass, even if not known to international audiences (Cockrell
2003: 42), and having launched Daniel Brühl as a European 'Shooting Star', *Good Bye
Lenin!* was primarily marketed as a popular comedy.

The film was seen by six million viewers in Germany and released in over thirty countries around the world. It was also successful with critics, winning a significant number
of awards at home and across Europe. Adding to eight German Film Awards, *Good Bye
Lenin!* was particularly successful at the 2004 European Film Awards ceremony, receiving an Audience Award, as well as Best Film, Best Actor and Best Screenplay prizes.
Randal Halle (2006: 256) noted 'the reviewers of *Good Bye Lenin!* repeatedly reassured
potential viewers that, although it might be hard to believe, this German film really
was funny!' The stress on genre rather than on language and nationality contributed
to *Good Bye Lenin!* being globally promoted not so much as a 'German' film, but more
as a 'universal' comedy. This is, for instance, the strategy adopted by the Pathé!/20th
Century Fox DVD edition released in the United Kingdom, and which features, on
the cover, the slogan 'funny, moving, charming and original'. The film's title has also
remained the same – in 'international' English across borders.

One way in which the film steers away from the national is by giving prominence
to the family strand of its narrative, which is here projected as a universal plot line. For
instance, *Good Bye Lenin!* was praised in *Variety* as 'the moving story of a son's uncon-
ditional love for his mother' (Cockrell 2003: 42). In one of the key sequences of the
film, afraid his mother will not recover from the shock of learning about the dramatic
changes Germany has undergone, Alex decides to bring her home from the hospital.
He forbids his sister Ariane (Maria Simon) to mention her new job at Burger King and
replaces the new (Westernized) furniture with the old one. It is through this cover-up
that *Good Bye Lenin!*'s plot develops, but while at first Alex's plan of absolute reclusion
seems to be working, outside the room the world has kept spinning. Although there is,
in *Good Bye Lenin!*, a clear parallel history, this is only plausible in the restricted environment of the mother's room. As in *Good Morning, Night*, where alternative versions
of history seem to inhabit only Chiara's mind, in *Good Bye Lenin!* fantasy is similarly
contained, in this case within the space of the mother's bedroom.

In a subsequent sequence, Christiane asks Alex to set the television in her room
(Figure 3.10). This presents a problem for Alex's narrative. However, it does not come
as a surprise, since television had been constantly present in *Good Bye Lenin!* The actual
first shot of the film, for instance, was of a television showing the cosmonaut Sigmund
Jähn. Television also literally contributes to German unification, bringing Eastern and
Western workers together, and showing how, through their efforts (installing new aeri-
als), the two nations gather to watch West Germany's performance in the 1990 FIFA
World Cup. The request for a television amplifies the space of Christiane's bedroom,

Figure 3.10 *Good Bye Lenin!*: The television in Christiane's room.

but what is seen by Alex as an inconvenience is soon demonstrated by his new work partner Denis (Florian Lukas), from West Berlin, to also be the solution. Television and the images it broadcasts are in *Good Morning, Night* a guarantor of realism. But in *Good Bye Lenin!* when controlled, television images allow for a creative reconstruction of past and present. From Alex's point of view, who is in turn considering his mother's perspective, television can be 'more authentic' than the real world outside.

Relying on his friend's editing skills, as well as on Denis's collection of old GDR television programmes, Alex initiates a funny, albeit not very credible, rewriting of German history. He shows Christiane previously transmitted news and shows, also being forced to create 'new' content. For instance, during Christiane's birthday party, a Coca-Cola banner is placed on a building in front of her window. Looking for a convincing (in his mother's eyes) explanation for this, Alex and Denis prepare a 'journalistic' piece, which informs the citizens of the GDR that Coca-Cola is in fact an Eastern recipe stolen by Western capitalists. Filming outside the Coca-Cola factory, Alex concludes: 'I realized that truth was a rather dubious concept'.

While Alex's truism is not particularly surprising in a film that operates a self-conscious rewriting of history, it can also be related to the overwhelming presence of television. Discussing what he calls a 'new memory', Andrew Hoskins (2004) has looked at the extent to which media, and television in particular, fabricate the past. As he argues, 'fundamental to the process of both individual and collective memories is that they are increasingly mediated. In this way our understanding of the past is "manufactured" rather than remembered' (336). This is particularly relevant for *Good Bye Lenin!*, a film where history can be manipulated only because it had previously been, and is once again, mediated: it is only through video (Alex and Denis' new recordings) and television (especially Denis' archive) that this particular German past can be re-created.

In *Good Bye Lenin!*, the distinction between 'real' and 'fake' is also importantly about time, and this has implications for the way in which history is told and perceived. In *Good Morning, Night*, television shared with Bellocchio's images, including the ones depicting the 'fantasy' strand, the same temporal sphere. But in *Good Bye Lenin!* the programmes showed to Christiane, at least the 'authentic' ones, are old – and Alex, as well as the spectator, are aware of this. The film's main humorous sequences thus rely not only on the East/West divide, but also on a past (East)/present (West) divide. In the first half of the film, the representation of the West is mostly positive (Ariane finds a job, Denis solves Alex's problems). However, *Good Bye Lenin!* also narrates Alex's disappointment with the new Germany and its politics of openness. Realizing that the process for German reunification is evolving too quickly, Alex soon rejects this new lifestyle. After his mother is released from the hospital, Alex's view of Western customs is ironic, when not dismissive. He despises Ariane and Rainer's (Alexander Beyer) belly dancing as a shallow interest for the 'Orient' (a Westerner 'fashion'). Coca-Cola trucks driving through the city and covering, in the frame, the traditional change of guard are, for Alex, a 'relentless victory of capitalism'. At first motivated by the narrative, and more specifically his mother's wish to watch television, Alex later deliberately brings the past into the present, because he wishes everything was more like before. Through this overlapping of both time frames, the film also becomes nostalgic.

Disparaging critiques of *Good Bye Lenin!* focused precisely on the extent to which such passionate feelings for the nation as it was 'in the olden days' were taken too far. The film is underpinned by a sense of *Ostalgie*, which is defined by Nora Fitzgerald as 'a phenomenon of memory, a desire to collect and obsess on things that vanished following the reunification of Germany' (cited in Deltcheva 2005: 202). In some of the funniest sequences of the film, Alex looks obsessively for these objects – for instance, in trash bins and at the flea market. Jars of pickles, packets of coffee, clothes, songs and even language (vividly caricaturized in Christiane's letters to the communist party leaders) are, in *Good Bye Lenin!* agents of nostalgia. Richard S. Esbenshade (1995: 85) is one of many critics that highlighted the negative aspect of the reification of such objects, arguing they represent 'the total commodification of memory', where ' "East-nostalgia" now has "hard-West" currency value'. Esbenshade likens these objects to the artistic practices represented in the heritage films analysed at the beginning of this chapter and denotes a rejection of what is perceived as a disrespectful use of the past.

Rather, these objects can be seen as functioning as a referent for audiences, who can historically situate key representational elements. They are also an integral part of a narrative that sees attitudes towards East and West shifting during the course of the film. Alex's belief in GDR values, if only opportunistic and momentary, is immediately dismissed by his sister and Rainer, as well as, later, by Alex himself. While at first Alex thrives in the possibility of returning to this recent past, soon he sees only the impossibility of this longing. In *Good Bye Lenin!*, *Ostalgie* functions as an emotional project (Alex revives it for his mother) and an aesthetic one (it becomes a 'pretty' memory, crucial to the film's style), but a project that seems condemned, and is in fact soon abandoned. Even if the GDR memory appears at first as visually pleasing, as 'quaint' and therefore interesting, the film makes it clear that this is no longer a valid historical period. In doing so, *Good Bye Lenin!* raises questions about the historical culture of nations in the former Eastern Bloc, today part of the European Union. The case of Romania, for instance, is examined later in this chapter.

In their presentation of the relationship between cinema, television and history, *Good Morning, Night* and *Good Bye Lenin!* offer a reflection on the way in which Europe's past is constructed, allowing for an examination of issues such as fantasy, authenticity and manipulation. By expanding the borders of what contributes to knowledge of and engagement with history (the 'fake' version in *Good Morning, Night*, the fantasy television sequences in *Good Bye Lenin!*), they are key examples of the increasing questioning of history taking place in contemporary European culture and film. This can be partly explained by the crisis the idea of Europe seems to be in: a Europe that is unable (or, as suggested in Chapter 1 in relation to the EU's work, unwilling) to define itself opens space for unceasing questions. The suspicion towards history is also related to the increasing attention given to memory.

From history to memory: Where were you when . . .?

The relationship between history and memory has been the object of a vast and expanding body of scholarly literature. According to Pierre Nora (1989: 8), 'memory and history, far from being synonymous, appear now to be in fundamental opposition'. For Nora, because of its personal nature, memory keeps the facts that suit it, whereas history, as an intellectual and secular production, calls for analysis and criticism. However, even if subjective (or precisely because of that, in an increasingly individualistic culture and society), for Elsaesser (1996: 145), memory 'has gained in value as a subject of public interest and interpretation', in contrast to history, which 'has become the very signifier of the inauthentic, merely designating what is left when the site of memory has been vacated'. *Good Morning, Night* and *Good Bye Lenin!* raise questions about the validity of history, instead placing memory at the centre of their narratives. *Good Morning, Night* uses television archives as collective memory (choosing not to have film reconstructions of key, and factual, historical events), whereas *Good Bye Lenin!* takes advantage of the malleability of television images, which potentially serve as fake history, to construct new memories. But an examination of the value of memory is not exclusive to films set in the past.

12:08 East of Bucharest, a Romanian film dealing with history but set in the present, is of primary relevance for the debates explored in this chapter, as memory is the main theme of the film's narrative. Set in the small city of Vaslui, the film is centred on the making of a debate for the local television about the town's involvement in the revolution of 1989, which started in the city of Timișoara and ended forty-two years of communist ruling in the country. Reviving the topic sixteen years after the revolution, the film raises important questions about collective memory, as well as the ongoing significance of historical events. Although this is not exactly a historical film (the story it tells takes place in the year in which the film was shot and released), it proves an excellent case study to end this chapter, as it also raises the issue of the European status of those (citizens and films) at the continent's borders (in this case, Romania) – a discussion that will be expanded in Chapter 4.

Shot in 2006, *12:08 East of Bucharest* was directed by Corneliu Porumboiu. Unsuccessful in securing public funding for another, bigger, project, Porumboiu set up the production house 42 Km Film and decided to make 'a small film among friends' (Pinto 2007). What started as a minor and very personal project was soon launched to international attention, as the film won the Golden Camera and the Europa Cinemas Label award at the Cannes Film Festival. Porumboiu's presence at the 2006 Cannes Film Festival followed the success of *Moartea domnului Lazarescu/The Death or Mr. Lazarescu* (winner of Un Certain Regard award in Cannes in 2005). Together with the subsequent *4 Months, 3 Weeks and 2 Days* (Golden Palm at Cannes in 2007), these have been seen as the key titles of the critically labelled Romanian New Wave.

Long shots, wide angles and the predominant use of a fixed camera, as well as the absence of non-diegetic music, are some of the key features that have been attributed to the Romanian New Wave. These are also noticeably prominent in *12:08 East of Bucharest*. The film revolves around three main characters, presented in a forty-minute initial sequence, which crosscuts between scenes with each of them. Virgil Jderescu (Teo Corban) is a television presenter who is organizing the show to commemorate the revolution. For a debate on whether there was or not a revolution in their small town (the original title of the film, *A fost sau n-a fost*, literally translates as 'Was there or wasn't there?') he wishes to include in the show, he invites Manescu (Ion Sapdaru), an alcoholic history teacher. As his other guest turns him down at the last minute, Jderescu convinces Piscoci (Mircea Andreescu), a retired old man who used to dress as Santa Claus for school and family Christmas celebrations, to also participate in the debate. In addition to setting up the narrative and introducing the protagonists of the film, this initial sequence highlights decadence as a key theme in *12:08 East of Bucharest*: from the start, we are presented with excessive drinking, unpaid debts and ageing, as well as poverty, racism and sexism.

Decadence might also be seen to define the relationship the nation establishes with its own history. After Manescu declares live that there was a revolution in his town, since he and his colleagues (conveniently dead or emigrated) were in the main square that morning, the programme proceeds with viewers calling in to refute his story. Accusations of Manescu's tendency to lie and drink bring the show to an embarrassing conclusion. The film denies this town's heroic narrative, questioning the veracity of history. Moreover, *12:08 East of Bucharest* dismisses the importance of the past more generally. While for Virgil the revolution was a crucial event, this is an irrelevant topic for many other characters. Before the start of the show, Virgil's lover, for instance, claims 'no one cares about it', to which he responds: 'what do you want me to do, a show about inflation and gypsy music?'

Although perceptions of Romania have shifted with the country's accession to the EU in 2007, much of the country's representation in the West is based on negative stereotypes, often centred on economic power (or lack thereof), as well as race. By alluding to 'gypsy culture' and therefore replicating hackneyed perceptions of Romanian culture, Virgil situates the film between a national and a universal sphere. Although some of the jokes are generated by language, not all references are nationally specific. For instance, when looking for a dictionary, Virgil's wife advises him to 'look behind the bearded man' (small cast busts we see on his book shelf), to which he replies: 'which one, Aristotle or Plato?'

Another feature that gives *12:08 East of Bucharest* a global dimension is the film's focus on individual stories – a feature common to many of the films examined in this chapter. The film is concerned with people 'just like us', although this is perhaps taken to an extreme, as the protagonists of *12:08 East of Bucharest* emerge as comical anti-heroes. No sacrifice is presented; on the contrary, expediency and opportunism are the attitudes highlighted. Revolution is here depicted as a human experience and the transition from a communist to a postcommunist Romania framed by dispassionate feelings – as demonstrated by the final call, of a mother whose son was killed in 1989 urging the participants of the television debate to go outside and see the snow that has started to fall.

The exact time of Ceauşescu's fleeing the country is what can determine whether or not there was a revolution in this town. If, as most viewers argue, people only came to the streets after that time to celebrate, then the revolution seems to have been confined to Timişoara and Bucharest. It is because the helicopter transporting Ceauşescu and his wife, along with four other supporters, was on television (in Romania, the revolution was televised) that this fact is not contested, and is instead accepted as unquestionably real. Television is here part of a double involvement in memory and history: it revives the memories of those who lived through the revolution (referring back to the images of Ceauşescu leaving in a helicopter); but it is also used to write history (since Virgil's show discards the possibility of a revolution in the town).

By refuting the idea that there was a revolution in this town, the film also seems to break with the past. *12:08 East of Bucharest* is set in 2006 and it offers mostly a contemporary view of Romania. The character of the Chinese immigrant Chen (George Guoqingyun), who is abused by a drunken Manescu, contributes to this modern depiction. Chen's ambiguous position within the community is further highlighted by his call to Virgil's show, at which point, in an ironic twist to the narrative, he strongly defends the history teacher, praising him for his honesty and kindness. Embarrassed, Virgil, does not however appreciate his call, claiming: 'I don't think the Romanian revolution is any of your business'. The inclusion of Chen and his role in the film hints at the contemporary situation of Romania, as many other European nations, with regards to migration – an issue further explored in the next chapter.

In its depiction and concern with the present, *12:08 East of Bucharest* also has implications for the representation of Europe more generally. Luisa Rivi (2007) argues that the collapse of the Eastern Bloc in 1989 brought about a European identity crisis. For her, 'Porumboiu's film interrogates the past in order to face a vacuum of identity that may well extend from Romania to the whole of Europe, where the West and the East are no longer poles of a safe and stable identification' (23). 'Western' references abound in *12:08 East of Bucharest* – for instance, Christmas trees, Christmas lights and mentions of the French Revolution. But whereas the replacement of national culture with Western references is generally accepted, the loss of the national to other cultures beyond Europe is condemned. The characters' interest in defining a national identity is, throughout the film, highly ambiguous.

Hence, Virgil orders the band in the studio to stop playing Latin American music and focus on traditional Romanian songs, and we witness the contempt for China in Virgil's hostile reception of Chen's call. While *Good Bye Lenin!* defined in clear terms the significance of these older points of reference, the boundaries between East and West are, in *12:08 East of Bucharest*, much more blurred. The West is also more welcoming in the latter – something which Alex in *Good Bye Lenin!* criticized, but which most characters in *12:08 East of Bucharest* seem to aspire to. Eastern Europe appears here no longer to be the 'other', but a region consolidating its position on the path to political integration, and the film's mobilization of the past, mediated through television, contributes to this perception.

In *Good Morning, Night, Good Bye Lenin!* and *12:08 East of Bucharest*, Europe emerges as a political project which is first drawn at national level. Politics is not just the theme of these films. These films bring history to a political domain by criticizing a uniform view of the past and stressing the value of alternative tales. At the same time, *Good Morning, Night, Good Bye Lenin!* and *12:08 East of Bucharest* question the role of television in the construction of collective history. Television can be unifying – literally in the cases of East and West Germany in *Good Bye Lenin!* It is also universally recognized (as a device and as a catalyst for history) by viewers across Europe and beyond. Contemporary events are, by nature, televised, but television also allows for the formation of alternative histories. In contemporary political films set in the past, self-questioning becomes one of the central features of the idea of Europe in European cinema.

This chapter confirms the important connection political institutions, scholars and film-makers have established between the idea of Europe and the European past. The fact that this is a continent with history defines Europe at least in discourses about itself: there is, in the idea of Europe, as in contemporary European cinema, an incessant return to history as a way to give the concept of Europe meaning, and to define its values. However, these films do not simply illustrate this connection; they also explore its groundings and implications. Such a questioning can be seen in all the films analysed here, although it is more visible in those about Europe's recent history. A predominance of self-reflexive films indicates a Europe dealing with an identity crisis. History becomes the privileged theme for a continent that wishes to go back in time (to its power position up to the early twentieth century), but it also, paradoxically, betrays Europe, by rendering visible some of the key problems it has been, and is still forced to deal with.

Heritage films contribute to the public conceptualization of Europe. Many of the historical titles released with the support of MEDIA, including those films examined here, work as statues or museums, offering European and global audiences pieces of living history, constructing narratives around key figures and art forms. In order to communicate this knowledge, and European history, more effectively, many contemporary European films focus on individual characters and protagonists. In *Good Morning Night, Good Bye Lenin!* and *12:08 East of Bucharest*, Europe's history is resized to a personal scale. Through their protagonists, these films highlight the subjectivity of history. In this sense, they follow contemporary historiographies, as they turn to personal accounts, which not only revise history but also complement it. The human character of the individuals depicted on screen is strongly underlined in all of the films examined in this chapter, as there is a focus on feelings and emotions, from admiration (*Girl with a Pearl Earring*) to love (*Becoming Jane*), passion and ambition (*La Vie en rose*) to sacrifice (*Sophie Scholl*).

A rescaling of historical narratives also takes place at another level, as these films go beyond their national spheres, albeit in different ways. This is the case of *La Vie en rose* (where French references are filtered for international audiences); of *Good Bye Lenin!* (its promotion being centred on a more universal family plot, but also on the film's genre, as a comedy); and, perhaps more obviously, of *Merry Christmas* (which stresses the unity of, rather than the divisions between, European nations). As required by a EU that wishes to become a global actor, these films also have a strong sense of universality. The idea of Europe as welcoming and all-encompassing that arises in *Girl with a Pearl Earring*, *Becoming Jane* and *La Vie en rose* – where the artistic lives of these films' protagonists frame them as appealing to visitors – resurfaces in the films about the First and Second World Wars in the form of Europeanness as universality.

Finally, all the films analysed in this chapter can be seen as 'quality' films (as desired by the European Commission), even if this status is achieved through different mechanisms. These include plot (the artistic focus of *Girl with a Pearl Earring*), production design (*Merry Christmas*), detailed historical reconstructions (*Sophie Scholl*) and budget (*Black Book*). This sense of quality is tied to a need to please all – and that is why so many films here are perceived as universal, in their style and contents. The Europeanness of the MEDIA films analysed in this chapter also lies in their significance as examples of a particular conception of contemporary European cinema. Even films that present a more negative idea of Europe (for instance, *Black Book*) can be used as a political tool of communication of the EU and of Europe more generally. Europe is visualized in contemporary cinema partly through film form, not just content. These films are important to assess the place of history and the past in the definition of the idea of Europe also because, in the MEDIA 'clips' and other forms of communication, they have been labelled as EU films. Being in line with, or disagreeing with the EU's political discourse, these films also offer insight into the way European institutions envision history.

This Is Europe: From Tourist Haven to Secured Fortress

If scholarly definitions of Europe often refer to the continent's history, much of the popular and institutional debate about the idea of Europe is centred on the contemporary era. Europe's meaning, for better or worse, is also about power and rights, borders and customs, many of these having undergone a major process of reflection across the continent in recent years. This chapter turns from the representation of Europe's past to a focus on Europe's present. It is structured into two main sections: European cities on the one hand; social realist films on the other. Urban space and social problems are not only key aspects of contemporary Europe; they are also intrinsically related. The two sections however have very different tones: first, I look at films that offer positive visions of Europe, echoing the celebratory tone of the heritage cinema examined in the previous chapter; then I analyse dystopian views of the continent. The first section begins by exploring the interconnections between European cities, cinema and tourism. Open to travellers from within and beyond the continent, European cities are cosmopolitan spaces. This chapter questions the place the European city occupies in an increasingly globalized world. The global outlook of Europe projected on screen also raises the issues of margins, limits and boundaries. Focused on social realist films, the second half of the chapter examines Europe's geographical, cultural and political borders. Starting with an analysis of the inner divisions of European cities, especially in relation to video surveillance, it explores topics such as multiculturalism, religious and linguistic difference and immigration, as well as their role in the construction of 'Fortress Europe'. By looking at the overlapping cinematic visions of tourism and migration, this chapter presents a picture of the spatial and social realities of the European continent, as well as the way in which these relate to the work of the European Union (EU) and the idea of Europe its institutions support.

The growing relevance of European cities off screen and on screen

Cities have occupied a central place in European life, from the Hellenistic period to the contemporary era. Today, they house the overwhelming majority of Europe's population and with it most political and social challenges. The urban sphere is the focus of a number of key EU policies, in areas such as employment, social exclusion and poverty, transport, energy, culture and youth. The importance of the city in the European context has meant that its social, political and cultural meanings have continually been questioned – a questioning that has gained momentum with globalization, as well as Europeanization. As Patrick Le Galès (2002: 5) puts it, '[T]he making of the European Union (EU) gives a different meaning to the term "European cities" ... They are now part of a polity in the making'.

As cities gain a prominent role as political entities, their place in a globalized world is also asserted through culture. Europe's space, and particularly its urban space, has long been one of the continent's most instantly recognizable features. Cities are important both for Europe's external promotion and for its internal definition. Two of the defining elements of 'a certain idea of Europe' proposed by George Steiner (2006) are deeply tied to the urban experience. As he suggests, cafés characterize the European metropolitan landscape. They are 'the place for intellectual debate' frequented by 'the *flâneur* and the poet' (29) – utterly urban, artistic and creative figures. At the same time, Europe, for Steiner, 'has been and is still today *walked*' (32; emphasis in the original). Europe is a place for thought on the one hand; a space characterized by narrow streets, footpaths and visitor routes on the other. Chapter 3 reflected on the importance of heritage for the construction of the idea of Europe. Although not exclusively, considering the strong association between heritage, nature and the countryside (Samuel 1994), the city is a key space where the heritage industry develops. A crucial element of Europe's cultural heritage, the city becomes in itself an item to protect, cherish and celebrate.

Given that cities are particularly useful for the political communication of the European project, EU cultural policies include important initiatives in the urban sector. The most prominent of these has been the 'European Capital of Culture', which celebrated its thirtieth anniversary in 2015. Athens was the first city to receive this title in 1985. On the one hand, the city was chosen because the programme was initiated by the star Melina Mercouri (at the time minister of culture for Greece) together with Jack Lang (French minister of culture between 1981 and 1986, 1988 and 1992). On the other, it carries a particular signification as the cradle of Western civilization. While the inception of the city as a participatory arena can be traced back to Ancient Greece (and to its designation as polis), one of the core values of the EU, humanism, was, as Lang (1985) wrote in a note to Mercouri, 'invented in your country circa 2,500 years ago'. Host to famous ancient monuments, including two UNESCO World Heritage Sites, Athens is one of the best examples of European cities which are also European heritage, and which must therefore be cherished and protected.

After Athens, over fifty cities have received the title of European Capital of Culture. By 2010, all EU member-states had hosted the event at least once. Not just actual capitals (for instance, Amsterdam, Berlin, Paris, Madrid, Stockholm and Prague) but also smaller and developing cities (Bologna, Salamanca, Patras, Pécs, Sibiu and Guimarães, among others) have been named European capitals of culture. Croatia, the EU's newest member, will designate the European Capital of Culture in 2020. This initiative has also been taken up by non-members; Turkey celebrated Istanbul as European Capital of Culture in 2010. The conflation of European urban space and European culture was particularly visible in the case of Athens, but Istanbul also constitutes a remarkable case study. By focusing on Muslim Europe, one of the aims of the initiative was, as stated in its official website, 'to take a giant step for mutual understanding' (Istanbul 2010 Agency). The religious composition of contemporary Europe, which, as discussed in Chapter 1, was particularly challenged at the time of the writing of the constitutional treaty in the early 2000s, is of course a key issue for European nations, as well as the EU more generally.

These 'capitals of culture' become not only part of a larger network, being placed in a map of Europe and rebranded as European, but also constitute a new form of heritage. At times, the initiative contradicts commonly accepted views of these cities, including their cinematic representation. Glasgow constitutes an interesting example, as is argued in the second half of this chapter. European capitals of culture aim to reposition cities in a new European sphere, which is similar to what the prominence of urban space in contemporary film often seeks to achieve. This chapter focuses on the way in which contemporary European cinema uses cities as defining elements of its Europeanness, at the same time putting forward a particular notion of Europe tied to urban space.

In line with the 'spatial turn' observed in other social sciences, interest in the relationship between cinema and the city has been expanding. As Mark Shiel and Tony Fitzmaurice (2003) note, these discussions are often articulated around the modern/postmodern opposition – a framework that, as Ewa Mazierska and Laura Rascaroli (2003: 8) observe, is generally translated into the Europe versus US dichotomy. Mazierska and Rascaroli argue that, even though European cities are 'less postmodern' than American cities, they are also characterized by a post-industrial landscape. Such landscapes can be seen in films like *La Haine/Hate* (Mathieu Kassovitz, 1995), *Los Lunes al Sol/Mondays in the Sun* (Fernando León de Aranoa, 2002) and *Red Road* (Andrea Arnold, 2006), among others; the latter film is examined later. Changes suffered by European cities in the postmodern era can also be analysed in relation to tourism and historical landscapes. These are discussed in the first half of this chapter.

Stephen Barber (2002: 106) claims that 'European film-makers now increasingly interrogate the very form of Europe, often perceiving its cities as existing in a process of erosion or disappearance'. This is in accordance with the perception of Europe's new marginality on the global stage, as well as an inherent self-questioning by European institutions and scholars (Chapter 1). This chapter is also concerned with how 'visible' European cities are in cinema – what is on screen and what is left out. Myrto Konstantarakos (2000: 4) notes that a recurrent topic in discussions about space and

European cinema 'is that of centrality and marginality and, more precisely, of exclusion and inclusion – a *leitmotif* one does not find in the filmmaking of other cultures with quite the same obsession'. Ever changing, urban space becomes the key sphere in which to reflect on Europe, both internally (in relation to the European integration process) and externally (with regards to globalization).

The role of the city in cinema takes several shapes: from being a location to starring as a character. This chapter looks at the different ways in which European cities are represented in contemporary film, cutting across genres, nationalities and film-makers. In the case studies examined, cities are prominent to different degrees; I pay attention to both the representation of urban space as such and that of particular places. I question not only the extent to which cities in contemporary cinema contribute to the idea of Europe, but also how the ideas that they propagate relate to the official discourse of the EU.

Cinematic postcards: From Europe with love

As symbols of Europe, cities are also tourist attractions. Not only the lifestyle and culture that characterizes them, but also key landmarks are at the centre of their global appeal. The power of cinema in the touristic promotion of cities has been noticed by local authorities all over Europe, which have not only instated local film commissions, but are also often co-producers of European and international films. The programme of many European capitals of culture has included the commissioning of feature films devoted to the metropolises celebrated, namely, *Lisbon Story* (Wim Wenders, 1994), set in the Portuguese capital, and *Of Time and the City* (Terence Davies, 2008), about the evolution of Liverpool. Examples of this growing importance can also be drawn from the private sector. For instance, *Somers Town* (Shane Meadows, 2008), a film depicting the urban development of London, was entirely funded by the high-speed rail company Eurostar.

In his discussion of the 'tourist gaze', John Urry (2001: 3) defines 'tourism' as a visual practice. Both the production (through photography or video) and consumption of images (postcards, paintings, fridge magnets and other souvenirs) are a key dimension of the visitor's experience. Naturally selective, postcards present general views of a given place (for instance, through panoramic shots) or focus on key elements (often a monument), condensing, in both cases, one or more potential meanings of that space. Because of their static nature, postcards reinforce ideas of cohesion and stability, giving cities a timeless feel.

Postcards also provide a pertinent concept for the way in which European cities feature in contemporary cinema. On the one hand, the notion of the 'cinematic postcard' refers to a film's content, as landmarks and well-known monuments are featured on screen, such as the Eiffel Tower (in Paris), the Houses of Parliament (in London) and the Sagrada Família Cathedral (in Barcelona). Often represented stereotypically, such icons contribute, on a primary level, to geographically situate particular films. At the same time, they offer a glossy image of such locations, adding to these films' aesthetic construction. On the other hand, attached to the practice of tourism and to someone visiting and therefore only temporarily inhabiting a given space, the idea of the postcard hints at a mode of address that is generally synthetic. Postcards are produced and consumed in a brief moment and aim for a widely accepted view of the place represented.

While the depiction of iconic landmarks on screen is not new, a contemporary surge has been taking place, tied to changes occurring both in European society and in cinema. First, this phenomenon illustrates the substantial growth of tourism and the development of the heritage industry, as well as an association of Europe with the arts as demonstrated by the European Capital of Culture initiative. Second, not only has film become, to a greater extent, a key element in the promotion of various sites, the medium itself has been transformed by the development of new technologies and the emergence of a postmodern aesthetics that, as some commentators have argued, privileges style over substance. Serge Daney (2007) established a connection between postcards and his love for cinema. However, as he put it, the postcard is 'the product of a modest and anonymous commercial production that doesn't aim in any way towards art' (62). Such a perceived lack of artistic value illustrates a broader way of thinking that generally disparages shots of iconic buildings and landscapes, in the same way that the 'postcard aesthetics' of the French film genre *cinéma du look*[1] were dismissed by critics for being pretty but superficial (see Vincendeau 1995b: 82).

But the postcard is an important metaphor for a particular mode of representation of European urban space in contemporary films, which should not be dismissed as clichéd. Rather, these visions carry significant implications for the understanding of European cinema, as well as the international perception of European cities. A considerable number of contemporary films include or work as cinematic postcards, projecting fixed and memorable images of a city on screen. *Paris* (2008), for instance, directed by French film-maker Cédric Klapisch, depicts in a large number of scenes the city's most recognizable landmarks. Its very first shot, an aerial view of the French capital, is followed, in the credits sequence, by the Eiffel Tower and other iconic monuments and neighbourhoods, such as the Sacré-Coeur, the Opera and Montmartre.

Many other contemporary European films are set in the French capital. This is no surprise given the predominance of French films in European cinema, as well as the status of Paris as a cinematic city. This is the most frequently filmed city in Europe and possibly the world. The body of literature on Paris in the cinema is also substantial and still growing. Writers approach the topic from the perspective of national and European cinema, stars, directors and key cinematic periods or movements, such as poetic realism, the French New Wave and, more recently, the *banlieue* film.[2] A detailed analysis of a number of contemporary European films also invites a discourse on the Europeanness of Paris, which emerges here as a transnational film location. This theme can be explored through a consideration of not only cinematic views often associated with tourism, but also a certain 'artistic' conception of film (Chapter 2).

In addition to Parisian architecture, some of the films released with the support of MEDIA reflect the cinematic status of the French capital by focusing on cultural aspects. As such, they work as *conceptual* rather than just *visual* postcards. In such cases, their meaning is not conveyed solely through the images on screen, but can also be found in the film's narrative, dialogue or credits. Here the function of the postcard is not so much to situate the film in spatial terms (although it still refers to a concrete geographical location) as in cultural terms, drawing on general perceptions of the feel, atmosphere and character of specific cities. *Paris*, for instance, not only features key landmarks in the presentation of the French capital, it also casts French stars that are, as Catherine Wheatley (2008: 74) suggests, 'themselves Parisian institutions', including Juliette Binoche and Romain Duris. *Belle toujours* (Manoel de Oliveira, 2006), another contemporary European film released with EU support, simultaneously mirrors the cinematic tradition of the city – it is a sequel to *Belle de jour* (Luis Buñuel, 1967) – and landmark Paris, using images of iconic buildings and neighbourhoods as transitions between sequences.

Similar transitions (including aerial views of Paris, as well as shots of Montmartre, the Pantheon and the Eiffel Tower) are used in the collective film *Paris je t'aime* (Olivier Assayas et al., 2006).[3] Following the tradition of *Paris vu par* (1965) and *Paris vu par ... vingt ans après* (1984),[4] *Paris je t'aime* presents a number of love stories set in different neighbourhoods of the French capital. Composed of short films directed by French and international high profile directors (Olivier Assayas, Joel and Ethan Coen, Isabel Coixet, Wes Craven, Tom Tykwer and Gus van Sant, to name just a few), the film is thus also, as noted by one critic, 'a guided tour to contemporary cinema' (Tobin 2006: 133).

In its use of French language (also maintained at international level, including in the United Kingdom and in the United States), the film's title already functions as a postcard, hinting at the stereotype of Paris as a romantic city. Through its eighteen segments, *Paris je t'aime* constitutes a catalogue of the different dimensions of love, from hetero- and homosexual romance, to the affection between father and daughter or mother and son.

The film also covers different stages in these relationships, from *coup de foudre* and falling in love to keeping the spark alive, fighting or breaking up. Emblematic depictions of the French capital, the short segments refer to a wider view of the city as the international capital of romance. Despite this, reviewers noted the avoidance of clichés in terms of the representation of landmarks, which, with the exception of the Eiffel Tower, do not figure in the film's eighteen segments, but only in the opening credits and transitions (see, for instance, Darke 2007; Morrison 2007; Rinaldi 2007). Similarly, the film explores other aspects of the city, beyond its romanticism. In *Paris je t'aime*, views of the city span from 'the city of lights, the city for lovers' (as read in a travel guide in the segment by the Coen brothers) to a more complex, global city, where there are people from different ages, sexualities and origins.

Directed by Julie Delpy (who also stars in the film), *2 Days in Paris* (2007) also draws on and questions two particular stereotypes of the French capital: Paris as a cinematic city and Paris as the city of love. The two main characters are Marion (played by Delpy) and Jack (Adam Goldberg). They are two Americans in Paris, even if one is 'more American' than the other: Marion has, like Delpy herself, double, American and French, nationality. There are references to Marlon Brando's performance in *Ultimo Tango a Parigi/Last Tango in Paris* (Bernardo Bertolucci, 1972) (Figure 4.1), as well as

Figure 4.1 Julie Delpy 'doing Brando' in *2 Days in Paris*.

to the French New Wave, as Jack tries on different sunglasses and asks Marion 'which are more Godard?' But whereas Venice is, as Marion states at the beginning of the film, 'the city where lovers go', the romantic aura of Paris is almost destroyed. Towards the end of the film Jack confesses: 'I want to remember the least romantic day in Parisian history'.

Centred on Marion and Jack's romance (or lack thereof), the film further explores the relationship between France and the United States. This is visually made clear in a shot that simultaneously frames a replica of the Statue of Liberty, at the Pont de Grenelle, and the Eiffel Tower – architectural symbols of New York and Paris, respectively. In *2 Days in Paris*, the French capital is also the city of galleries and of political art. In one of the film's key scenes, Marion and Jack visit a very sexually explicit (and by consequence 'exotic') exhibition, which is in line with an American stereotypical view of France and of Europe more generally. As Vanessa Schwartz (2007: 107) has argued, from an American perspective, 'France's "particularity" seem[s] to be sex'.

By quoting the French capital in their titles, these two films directly signal widespread connotations of Paris, especially for international (and in this case American) audiences, who thus seem to appear at the recipient end of conceptual and visual postcards. Just like *Paris je t'aime*, *2 Days in Paris* also had more viewers in the United States than in France.[5] Both films offer a depiction of Europe as a travel destination, through a focus on the figure of the tourist, namely, Jack in *2 Days in Paris* and the main characters of two segments from *Paris je t'aime*. The sketch directed by Joel and Ethan Coen, for instance, is set in the Tuileries Metro station and focuses on a tourist (Steve Buscemi) who reads passages from his travel guide as he waits for a train. Advised by his book to avoid eye contact, he inadvertently looks up to meet the gaze of a young woman on the opposite platform. As her boyfriend notices, the couple walks up to Buscemi's character to confront him. In the last segment of the film, directed by

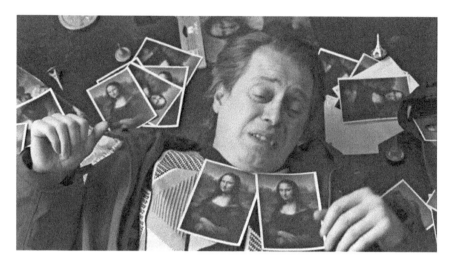

Figure 4.2 Defeated tourists in *Paris je t'aime*: Steve Buscemi floored by Mona Lisa postcards.

Alexander Payne, Carol (Margo Martindale), a postwoman from Denver, describes her recent visit to Paris and her love for the city. However, Carol is presented throughout as alienated, narrating her disappointment with Paris and her failed attempts to understand the city's culture or blend in.

Just as Jack has a miserable time during those two days in Paris, so do these segments present a negative view of tourists and, to a certain extent, make fun of them. In the Coen Brothers' segment, Buscemi's character is violently beaten up and ends up on the floor (Figure 4.2). Shot from a high angle, we see him covered by postcards of the Mona Lisa, as the French couple empty his souvenir bag on him. Carol, in turn, is shown defeated from the first time we see her on screen, in an uncharacteristic and cold hotel room. Her voice-over, in the narration, tells us how, after five days in Paris, she is still trying to overcome jet lag. She is further depicted as a naïve and ignorant tourist, not only through the music that accompanies the segment, but also as she claims it is Simon Bolívar rather than Simone de Beauvoir who is buried next to Jean-Paul Sartre in the Cemetery of Montparnasse.

Paradoxically, while these films appeal to those interested in visiting the places they depict, by criticizing the figure of the tourist, they stress the existence of a(nother) city that goes beyond clichés. Unlike the tourist represented on screen, the knowing viewer understands the joke surrounding the confusion between Bolívar and Beauvoir reflecting on his knowledge of 'authentic' Paris and Parisian culture. In their demeaning tones, both sequences illustrate Dean MacCannell's (1999: 9) claim that 'it is intellectually chic nowadays to deride tourists'. As he goes on to suggest, from this perspective, 'the touristic experience that comes out of the tourist setting is based on inauthenticity and as such it is superficial when compared with careful study. It is morally inferior to mere experience' (102). Hence, although Carol in *Paris je t'aime* tries to experience

Figure 4.3 Defeated tourists in *Paris je t'aime*: Carol tries to experience French cuisine.

'true' local culture, when she speaks French, people reply in English; and when she asks for restaurant tips, she ends up eating burgers and Chinese food (Figure 4.3). Similarly, in *2 Days in Paris*, Jack's first view of the city ('oh, look at the light! It's like a postcard of Paris!', he exclaims) is mediated through a taxi window, since he refuses to take the metro or a bus as he is afraid of terrorist attacks.

To a certain extent, this ridiculing view of the tourist is nuanced in *2 Days in Paris*. Early on in the film Jack gives wrong directions to an American excursion group, suggesting his interest in the city is superior to those visiting only to see the Louvre. Jack thus seems to be engaging in what Urry (2001: 57) has named the 'romantic' tourist gaze, ever growing in contemporary tourism, and through which 'more and more people wish to isolate themselves from the existing patterns of mass tourism'. The dichotomy between real and authentic thus finds a parallel in that of the citizen versus the tourist, as well as in the opposition between high and low forms of culture.

Both films nevertheless highlight the importance of the tourist for Paris and for European cities more generally, confirming these spaces' dimension as popular travel destinations. They present comprehensive pictures of the behaviour of the tourist in Europe, and of what people do when visiting. Activities include, as suggested by Steiner, walking (through narrow streets in *2 Days in Paris*, through sunny courtyards and parks in *Paris je t'aime*), as well as eating (exotically, as in the scene with the rabbit in *2 Days in Paris*; 'globally', as in Carol's meals in *Paris je t'aime*), going to museums such as the Louvre and buying souvenirs (the Mona Lisa postcards also in *Paris je t'aime*). *2 Days in Paris* and *Paris je t'aime* further highlight an association of Paris and Europe more generally with romance, as all characters find love in/for the city – a notion that echoes the feeling conveyed by the 2007 MEDIA 'clips' (Chapter 2). At the same time, they denote an ideal, and thus literally romantic, perception of Europe, characterized by its intellectual life and the importance of art. European cities are touristic destinations with a 'twist': their intrinsic connection to art and culture. As hinted in Chapter 3, Europe's association with a sense of exclusivity, quality and elevation is not however at odds with an encouragement of mass tourism.

European cities and their art (cinema)

Although not filmed as often as Paris, London is the setting of a large number of contemporary European films, including, among those supported by MEDIA, *Happy-Go-Lucky* (Mike Leigh, 2008), *Irina Palm* (Sam Garbarski, 2007) and *Match Point* (Woody Allen, 2005). *Match Point* is centred on Chris (Jonathan Rhys Meyers), a tennis instructor who, working in an upmarket club in London, becomes engaged to Chloe (Emily Mortimer), the sister of one of his clients named Tom (Matthew Goode). The film was watched by seven million viewers in Europe (not so much in the United Kingdom, mostly in France, Spain and Italy).[6] It won awards in Spain (Goya) and Italy (David Donatello) as the 2006 Best European Film. Although this appears as a curious award given the film-maker's nationality, *Match Point* is an international co-production between the United States and a series of European nations – which hints at the internationality of European cinema in the contemporary era. *Match Point* was also well received after a screening in Cannes, but although for Allen, 'it turned out to be the best film I've ever made' (cited in Matloff 2006: 100), British critics were not as supportive.

The negative reception of *Match Point* in the United Kingdom was mostly perceived as a reaction to its 'touristic' depiction of London (Fuller 2006: 18), which was dismissed as superficial. *Match Point*'s first iconic image of London showcases the Royal Opera House in Covent Garden. In the earlier moments of the film a montage sequence that intends to show the development of Chris and Chloe's relationship features the London Eye and the Saatchi Gallery (located, at the time of the film's shooting, by the river Thames; currently situated in the affluent neighbourhood of Chelsea). The camera tilts down to allow us to read the name of the gallery and then shows Chris and Chloe leaving the building. As they walk out of the frame to the left, the film cuts to a wide shot of the couple strolling on the riverbank, leaning on the rail to admire the Thames and the Houses of Parliament (Figure 4.4). The sequence ends with a shot of Chris and Chloe walking through the Mall. At one point, Chris stops talking to Chloe to look back at the Palace Guards in their internationally recognized uniforms. He thus puts the action on hold to fully contemplate a typical London landmark, reproduced ad infinitum on postcards. Covent Garden, the London Eye, the Thames and the Houses of Parliament are part of what Charlotte Brunsdon (2007: 22) has called a 'landmark iconography ... historically formed'.

Match Point might be using these landmarks to orientate the spectator, but they also contribute to a particular view of the city. The first time the city is mentioned in the dialogue is as 'expensive' London. One of the key themes in the film is the class system – a theme that is central to the understanding of British national culture and cinema (Hill 1999; Dave 2006) and one that, as the narrative evolves, stresses the opposition between

Figure 4.4 London's 'landmark iconography' in *Match Point*.

different groups of characters. The exploration of the issue of class, generally associated with exclusivity and the world of high art, is also, as we will see, an important way in which this film echoes a traditional, 'prestigious' vision of Europe and its cinema. The exclusive tennis club where Chris finds a job at the beginning of the film is in contrast with the cockney accent of the estate agent that shows him a cheap and small central London flat, the main features of which are a sofa bed, a second-hand wok and a 'telly'. Chris and Nola (Scarlett Johansson), an aspiring actress, are in stark contrast to 'posh London', that of Chloe and her family, of truffles and caviar (which Chris refuses in a restaurant, instead ordering roast chicken). Although not tourists (since they are working) in *Match Point* Chris and Nola are outsiders. Constantly referred to as the 'Irish' and the 'American', they are, respectively, an underpaid tennis instructor (albeit then a junior financial investor) and a struggling actress, explicitly positioned outside the British upper-class stratum. The fact that the film ends up badly for Chris and Nola also contributes to the class distinction stressed throughout.

This distinction is also made visually, as the private spaces they inhabit are utterly different, from Chris and Chloe's new flat on the Embankment, with a stunning view of the Thames, to Nola's new flat, which has mice. Testifying to the centrality of space in the film – its location is, very clearly, London, represented both in terms of physical landmarks and cultural stereotypes – in *Match Point* the characters are framed in wide shots that show them in context, in the setting of the action. This is the case for the presentation of Chris's flat mentioned earlier, as well as, for instance, of his new office after he accepts a job in the company Chloe's father owns. When Chris first visits his new workplace, a low angle shot of the 'Gherkin' (the popular nickname for an office block on St. Mary Axe in the City of London) emphasizes the majesty of this building. Inside, the camera pans around the room, to show, through massive glass windows, other impressive high-rise buildings in the financial district of the British capital. In addition to narrative, the film's cinematography further highlights the richness or poorness of settings and characters alike.

In the travel section of *The New York Times*, an article entitled 'The London of "Match Point"' comments on the impact of this film for a cinematic vision of the city, listing a number of its locations and proposing a film-related tour around the British capital (Cameron 2006). *Match Point* thus also shows that while cinematic postcards are generally dismissed by critics – particularly those writing for cinephile publications such as *Sight and Sound* and *Cahiers du Cinéma* – they contribute to the promotion of cities and of Europe more generally. 'Movie maps' for London visitors are available online, related to films such as *Closer* (Mike Nichols, 2004), *Bridget Jones: The Edge of Reason* (Beeban Kidron, 2004), *Love Actually* (Richard Curtis, 2003) and *Match Point*. The movie map for *Match Point* includes some of the sites mentioned earlier, namely, the Royal Opera House, as well as Tate Modern, which Chloe and Chris visit later in the film. The city's cultural venues are especially emphasized in this film. Chris also confesses his joy in having moved to London, telling Tom he had never seen so much art or theatre. Six minutes into *Match Point* we are watching *La traviata* performed at the Royal Opera House. The connection between European cities and the world of art is very clearly stressed, and at least initially presented in a positive light.

Les Roberts (2010: 185) has discussed the impact of movie maps in a number of cities around the world, arguing they demonstrate 'the increasingly co-extensive and economically contingent geographies of tourism and film, as well as the growing inter-penetration of the two industries in the way film locations are being promoted and consumed as sites of spectacle and attraction'. The idea of attraction is central to the understanding of the interconnections between cinema, tourism and the international promotion of Europe. In this sense, the postcard becomes not so much a souvenir for someone who has visited a given space, but more a teaser for those who will potentially travel – in line with what Urry (2001: 3) describes as anticipation. Films such as the ones analysed so far work as previews of Europe. As suggested by Roberts, there is in movie maps, as in the films they refer to, a sense of spectacle. This is, by consequence, a particular, positive and alluring view of Europe.

Similarly, an article published in the Spanish daily *ABC*, 'Barcelona según el cine' (translated as 'Barcelona according to the cinema'), discusses a new service offered by the city council (Güell 2008). A web page lists a series of locations featured in contem-porary films, creating new touristic routes. While a general view of cities is marketed internationally through initiatives such as the one launched by the Barcelona council, cinematic representations of cities contribute to a commodification of the urban space, which becomes a modular product that can be itemized for tourist consumption. Although never a European capital of culture, Barcelona was given international atten-tion as the host of the 1992 Olympic Games. It is now one of the most visited cities in Europe, being promoted through its Mediterranean heritage, art nouveau architecture (especially in relation to the work of Gaudí) and as a centre for Catalan culture.

In addition to *Perfume* (Tom Tykwer, 2006), *Salvador* (Manuel Huerga, 2006), *Pot Luck* and *Vicky Cristina Barcelona* (Woody Allen, 2008), one of the films included in the list on the council's web page is Pedro Almodóvar's *All About My Mother*. The film was successful with critics and audiences alike. It was seen by almost two million viewers in France, two million in Spain and a total of seven million in Europe, and was awarded an Oscar, a BAFTA, a Golden Globe and a César as Best Foreign Film. Almodóvar won the prize for Best Director at the Cannes Film Festival for *All About My Mother* and a European Film Award in 1999 for Best Film.

Despite Almodóvar's connection to Madrid, the Spanish capital is more visible in other films supported by MEDIA – for instance, *Caótica Ana/Chaotic Ana* (Julio Medem, 2007). While *All About My Mother* actually begins in Madrid, there are no recognizable images of the city, and for the most part, the action takes place indoors. By contrast, Barcelona is introduced by a spectacular aerial view of the city. Ismaël Lô's 'Tajabone' song begins as a soft guitar while the film's protagonist Manuela (Cecilia Roth) is on a train. As the harmonica is played and the music's intensity increases, a helicopter shot shows Barcelona at night, seen from Mount Tibidabo. In the following shot, a taxi drives through the Monument to Colón; the film then cuts to Manuela looking at one of the key landmarks of the city, the Sagrada Família Cathedral, from the taxi window. The music is moving and nostalgic, appropriate for someone returning to a place dear to them after a long absence; in this sequence, Almodóvar invests the city with a strong emotional charge.

Other iconic places in Barcelona are mentioned throughout the film, including la Barceloneta, the run-down neighbourhood of Raval (where many art-nouveau buildings can be found), the imposing Plaza del Duc de Medinaceli, the cemetery of Montjuic and a number of theatres. Barcelona's art-nouveau buildings, as well as décor, are vividly on display in a film that tells a story about artists and an artistic milieu. Manuela's son Esteban, who dies after going to the theatre with his mother, dreamt of being a writer. Madrid and Barcelona are linked by their theatres, as well as by the performance of the same play: *A Streetcar named Desire* by Tennessee Williams (1947). The connection to the world of culture goes beyond the film's plot. *All About My Mother* has been examined in relation to the intertextual links it establishes not only with stage performers, but also with earlier periods of film history, especially its reworking of classical Hollywood melodrama, both in terms of content and style (see, for instance, Allinson 2009).

The representation of key landmarks on screen allows for admiration, and for visual pleasure in looking at such impressive monuments. This is achieved through careful cinematography and emotional music, particularly in the shot of the Sagrada Família that opens Almodóvar's view of Barcelona. The postcards created in *Match Point* and *All About My Mother* give these cities an artistic aura. The promotion of these cinematic cities is thus also tied to an idea of quality. As is the case with postcards, these films' representation of London and Barcelona, respectively, is selective. While Almodóvar leaves aside the political intricacies of the Catalan capital, Allen represents an exclusively traditional London. Chris simultaneously explores London (especially its artistic circuits) and the lives of the British upper class (visiting the tennis club, expensive restaurants and the country house). Both are selective environments, linked in the film through dialogue and music. In the montage sequence described earlier, Chris and Chloe's walk through galleries is accompanied by *Mia piccirella*, an aria from

Carlos Gome's *Salvator Rosa* that reoccurs in the film. The music begins as they leave the Saatchi Gallery. Ironically, it continues when they go into Chris's rundown flat. He is, at the beginning of the film, defined by his lack of money and social prestige, but through art (reading Dostoyevsky in his flat, attending the opera and visiting galleries with Chloe), Chris enters the upper-class circuit.

Woody Allen's other European city films also illustrate very clearly this idea of exclusivity, enacting the connection between art and the upper classes. In addition to the characters and locations of *Match Point* (an actress, a tennis instructor, private clubs, expensive restaurants, luxurious cottages and the Royal Opera House), we should note those in *Vicky, Cristina, Barcelona*: a master's student, painters, photographers and other artists, spending time at the university, art galleries and trendy bars. Something similar occurs in Allen's *Midnight in Paris* (2011), which features a long list of top international artistic figures from history, including American writers Ernest Hemingway, F. Scott Fitzgerald and Gertrude Stein, as well as European painters Pablo Picasso, Salvador Dalí and Edgar Degas, even if here the main character, a scriptwriter, is placed in opposition to a 'pretentious' scholar.

A connection between art and superiority can also be made if we look at these films' directors. *Match Point* in particular is used to 'sell' London, but the film is paradoxically praised as a symbol of quality and art cinema because of its auteur. The glossy dimension of the postcard is paired with a glamorous view of cinema, with an impact not only on the cities represented, but also on the positioning of the film in question, conveyed through the figure of the star director. The status of Woody Allen as a recognized auteur confirms European cinema's ties to notions of quality and prestige – even if he is not a European director. It should be noted here, however, that Allen's 'intellectual' image, as well as his long-standing critical recognition in Europe, go some way towards explaining his easy association with the continent. Similarly, Barcelona becomes a European city of culture through the identification with one of the key European auteurs: Pedro Almodóvar. In a short article entitled 'The power of Pedro', for instance, a critic for *Sight and Sound* highlights the popularity of recent works by the Spanish film-maker, as well as his leading position within contemporary cinema (Gant 2006).

These two films highlight the importance of auteurs not only for European cinema but also for European cities. Barcelona's architecture and popular culture, together with London's wealthy and artistic circuits (the tennis club, the opera and museums) contribute to the creation of an image of a cultural Europe – echoing the aims of the EU's European Capital of Culture programme. Significantly, the imagined city is attributed a special meaning because of a prestigious auteur's view. Allen and Almodóvar emerge as 'qualified' tourists (Allen more obviously, but Almodóvar also because he is more readily associated with Madrid than Barcelona). Their views are praised, rather than ridiculed as in the previous section, even though they are just as selective.

These films constitute cinematic postcards through the inclusion of on-screen representations of monuments and landmarks, as well as through their titles (romance in *Paris, je t'aime*), plots (the artistic milieu of *Match Point*) and the promotion of their directors (for instance, Almodóvar). Functioning as souvenirs or teasers, these postcards update the experience of the visitor, or generate interest in potential visitors. As such, they stress the important link between tourism and knowledge. To visit a place is to get to know it (even if partially); to visit Europe is thus to learn about it. Cinematic postcards are sent from Europe and with love, both literally (as in the association between Paris and romance) and symbolically, through a positive feeling that stresses an emotional connection to the continent. Knowledge and emotion are, as in the films discussed in Chapter 3, equally crucial for the production of cinematic visions of contemporary Europe.

The concept of the cinematic postcard problematizes images of iconic landmarks in cinema, as well as the discourses circulating around them, in relation to the notions of quality and authenticity. These films characterize European cities as simultaneously old and historical (and as such prestigious touristic attractions) and modern and developed (and therefore spaces for consumption). Iconic views of European cities are in keeping with the idea of European urban space as a tourist space, as well as a cultural space. Cinematic postcards are tied to a sense of superiority and high-art, which is in line with the idea of Europe that positions the continent as the cradle of art and culture, as well as with perceptions of European film that leave aside popular cultural forms. Paradoxically, however, they are also used in the promotion of Europe, namely, in the mainstream realm of tourism – especially in the case of movie maps and movie tours. As with the notion of popular art cinema (Chapter 2) and the positioning of heritage films (Chapter 3), the films examined in this chapter also put forward a middlebrow idea of Europeanness. They are at the same time 'serious' and consensual, quality films that are about mainstream culture, and appeal to universal audiences too. As contemporary European films present tourism as paradoxically good (through the view of an auteur) and bad (because it is inadequate and massified), economically important and culturally limited, they highlight the existence of a European notion of popular quality that underpins the promotion of cities as well as film. Noting the need to go beyond an elitist definition of Europe, the EU aims to position the idea of Europeanness increasingly closer to the notion of universality. Openness, and not just distinctiveness, also marks the nature of Europe's urban space, as well as its cinematic representation.

Cosmopolitanism and universality in European cities

Unlike the films discussed so far, which are case studies for the depiction on screen of individual cities, many contemporary films are set in more than one place, establishing narrative and visual links between European metropolises. Other visitors and travellers, figures in between the tourist and the citizen inhabit contemporary Europe. In addition to the migrant, examined in further detail towards the end of this chapter, a key example is the Erasmus student, an idiosyncratic kind of traveller within Europe. *Pot Luck*, for instance, represents different European cities. The film tells the story of Xavier (Romain Duris), who moves from Paris to Barcelona, as part of the student exchange programme Erasmus. A European Commission initiative, Erasmus was launched in 1987 and has funded more than two million exchange students all over

Europe. Hoping to 'give students a better sense of what it means to be a European citizen' (in the words of the European Commission[7]), the programme is aimed at youngsters who will, like Xavier, meet people from all corners of Europe. European identity emerges here mostly through comparisons, as students are incited to recognize the differences, and more importantly, similarities, between their cultures and that of young people from other corners of the continent. Initiatives such as the Erasmus programme have been praised for their contribution to the formation of a European cultural idea by commentators including Umberto Eco (in Riotta 2012), as noted in the introduction to this book.

Pot Luck was watched by almost three million viewers in France. The film's popularity as an 'Erasmus film' has been accompanied by discussions of its stereotypical representation of national cultures, as well as of the cities where it is set: Paris and Barcelona (see, for instance, Ezra and Sanchéz 2005). As in his 2008 film *Paris*, Klapisch's *Pot Luck* begins with a 'postcard' image of the French capital. At the start of *Pot Luck* Xavier meets a friend of his father's to discuss his future and employment options. In an office located in central Paris, his father's friend shows Xavier the view from his window, pointing at the Sacré-Coeur and the Eiffel Tower. These icons clearly present a stereotypical view of the French capital – a perspective also adopted later in the film to represent foreign cultures. When asked if he knows Spain, Xavier replies he has been to Ibiza (a common touristic destination) and '*habla un poquito español*' ('speaks a little Spanish'). However, after landing in Barcelona, he reacts angrily to the efforts of a French couple that try to tell him about the city, which he hopes to discover on his own.

As Xavier arrives in the city centre, the camera is more focused on him than on Barcelona. A medium close-up of Xavier stresses the importance, for this film, of his perspective. This is matched by the voice-over, which reflects on the experience of exploring an unknown city, when everything is new and nothing makes sense. Dialogue also contributes to the view of Xavier as an outsider. When he has to leave the flat of a friend of his mother's, where he had planned to stay during his first week in Barcelona, Xavier calls Jean-Michel, the French man he met at the airport. On the street, a group of kids imitate the sounds he makes (speaking French) and follow him around, saying: '*vete a tu país*' ('go home to your country'). When he receives Xavier, Jean-Michel notes that 'we French have to help each other'. Xavier defensively agrees and nods, defeated.

As an outsider, Xavier's knowledge of Barcelona is initially limited to some of the iconic landmarks of the city, including Parc Güell and the Sagrada Família. Throughout *Pot Luck*, Xavier's relationship with the city remains dual: he is 'in' (knows the names of some places, recognizes routes and buildings), yet he is also 'out'. For instance, he is clearly still thinking of home when he asks, at a beach in Sitges, pointing at the sea: '*C'est où la France? Par la?*' ('Where is France? In that direction?') (Figure 4.5). In spatial terms, the film oscillates between a defence of authenticity (wanting to know the 'real' Barcelona) and the perpetuation of stereotypes (including in his 'to see before leaving' list places such as Montjuic).

Xavier's temporary condition in Barcelona increases the tension between a superficial and a 'true' knowledge of the city. By the end of the film, he is no longer a tourist

Figure 4.5 Missing home in *Pot Luck*: *C'est où la France?*

(unlike the brother of his British flatmate who comes to visit), but a citizen, albeit from a different origin. In the final sequences of *Pot Luck* Xavier speaks Spanish fluently. He walks alone in Barcelona; he knows the streets and shortcuts that allow him to run home. His nationality, like his class, strongly contributes to his integration, in contrast with an increasing number of migrants in Europe, as will be discussed in this chapter. Back home in Paris, Xavier explores his status as both a 'local' and a tourist. After having a drink in Montmartre, a reference to *Amelie* – Audrey Tautou also featuring in a subplot in *Pot Luck* – he goes to a street 'where Parisians never go'. He sees himself as 'a foreigner among foreigners' and meets other Erasmus students, feeling at the same time at home and out of place.

Lost in spaces and cultures that only partially belong to him, Xavier concludes 'I am not me, but everyone', referring to his flatmates from Barcelona. He is, he claims, French, Spanish, English and Danish. He is like Europe: 'a real mess'. Space and identity (a topic previously approached in the film in a discussion between students from different nationalities, and that illustrates Europe's 'café culture') conflate in this scene to literally make a point about the unity of Europe as a synthesis of different cultures. Paris, like Barcelona (and potentially the other cities where the remaining characters live), is shown to be truly cosmopolitan. In *Pot Luck*, these cities allow those who inhabit them, national or not, to feel they belong to Europe's urban space. At the same time, they can feel that they are connected to 'strangers' through shared values and emotions.

Following the success of *Pot Luck*, the sequel *Les Poupées Russes/Russian Dolls* (Cédric Klapisch, 2005) was released three years later. With most of the same characters and still centred on Xavier, *Russian Dolls* was however less well received. Cécile de France won another César for her performance as Isabelle, the Belgian student Xavier meets in Barcelona. But critics dismissed the film, invoking problems with its narrative.

Spencer (2006: 67), for instance, discusses its looseness, faced with the constant change of locations. As she argues, despite being 'crowded with characters and incidents', the film is 'all story but no plot'. *Russian Dolls* refers to *Pot Luck* in its very first scene, with a close-up of each of the main characters waiting to cross the road. The film then cuts to a long shot of the whole group when Xavier mentions 'St. Petersburg', situating us geographically. Space is, once again, a key element of the film's narrative.

Despite this early image of Russia, like *Pot Luck*, *Russian Dolls* also begins in Paris. Alluding to Xavier's interview in the previous film, a panoramic shot that includes in its sights the Eiffel Tower and the river Seine clearly situates this sequel in the French capital. The camera zooms in on a modern building to the sound of Marc-Antoine Charpentier's *Prelude to Te Deum*, the Eurovision Song Contest theme that was associated with the EU in *Pot Luck* (see also Chapter 1). This time, Xavier is at the headquarters of TV France, applying for a job as a soap opera writer. The broad topic of the show is 'love', a theme the producer believes will have a strong commercial potential since, as he concludes, 'we all love postcards'.

As it negotiates notions of authenticity, *Russian Dolls* also explores the dichotomy between the local and the global. The first part of the film is set in the French capital. Locations include residential flats, shops and cafés – relatively 'familiar' spaces, which fit within a 'neighbourhood' view of Paris. By contrast, Martine (Audrey Tautou) tells Xavier about the World Social Forum held in Porto Alegre in Brazil and how 'it really makes you feel connected to the planet'. In the background, the camera shows a map of France, next to a Chinese poster on her kitchen wall (Figure 4.6). Multiple levels are also constructed visually, either through split screens or through longer, more complex shots. In a later sequence, as Xavier storms out of Martine's flat, he answers the phone, now on the street. The camera zooms in, going past his phone and towards her balcony, to show them both in the same shot. This strategy is repeated later on, with Celia, a

Figure 4.6 *Russian Dolls*: The local and the global.

model whose biography Xavier is hired to ghost write. This visual composition, allied to the movement within the frame, stresses not only that reality is split into different levels, but also that these characters, as potentially anyone in contemporary European cities, are connected through communication devices. On the one hand, Paris is presented as a global city (Sassen 2001), as economic transformations caused by globalization are alluded to in the film. On the other, a reflection on the implications of this fact is conspicuously absent, particularly in terms of class and race.

To add to this tension between the local, the national and the global, the European dimension contributes to the transnational feel of *Russian Dolls*. An hour into the film, Xavier returns to TV France, where he is told that, through a European programme entitled Eurosat 2000, the show he has been working on will start to be co-produced by the British channel BBC 2. As Xavier claims he can speak English, the film cuts to a dialogue in English and then to a shot of the Gare du Nord in Paris (Figure 4.7). William (Kevin Bishop) is the first 'foreign' character to be introduced (in the sense of a tourist, not an expatriate, as is the case for Isabelle, a Belgian national living in France). William is, as he was in *Pot Luck*, a character full of clichés. Hence, as he leaves the train station, he shouts '*Bonjour Paris!*' (another cinematic reference, this time to *Funny Face* [Stanley Donen, 1957]) and '*Je veux des escargots et du vin rouge!*'. At the same time, William also brings into the film's narrative – so far, entirely set in Paris – images of other countries, including the Royal Albert Hall in London and a canal in St. Petersburg. In doing so, the sequence that introduces William in *Russian Dolls* highlights the notions of movement, travelling and flux that, as these films show, are central for the definition of globalized Europe.

The introduction of this European dimension also accelerates the pace of the narrative. After Xavier returns to TV France and he is told he can go to London, the film cuts to a shot of Waterloo Station, where Wendy (Kelly Reilly) is waiting for him (Figure 4.8). The film's view of London, as had been the case with the presentation of Paris, alternates between the landmark and the universal city – between red buses, Piccadilly and Oxford Street (local), references to English breakfast (national) and mentions of a Pakistani deli (global). After London, Xavier, Wendy and the remaining characters that figured in *Pot Luck* go to St. Petersburg, to attend William's wedding.

Commenting on Klapisch's Europeanist impulses, Sylvie Blum-Reid specifically reads *Russian Dolls* against the background of the European integration process. Although Russia's belonging to Europe is debatable, for Blum-Reid (2009: 4), 'the film programmatically addresses the need to spread a larger Europe as far east as Russia, expanding both East and South'. *Russian Dolls* stretches the traditional view of Europe by highlighting the similarities that exist between the European cities where it takes place: Paris, London and St. Petersburg. As in *Pot Luck*, parallels are drawn between different cities – in this case, also visually, as *Russian Dolls* cuts from William waiting by the canal in St. Petersburg to William and Xavier walking by the canal in Paris. Hence, in St. Petersburg, Xavier and Wendy behave just like they had in Paris and London. William is now the 'guide', pointing to squares, buildings and the river as they ride the tram (just as Wendy had done in London, from a double-decker). Public

Figure 4.7 Similarities in *Russian Dolls*: Gare du Nord in Paris.

Figure 4.8 Similarities in *Russian Dolls*: Waterloo Station in London.

means of transport, international train stations, as well as bars and discos (or pubs, in the British inflection), are common to Paris, London and St. Petersburg.

Such parallelisms seem to confirm Mazierska and Rascaroli's (2003: 19) claim that, 'as a consequence of both its fragmentation and its cosmopolitanism, the city partly loses its individual identity, and looks more and more like any other city in the world – or, at least, in Europe'. But although the film draws comparisons between these cities, it positions them as global rather than as European. The latter aspect is developed exclusively through plot, as a sequel to an 'Erasmus' film, through the French and British co-produced television show and finally William's wedding.[8]

At the same time, the fact that Paris, London and St. Petersburg are presented not simply as transnational, but also as European, suggests cosmopolitanism is a particular feature of Europe. As discussed in Chapter 1, European identity is seen as cosmopolitan because it invites its citizens to feel connected to other countries and cultures through a positive association with inclusion and acceptance of difference. Hinted at in narrative terms towards the end of *Pot Luck*, the idea of cosmopolitanism is recovered in *Russian Dolls*, when, in St. Petersburg, all characters make a toast in different languages, wishing their best to the newlyweds. The cities depicted in these films are European as well as universal, just as European citizens are part of a globalized world. As Stephanie H. Donald, Eleonore Kofman and Catherine Kevin (2009: 3) put it, cosmopolitanism can be seen as 'a process of the human imagination, that is, an affective disposition that inflects social and political relationships', as 'a wishful thought, a dream of a better world'. Films such as *Pot Luck* and *Russian Dolls* insist not only on commonality, but also on the highly positive features of this feeling and its political contours, and thus may be seen as 'wishful thinking' too. The idea of 'Europeanness as universality' discussed in Chapter 3 re-emerges in European city films, particularly those directed by Klapisch, a true supporter of the European integration process as noted by Blum-Reid (2009: 4).

From the perspective of Klapisch's films, cosmopolitanism, especially in its European guise, is something to pursue, rather than to question. However, as Tim Bergfelder argues, cosmopolitanism can be problematic if understood as a totalizing universalism. As Bergfelder (2012: 63) notes, '[C]osmopolitanism's historical closeness to Euro-centrism has also been criticized'. The opposition between a cosmopolitanism that respects difference and one that overlooks it is analysed in greater detail later in this chapter. *Pot Luck*, like *Russian Dolls*, ignores not only those outside Europe's borders, but also those who, living within 'Fortress Europe', yet unlike white middle-class Xavier and his fellow Erasmus students, face the power of exclusion. Tourism and cosmopolitanism, rather than being in opposition, become part of the same phenomenon that allows a number of global citizens (but not all) to travel freely, mostly without hindrance from linguistic or political barriers. The European traveller, because of his or her cosmopolitan status, becomes the 'right kind' of tourist – even when he is, like Xavier, more than just a short-term visitor. The cosmopolitan view of Europe put forward by these films thus denotes a real but partial reflection of the continent. In addition to picturing key landmarks, Klapisch's presentation of people from different countries happily living together is in itself a postcard; it is a snapshot, a glossy and optimistic view, hiding complex, darker, layers.

Another film directed by Klapisch instead presents the other side of the European global city. *Paris* marks the return of the director to his city after the European co-productions analysed before. Less successful than his two previous films, it was nevertheless seen by 1.7 million viewers in France. The film follows different characters, interrelating a number of stories set in the French capital. Its main narrative is focused on Pierre (Romain Duris), a dancer who is diagnosed with a serious health condition and, waiting at home for a heart transplant, spends his days looking down at the Parisian streets from his balcony. The city emerges as a space of dualities, from the market Pierre's sister Élise (Juliette Binoche) visits on a weekly basis (invested with the meanings of happiness and the local) to the immigrants she interviews at work (signifying anguish and the global). A sense of struggle connects the different characters, showing Paris as a globalized metropolis, where the inequalities of contemporary society come into view. Visions of the French capital are presented through two main discourses: tourism and cultural diversity. Montmartre (where a couple sits drinking champagne, claiming 'let's act like dumb tourists') is thus positioned in deep contrast with the 'real', multicultural city, including a bakery owner's comments on an 'Arab' girl who applies for a job in her shop.

Paris makes a further detour through Africa, telling the journey of an illegal immigrant from Cameroon to Paris. The immigrant is significantly unnamed. Despite playing an important role in this sequence of the film, he emerges here as a secondary character. *Paris* thus makes a point about the presumed insignificance (when not invisibility) of those who do not belong to Europe, generally cast as second-class people and less important figures. The film shows him working at a holiday resort in Africa and wearing a French national team football T-shirt with Zidane's name on it. France is here a point of identification, not in the present or in reality, but as a wishful thought too. Later, through editing, the film combines a shot of a luxurious setting in Paris with the back of a truck on its way to Europe. Baroque music links the two shots, but whereas hues of gold define the first location, the latter is dire and poor. In *Paris*, disparity, rather than commonality, defines the relationships between characters of different ethnic and racial backgrounds, and citizens are not all alike, or even all citizens.

The film ends with the Cameroonian, who travelled to Paris on the back of the truck shown before, standing on a bridge across from Notre Dame. Holding in his hand a postcard he had been sent from Paris, he compares the real cathedral with its pictorial representation. As this scene literally shows, in addition to using culture as a selling point, postcards, and by consequence, cinematic postcards, contribute to the debate about globalization and Europeanization that has characterized the study of cinema and the city.

While the plot line of the Cameroonian adds migration to the trajectories of tourism and cosmopolitanism discussed so far, it also superimposes them, showing not only that they overlap, but also that they are equally crucial for an understanding of global European cities. Visions of cosmopolitan Europe raise important questions about whether the supposed universality of the idea of Europe is not in fact challenged by an exclusive perception of the continent. Cinematic postcards question a paradox at the core of the EU's contemporary work with regard to the cultural placing of the continent within a universal sphere, but a simultaneous political project to delineate Europe's borders, therefore effectively closing it to the globe.

Paris encapsulates both positive and negative readings of Europe's metropolises. As the film shows, at the same time as European cities are praised for their history, beauty and culture, they are also an important location regarding the development (and resolution) of social problems. While cinematic postcards are imbued with an optimistic feeling, many contemporary films are very critical of Europe's current state. The films analysed in the second half of this chapter stress this other side of the European city, as a space, at least at first glance, not for integration but exclusion, not for happy cosmopolitanism but unfair globalization. I look at 'state-of-the-nation' films – an expression borrowed from John Hill's (1999) taxonomy for 1980s British cinema – although I am not concerned with the nation as such, but with the implications the issues represented on screen carry for the definition of the European city and European society more generally. My focus is primarily on the matter of Europe's borders. Whereas the majority of the films analysed to this point take place in the city centre, those considered from here on are set at the margins, geographically and/or metaphorically, of large European cities.

Under surveillance: Europe's urban dystopias

Before moving to look more closely at Europe's external borders, this chapter examines the inner divisions of European cities, particularly in relation to video surveillance. A significant number of contemporary European films deal with the topic of surveillance. These include, among those released with the support of MEDIA, *La Zona/The Zone* (Rodrigo Plá, 2007), set in Mexico City; *Red Road* (Andrea Arnold, 2006), set in Glasgow; and *Caché/Hidden* (Michael Haneke, 2005), set in Paris. Rising interest in this theme highlights changes in the regulation of national and international security. A component of policies on terrorism and immigration (a topic to which I return at the end of this chapter), surveillance is depicted in these films as an urban problem. Although surveillance is of course also a feature of touristic spaces, cinematic narratives generally associate it with marginal urban locations. Its presence hints at a negative view of the city, perceived as unsafe and in need of monitoring. Surveillance itself mobilizes impulses often viewed negatively, namely, voyeurism. Through their narratives, films such as the ones mentioned earlier bring to the fore the issues of exclusion and inclusion in contemporary European cities, putting forward a dystopian vision of urban space.

A key example of the cinematic articulation between inner divisions in Europe and urban marginalization can be seen in *Red Road*. A British and Danish co-production, this is Andrea Arnold's first feature film and the first to emerge out of Lars von Trier's 'Advanced Party' project (see Hjort 2010). Awarded a number of accolades, including a Jury Prize at Cannes, *Red Road* achieved considerable critical success. This was not however matched at the box-office; the film was seen by 150,000 viewers only across Europe. Nevertheless, as my analysis will show, *Red Road*'s representation of urban space makes it an invaluable case study for the understanding of the cinematic visions of Europe supported by the EU.

The film tells the story of Jackie (Kate Dickie), who is a closed-circuit television (CCTV) operator. In one of her shifts, she recognizes a man she had not seen for a long time. Clyde (Tony Curran) has just been released from jail, having killed, as we later find out, Jackie's husband and daughter in a car accident. Jackie starts spying on Clyde, using the CCTV system at work. She finds out where he lives (the Red Road flat complex, which gives the film its title) and decides to approach him in order to get revenge.

Red Road is set in Glasgow, a city that has an important tradition of cinematic representation. For instance, Elizabeth Lebas (2005: 29) extensively documented the work of the Glasgow Film Corporation (active between 1920 and 1978) as offering, for the most part of the twentieth century, a view of the city focused on 'radical social policies of national reconstruction, particularly those promoting public health, public housing and public education'. *Red Road* seems to be built on a predetermined vision of Glasgow that reflects the difficult and problematic image denounced by the documentaries produced by the local authority, as well as by subsequent fiction films. Like, for example, Liverpool and Manchester, Glasgow faced a major decline after the Second World War and became a post-industrial city. In the post-war era, the city and its neighbouring towns became the perfect location for stories of an impoverished working class and its decaying houses – as depicted, for instance, in Ken Loach's *Sweet Sixteen* (2002).

More recently, however, a new view of the Scottish city has emerged. After hosting the European Capital of Culture initiative in 1990, Glasgow was named UNESCO City of Music in 2008. The city also hosted the Commonwealth Games in 2014. As acknowledged in a report about the celebration of Glasgow as European Capital of Culture in 1990, 'from a declining industrial centre with widespread pessimism about its future, Glasgow has been transformed into a forward thinking city with a population of 600,000 and is currently one of the "hippest" spots in Europe' (Glasgow Development Agency 1992: 12). This notion is consistent with the 'Glasgow, Scotland with style' brand launched by the Glasgow City Marketing Bureau in 2004 – and which follows in the footsteps of the 'Glasgow's Miles Better' campaign of the 1980s. However, this supposed new image has not replaced, but coexists, with past perceptions of the city. The 2004 brand's focus on 'style' is in stark contrast with Glasgow's ongoing social problems, including low life expectancy, high unemployment rates and growing complaints about social harassment and discrimination (Scott 2004).

In view of such contrasts, Glasgow is a particularly interesting cinematic location. The more modern view of the city is depicted, for instance, in *Ae fond kiss* (Ken Loach, 2004), examined later in this chapter. In turn, *Red Road* privileges the decaying perception of Glasgow – even if this is more of a conceptual, rather than a visual, perspective of the city. Although *Red Road* was co-funded by the Glasgow Film Office, it shows very little of the actual space of the city. Overall, the narrative feels claustrophobic, with the majority of scenes taking place indoors, in the CCTV room at work, in Jackie's flat or in her friend's car. The images played in the CCTV control room show buses, streets that are busy during the day and deserted at night, houses, shops and office buildings. These could be located in any other city in Scotland, in the United Kingdom or in Europe. The only distinguishable space is in fact the central and most striking location of the film: the Red Road flat complex.

Formed of eight high-rise towers, the estate was built in 1969. In the summer of 2012 one of the towers was demolished; the remaining buildings are planned to be pulled down in coming years. Initially, the demolition of the towers was to be included in the opening ceremony of the Commonwealth Games in 2014. This idea was abandoned after protesters strongly argued against the demolishing of homes for entertainment; the plan was, according to demonstrators, hugely disrespectful towards those living in Red Road. Most of the inhabitants of Red Road are immigrants who face ever-decaying living conditions. Known for high levels of crime, this is depicted as a dangerous and deprived area in the film. Jackie assumes it to be a conglomerate of 'ex-prisoner flats'. We first see the blocks of flats through surveillance images; the buildings are so wide, and especially so tall, that Jackie needs to move the camera from side to side and up and down to see the entire estate. Despite these dimensions, the presentation of the Red Road estate feels claustrophobic. When Jackie first goes to Red Road, we see the towers from a bus window. The rigid frame reinforces the enclosed nature of that space.

The tower blocks are a territory of their own, with clearly defined boundaries. Hence, when Jackie first tries to enter one of the Red Road towers, she is stopped by a concierge. Just as this space is noticeably made distant from the city centre, so do its inhabitants feel detached from the outside world. *Red Road* is a film about the loss of family and the notion of (in)justice, as well as of a compromised future: the Red Road flats are a decaying space where people are stuck; they are lost, with no employment or future perspectives. Such sense of detachment is highlighted in a scene when Clyde's friend opens the window from their high rise flat to look at the view and feel the wind. This prevents them from breathing or feeling closer to other locations outside the estate, pushing them back in, as the wind quite literally sweeps their faces. The outsiders of European society are kept at the margins by the inner divisions of European cities: architecturally, when one considers the Red Road flats, visually when we look at the role played by video surveillance. The idea of Europe emerges here as divisive rather than all-encompassing.

Also present in Arnold's subsequent feature *Fish Tank* (2009), tower blocks appear in a large number of British as well as European films, such as *Gomorra/Gomorrah* (Matteo Garrone, 2008), *12:08 East of Bucharest* and *Lilja 4-Ever/Lilya 4-Ever* (Lukas Moodysson, 2002). Housing problems and urban sprawling are pan-European concerns. Equally, a realistic treatment of social issues is a strong component of European art cinema. Another film released with the support of MEDIA and which represents Europe's urban space under surveillance is *Hidden*, which stresses geographical, class and ethnic borders in a non-romanticized Paris. The film was awarded Best Director, the FIPRESCI and the Ecumenical Jury prizes at the Cannes Film Festival in 2005. It also won a number of European Film Awards, including Best Director for Michael Haneke. Watched by 1.7 million viewers across Europe, *Hidden* generated a vast number of reviews, articles and scholarly essays across Europe and beyond, including 'The Caché dossier' published in the journal *Screen* in 2007. Together with *Amelie*, *Hidden* is probably one of the most widely discussed European films of the contemporary era. It is therefore particularly interesting to note the overwhelmingly opposed views of Paris the two films present. [9]

Hidden tells the story of an upper-middle-class couple, Georges (Daniel Auteuil) and Anne (Juliette Binoche), who have an anonymous videotape containing images of their house delivered to their doorstep. After the first tape, a second one arrives, followed by letters, delivered to Georges' office and to their son's school, as well as by unidentified phone calls. Developing as a thriller, the film then unravels a plot connected to the Algerian War, in particular the Paris massacre of 1961. In addition to referring to a particular historical period, *Hidden* is also concerned with today's Paris, albeit in a much more negative way than a number of films analysed before.

The film's narrative is divided between two major locations: a quiet residential inner-city area (the *quartier des fleurs* in the fourteenth arrondissement) and the HLM (*habitation a loyer modéré* or council flats) of the North-East *banlieue* of Romainville, at a distance of more than seven kilometres from the city centre. While obvious comparisons can be drawn between Georges' discreetly elegant house and the buildings in the *banlieue* (in terms of location, size and decoration), both habitats are similar insofar as they are clearly isolated from the outside. The flats of Romainville are located in a deserted area of Paris; Georges and Anna's home, although in a residential area and well connected, has two doors and is very much protected. Surrounded by books, the bourgeois couple lives in the comfort of their house. Comfort is also what characterizes other locations in the film where we see them, such as the swimming pool, the television studio where Georges works or the stylish bookshop where Anna attends a reception. These are selective and exclusive settings, separated from the outside world and the rest of the city. As is the case with *Red Road*, *Hidden* highlights the boundaries that separate specific areas both in the centre (geographically) and at the margins (including metaphorically) of European cities.

Ignoring the key landmarks of the French capital represented in the films analysed in the first half of this chapter, *Hidden* could be seen to depict, to use Susan Hayward's (2000: 23) terms, a 'real' Paris more that an 'imagined' one. Of course, the Eiffel Tower is just as real as the Parisian *banlieue*. The value attributed to locations such as the ones featuring in *Hidden* echoes the dismissal of touristic spaces as inauthentic. Non-touristic spaces emerge as genuine, also because, rather than presenting an apparently superficial view of European culture, they more immediately showcase the complexities of contemporary Europe. Whereas Europe's cinematic postcards emphasize a sense of harmony within the continent, the locations of *Red Road* and *Hidden* stress the inequalities that characterize the cities in which their narratives are set. By showing the darker sides of Glasgow and Paris, both films put forward a dystopian vision of the metropolis in Europe. Even surveillance is not presented as contributing to the security of the city's inhabitants; rather, it endangers their lives. In *Hidden*, it brings back compromising memories of Georges' past; in *Red Road*, it is used to convict Clyde of a crime he did not commit. Video images enclose characters in specific spaces, with clearly defined limitations. CCTV footage not only highlights geographical boundaries within the city, it is also in itself a kind of border, in both cases, to the past.

At the same time, both cinematic postcards and surveillance footage of marginal locations of European cities, including those depicted in *Red Road* and *Hidden*, are equally partial visions of Europe. Just as postcards are selective, so is video surveillance; the two types of images show only one apparently discrete section of European cities. Against the glossy and glamorous representation of cinematic postcards, the contained zones of European cities showcased here are not characterized by discovery or celebration, but exclusion and desolation. *Paris*, examined earlier, hints at the potential encounters between separate areas of the global European city. By contrast, *Red Road* and *Hidden* enact the crossing of borders only to show its devastating effects. Europe is often defined in relation to these two extremes too: either as a totalizing dream, especially in the eyes of institutions such as the EU, or as an unbalanced mix of isolated units, according to many critics of the European integration process. Departing from a focus on divisive surveillance and moving to the exploration of the potential abolition of borders, the next section examines films where the boundaries are not physical but cultural. I analyse cinematic visions of multicultural European cities. At stake here are also religious, ethnic and linguistic differences.

Europe's cultural borders: Multiculturalism and intercultural dialogue

As noted in a EU report on urban development, '[T]he demographic change and migration challenge is one of the most important issues confronting European cities and regions today and in the future' (European Commission 2009: 47). Consequences of this change include overpopulated and ageing cities, as well as unregulated urban sprawl and housing problems, as depicted in *Red Road* and *Hidden*. A shift in the global migration flux should also be considered: Europe is increasingly perceived as a destination rather than a point of departure. Even traditional emigration states, such as Spain, Greece and Portugal, are today the targets from migrants from all over the world, including other parts of Europe.[10]

The European Commission (2009: 47) report goes on to stress that 'the population of non-EU residents in cities can be as high as 23 per cent in France and 16 per cent in Germany. The average non-national population in the EU Member States is about 5.5 per cent of the total population'. In European cinematic cities such as Barcelona in *Pot Luck*, Xavier's life is presented as 'multicultural' when he sits with colleagues from Spain, Belgium and Senegal. However, as Ella Shohat and Robert Stam (2003) note, the term 'multiculturalism' has many different significances and connotations. For them, it is important to distinguish between the multicultural fact and the multicultural project. Whereas the former points at the heterogeneity of the characters depicted in *Pot Luck*, the latter aims to rewrite 'world history and contemporary social life from a decolonizing and antiracial perspective' (7).

Particular EU policies illustrate Shohat and Stam's conception of multiculturalism as a project, albeit in a negative way. These have been strongly criticized for their Eurocentrism – as also hinted at by Bergfelder's (2012) views on cosmopolitanism discussed earlier. For instance, the European Commission nominated 2008 as the European Year of Intercultural Dialogue (EYID). As stated in the programme's official website, the EYID 'recognizes that Europe's great cultural diversity represents a unique advantage. It will encourage all those living in Europe to explore the benefits of our rich cultural heritage and opportunities to learn from different cultural traditions' (European Commission 2008). The EU's view of multiculturalism suggests this is an increasingly visible phenomenon, at the same time as it highlights the intercultural nature of

Europe's history. Including the use of words such as advantage and opportunities this quotation points to a utopian perspective. Even though this has been challenged by many involved in and commenting on the European integration process, this quotation is also a good example of the Commission's positive attitude, which encourages dialogue, and puts forward the notion of understanding as one of the keywords for successful integration.

Such values, as well as a similar positive tone, are also explored in one of the many films supported by MEDIA that address the topic of multiculturalism: *Seres Queridos/ Only Human* (Dominic Harari and Teresa Pelegri, 2004). The film tells the story of Leni (Marián Aguilera), who introduces her Palestinian boyfriend Rafi (Guillermo Toledo) to her Jewish family. A comedy, the film takes place in Madrid in the space of one evening. It follows a series of events that lead Leni to reveal the truth about Rafi's origins, narrating the chaos that unfolds. Despite its generally positive outlook, the film's view of multicultural Europe is ambiguous. *Only Human* also criticizes political strategies for multiculturalism, explicitly referring to the European Commission in one particular scene. Finding Leni and Rafi's luggage in the building's hall, one of the neighbours rings their flat to complain. When Leni's younger brother opens the door and mechanically answers with a number of Sabbath rules (claiming, for instance, that he cannot carry the luggage back to their house as it is forbidden to work on the Jewish weekly day of rest), the neighbour dismisses his fundamentalist claims and replies: 'to be part of this community, you must be normal'. When he turns around, going down the stairs to his house, the camera focuses the yellow euro logo (€) on the back of his blue tracksuit (Figure 4.9). Later on, when a shot is fired and accidentally hits the ceiling of his flat, the neighbour comes up the stairs reading the building's regulations out loud, thus parodying the EU's bureaucratic nature. Trying to achieve 'normality' by 'flattening' multiculturalism is a common criticism of EU policies, which are often seen as Euro-centric and homogeneous.

Figure 4.9 Defending 'normality' in *Only Human*.

Normality is of course an elusive term. In *Only Human*, despite having lived in Spain for twelve years and speaking perfect Spanish, Rafi is portrayed as an outsider; this is based more on religion than on language or other cultural references. Rafi sounds Spanish, but there is still something 'strange' about him – especially his religion: Islam. However, the family of the Jewish Leni is also portrayed as 'weird'. In the film's initial sequences, we are introduced to Leni's sister, a nymphomaniac; her brother, a recently converted orthodox Jew; her six-year-old niece who believes she is pregnant; and her grandfather, a war veteran who loads and shoots a rifle inside the house even though he is blind.

At first glance, *Only Human* seems to stress diversity rather than unity – to echo the EU's motto. However, presenting these characters as just as 'different' as Rafi (him in terms of nationality and religion), the film moves from a stress on cultural borders to a depiction of humanism. All characters are shown to behave strangely, and this is what makes them equal; diversity leads to a sense of unity allowed by universality. The film's international title, *Only Human*, hints at the importance of seeing people as individuals not defined by their race, class or religion – something not present in its original title, *Seres Queridos*, literally translated as 'loved beings'. In the film's international title, humanity replaces the idea of love. Europe is here presented as truly cosmopolitan, in the sense that the term suggests individuals from all over the world are connected and empathize with each other – as in Kwame Anthony Appiah's (2007) view of cosmopolitanism discussed in Chapter 1.

Similarly, in *Ae fond kiss* we are presented with a cosmopolitan view of Glasgow separated by religion but unified by love. The film tells the story of Casim (Atta Yaqub), an entrepreneur of Pakistani origin, and Roisin (Eva Birthistle), a music teacher at a Catholic school, who fall in love and are faced with conservatism both from his family and from her employers. The film is the fifth collaboration of director Ken Loach with screenwriter Paul Laverty. Released in 2004, *Only Human* ominously preceded the Madrid train bombings that took place that same year and that meant many Arabs were discriminated against after the attack – just as Rafi is at key points in the film. By comparison, Laverty has stated in interviews that *Ae fond kiss* originated from his reflection on 9/11 and the way Pakistani people were treated in the United States and in the United Kingdom after these events (in Mottram 2004: 23). Pakistani immigrants in the United Kingdom have been widely depicted on screen in previous decades (for instance, in Stephen Frears' 1985 film *My Beautiful Laundrette*), but the issue clearly has contemporary resonance. *Ae fond kiss* was watched by 1.4 million people all over Europe. It won a prize of the Ecumenical Jury at the Berlin Film Festival in 2004 and a César as Best European Union Film in the same year.

In conjunction with *My Name Is Joe* (1998) and *Sweet Sixteen*, *Ae fond kiss* has also been seen as part of Loach's Glaswegian trilogy. Rather than privileging the social realist strand of Glasgow's cinematic history like *Red Road*, for David Martin-Jones (2009: 182), *Ae fond kiss* 'goes out of its way to represent post-industrial Glasgow as a city of ethnic and cultural diversity, despite the problematic relations that can arise when immigrant traditions meet Western modernity'. While it does not shy away from the problems that stem from religious and racial conflicts, *Ae fond kiss* presents

Glasgow's ethnic diversity as, more than politically correct, almost trendy, in line with the previously mentioned 'Glasgow: Scotland with style' 2004 brand. Characters often meet in elegant bars and clubs and both Roisin and Casim's friend live in modern, fashionable houses.

Unlike in *Red Road*, in *Ae fond kiss* the city's inner boundaries are not in evidence. While cultural borders are visible in society more generally, the film does not construct an urban dystopia, as characters move freely all around town. Mobility characterizes Glasgow as an open metropolis, which is in contrast with the divided Glasgow discussed earlier. The style of *Ae fond kiss*, particularly the use of sound, also contributes to a unified view of the city. This can be seen, for instance, in relation to dialogue (especially in its initial sequence at school, when Casim's sister argues against the West's simplification of Muslims), as well as to the use of language as an idiom (Roisin and Casim use each other's language to show intimacy and demonstrate their knowledge of their respective cultures).

Music also plays a significant part in the presentation of a unified cosmopolitan Glasgow. Diegetic music often carries on from a sequence where it is narratively motivated to others where it works as soundtrack, or begins as a backdrop and then continues to a sequence that shows its on-screen source. For example, the Scottish folk song 'Ae fond kiss' (by Robert Burns), interpreted by a student during Roisin's lesson, accompanies the first shot of Casim's house, thus linking for the first time the two lovers. Confirmation of their relationship also comes through music, as, after helping to move Roisin's grand piano to her flat, Casim listens to her playing, smiling, in love. As an element of the film's form that pervades and links sequences, music can be seen to symbolize their multi-ethnic union, as a universal language that allows the borders of their cultures to become more permeable.

The presentation of music as universal language makes *Ae fond kiss* similar to *Merry Christmas*. However, through a focus on religion, both *Only Human* and *Ae fond kiss* show the socio-temporal change that has occurred in Europe, for instance, since the First World War. Contemporary Europe is no longer exclusively white and Christian (if it ever was) – one of Europe's most debatable historical features as discussed in Chapter 1. The protagonists of *Only Human* and *Ae fond kiss* come from middle-class backgrounds and try to address multicultural, multilingual, multi-ethnic and multireligious issues in an enlightened way, through discussion and dialogue. In *Only Human* words like 'tolerance' are often spoken. In *Ae fond kiss* this is particularly visible in a scene in Spain, where Roisin and Casim enjoy a romantic break and, sitting in a café, ask each other what stories 'they' have, comparing the Bible with the Koran. The couple are comfortable in their roles as cosmopolitan European citizens, who can easily travel outside the United Kingdom – just as Leni and Rafi are prepared to face centuries of cultural battles to build a new intercultural family.

The cultural differences accentuated in *Only Human* and *Ae fond kiss* do not prevent these films from depicting an essentially borderless, undivided urban space (and, by consequence, Europe), which is brought together by a cosmopolitan wish to be tolerant and culturally open. *Only Human* and *Ae fond kiss* privilege similarity, rather than difference, in the encounters taking place in Europe between people from diverse backgrounds, even if, in order to do so, they begin by displaying stereotypical views of particular communities. This is similar to the way in which, as argued in Chapter 3, many contemporary European films depicting transnational encounters often start by stressing essentialist visions of the nation.

Dialogue and language as privileged means of understanding are also explored in *The Class*, another film released with MEDIA support. The film narrates one year in the life of a teacher and his teenage students in a school in Belleville, a multi-ethnic Parisian neighbourhood. Popular with critics and audiences alike, *The Class* was watched by 1.5 million viewers in France and a total of two million people all over Europe. It won the Golden Palm at the Cannes Film Festival in 2008 and was nominated for an Oscar as Best Foreign Film. In addition to launching a public discussion about education in France and abroad, *The Class* also fuelled debates on interracial mix and integration. Although for an Italian critic, it reflects 'all peripheral schools of big European cities' (Frasca 2008: 3), as Vincendeau (2009: 36) suggests, the film engages with the theme of Frenchness, asking what it means to be French today. As such, it echoes former president Nicolas Sarkozy's project on this topic (launched in 2009), which involved the creation of a Ministry for Immigration and National Identity, and which was met with strong political and popular opposition. However, unlike this initiative, *The Class* does not aim at an essentialist idea of French culture or even of multiculturalism, rather playing out contrasting views of students from European, Asian and African backgrounds.

The film's focus is on language, which is central for any policy on national identity. It is thus no coincidence that the main character is a teacher of French language and literature, in addition to the fact that the actor who plays him, François Bégaudeau, is a former French teacher in a similar 'real' school and wrote the book on which the film is based. On the one hand, *The Class* highlights the importance of what people say, thus exploring the value of discourse. For instance, the students challenge the precision of the teacher when instead of 'one hour' he should have said 'fifty minutes', playing with the actual meaning of words. On the other hand, the film's dialogue hints at how people say what they say. This can be seen in terms of connotations (as they discuss whether or not 'homosexual' is an insult); the use of expressions and sayings (for instance, 'the penny drops' idiom is used in the English subtitling of the film's DVD edition launched by Artificial Eye); the cultural references available to these students (who know about Austria but cannot locate it on a map); and the idea of register (which they relate to age and class). The idea of Europe is not just defined through meaning, but also tone. It is important for institutions such as the EU, criticized for their lack of legitimacy, to explore different strands of communication and try new ways to reach out to the citizens they represent.

At the same time however, the film also highlights the limits of communication. The teacher claims that 'everyone is free to express themselves as long as they are polite', but then uses a very strong word to describe two students, leading to the climax of the film. Whereas *Ae fond kiss* uses music and dialogue to create links between different cultures, *The Class* highlights the power as well as the shortcomings (or potential danger, precisely because of its strength) of language in a multicultural society. *The Class* demonstrates the importance of language and the issues surrounding its usages to emphasize a compromised European project that does not treat all citizens equally. This is especially significant as language is here allied to questions of class and privilege; the film is centred on a middle-class white teacher that addresses a class of working-class, ethnically diverse students.

EU cultural policy also places a strong emphasis on this issue, with multilingualism being one of the key working areas of the European Commission division in charge of the education and culture sectors. However, just as in *The Class* a number of students complain when the teacher uses 'Bill' (referring to a famous American president) as an example of a foreign name, proposing instead Aïssata or Fatou, so does multilingualism for the EU involve an exclusively Western and Euro-centric perspective. This scene, like EU policy, highlights the importance of defining what 'sounds European' in opposition to what does not belong to Europe's linguistic heritage. Similarly, EU initiatives in this area protect regional languages, such as Welsh or Catalan, but ignore the many Asian or African languages now spoken throughout the continent.

From Nicolas Sarkozy's project on what it means to be French to the rise of right-wing extremist parties and political associations across the continent, discussions about who belongs to and who should be excluded from Europe are central to the future of the EU. Angela Merkel's claim in October 2010 that multiculturalism has failed in Germany and similar remarks made by British prime minister David Cameron a few months later have fuelled topical debates on Europe's stand on immigration and integration. The historical results parties advocating racist and xenophobic policies achieved in the European Parliament elections in May 2014 confirmed the relevance of this debate for twenty-first-century Europe. While a growing number of voters support measures to increase border controls and effectively close Europe to 'foreigners', many other Europeans show their availability to host refugees, especially those fleeing Syria since 2011. Whereas *Only Human, Ae fond kiss* and *The Class* address the meaning of Europe from an internal perspective, the next section looks at the continent's external borders, in cultural and political terms. In doing so, it explores the importance of movement and mobility for the constitution of European cities. As many see the continent as a destination, my analysis also explores the EU's role as the guarantor of 'Fortress Europe'.

Entering, leaving and living in Fortress Europe

Coined during the 1940s and originally referring to a Nazi plan for European occupation, 'Fortress Europe' is today associated with European immigration. Also the title of a film (*Tvrdjava Evropa* [Zelimir Zilnik, 2005]), the expression signals the efforts of national governments and pan-European bodies to control Europe's boundaries. 'Fortress Europe' is also often used dismissively by critics, who highlight one of the most serious consequences of the definition of such boundaries: the difficulties and risks many face trying to illegally cross them. The difference between those 'with papers' and those without (or between the privileged Europeans and 'the others') is made very clear in a number of contemporary European films.

This is, for instance, the case of *Exils/Exiles* (Tony Gatlif, 2004). Awarded the Best Director prize at the Cannes Film Festival in 2004, the film tells the story of Zano (Romain Duris) and Naima (Lubna Azabal), a young couple who leave Paris for Algiers, walking, hitchhiking and travelling by train through France, Spain and the north of Africa. On the one hand, Zano and Naima are seen as strangers because they come from the city. Walking through fields and small villages in Andalusia, Naima regrets having left her mobile phone at home; later on, Zano calls her attention to peas, 'that green thing there', which she is incapable of recognizing. On the other hand, and more significantly, the fact that they are European citizens leaving the continent is in contrast with the voyages of many migrants who every day try to enter 'Fortress Europe'. For instance, in a key scene in the film, Zano and Naima calmly walk through the Spanish border, whereas two Algerian people they had met on the road must hide in the back of a truck.

In their editorial for the first issue of the journal *Mobilities*, Kevin Hannam, Mimi Sheller and John Urry (2006: 1) denote the prominence of studies of movement and spatiality across social sciences and the emergence of what they call a 'mobility turn'. As defined by their work, the study of mobility allows for an understanding of a complex Europe since, as they go on to suggest, it 'involves examining many consequences for different peoples and places located in what we might call the fast and slow lanes of social life' (11). *Exiles* and the particular sequence examined earlier denote the emergence of what Hannam, Sheller and Urry (2006: 6) define as a ' "kinetic elite" whose ease of mobility differentiates them from the low-speed, low-mobility majority'. However, as this section will show, it is not so much mobility per se but the legal status of this movement that distinguishes the citizen from the 'other', the tourist from the migrant.

Other contemporary films represent similar clandestine journeys, not from, but to Europe. These are often set in marginal spaces, within the city and within Europe more generally. *Lilya 4-Ever*, for instance, depicts a series of anonymous urban locations, from Eastern European derelict buildings to tall and isolated tower blocks in Malmö, Sweden. The film tells the story of Lilya (Oksana Akinshina), a young woman abandoned by her mother 'somewhere in the former Soviet Union'. With no money or interest in school, Lilya is promised a job in Sweden by handsome Andrei (Pavel Ponomaryov). However, after arriving in Malmö, she is locked in a flat and forced to work as a prostitute.

In addition to *Lilya 4-Ever*, films such as *25 Degrés en Hiver/25 Degrees in Winter* (Stéphane Vuillet, 2004), *Lichter/Distant Lights* (Hans-Christian Schmid, 2003), *Last Resort* (Pawel Pawlikowski, 2000) and *Transe/Trance* (Teresa Villaverde, 2006) approach similar issues. These films highlight internal divisions within the continent, as if some regions were 'more European' than others. Widely discussed as an example of the cinematic treatment of migration, globalization, neo-liberalism and human trafficking, *Lilya 4-Ever* also highlights the political limitations of Europe. It is because she has a passport (albeit a fake one) that Lilya is able to leave her impoverished town to travel to Sweden, which she sees as a definite improvement. However, it is also because her passport is taken away from her by those controlling her that Lilya is incapable of escaping.

Deprived of a document and of an official identity, she becomes a non-citizen, losing her rights.

Whereas *Lilya 4-Ever* denounces the barbaric commodification of trafficked women across Europe, *Princesas/Princesses* (Fernando León de Aranoa, 2005), another story set in the world of prostitution, further highlights the issue of racism in contemporary Europe. The film's main characters are Caye (Candela Peña), a Spanish middle-class prostitute, and Zulema (Micaela Nevárez), a Dominican illegal immigrant recently arrived in Madrid and forced to turn to prostitution. Watching the 'new girls' from the window of a hair salon, Caye and other Spanish prostitutes clearly mark the difference between them and 'the others', seen as competition because of the cheap prices they offer. Derogatory views of these women include comments about the way they walk, the fact that they 'smell' because 'they have different hormones' and that 'they don't wash' for cultural and religious reasons. Caye's friends more than once call the police, trying to get the immigrant women arrested and possibly deported.

The opposition between the Spanish prostitutes and the immigrants is constructed through shots of or with windows. In *Princesses*, windows become a motif to suggest that characters are trying to break free (as was also the case for Lilya). As the narrative progresses, Caye and Zulema become friends. But although there is a transformation in Caye (who becomes less bigoted and more humane, even if this is met with disapproval from her friends at the salon), no solution is presented for Zulema's troubles. Hence, when the two women sit in a café, discussing their dreams and plans for the future, they nostalgically look outside the window, as if imagining a place beyond the one they inhabit (Figure 4.10). Then, they go window-shopping, as Zulema looks for a birthday gift for her son, still in the Dominican Republic. The camera films them from inside the shop, clearly positioning them 'outside'. Finally, Caye watches Zulema calling

Figure 4.10 Windows as boundaries in *Princesses*.

her family from a glass phone booth, with the scene stressing the physical boundaries that affect Zulema's situation.

Zulema's origins, as was the case with Lilya's background in the previous film, are here presented as limitations. Throughout *Princesses*, Zulema tries at all costs to get a work permit; she feels her nationality is a shortcoming that prevents her from legally integrating within guarded Europe. Just as in *Lilya 4-Ever*, passports and permits become here a symbol of the continent's fear of the other, of racism and xenophobia. As leitmotifs, they also link the topics of tourism and migration, clearly dividing those who are in possession of such documents and as such belong (even if only temporarily) to Europe, being positively identified as tourists, and those who remain outside the community, negatively distanced as migrants. As such, these films highlight the existence of a two-tiered Europe that welcomes those visiting but denies entrance to those looking for work or better living conditions.

Conversely, the theme of (a European) nationality as empowerment is explored in *Le Silence de Lorna/The Silence of Lorna* (Jean-Pierre Dardenne, Luc Dardenne, 2008). The film tells the story of an Albanian immigrant who successfully applies for Belgian citizenship after a sham marriage with a junkie from Liège. After winning the Golden Palm at the Cannes Film Festival in 1999 for *Rosetta* and in 2005 for *L'enfant/The Child*, writers-directors Jean-Pierre and Luc Dardenne won the Best Screenplay prize for *The Silence of Lorna* at the 2008 edition of French festival. The film begins with a scene in a bank, where we see Lorna (Arta Dobroshi) asking for an appointment with the manager, revealing: 'I'll be Belgian soon, I'll be able to do it'. Referring to a loan application, she immediately states the importance of having a piece of paper officially attesting to her belonging to a European country. Citizenship signifies a new life and new opportunities. The setting of this initial scene highlights the importance of money (which often buys such documents) and transactions (at times of people themselves, trafficked as goods) for the situation of many immigrants trying to start a new life in Europe.

But, more importantly, the way Lorna phrases her request also stresses the fact that as a EU citizen she has rights – something that neither Lilya nor Zulema, in the films discussed earlier, could enjoy. To some extent, however, these rights are limited through language. Lorna's silence binds her to the plans, wishes and demands of other people. It also traps her in her own guilt about having agreed to be part of a plot that involves killing her husband with an overdose.

On the other hand, unlike Lilya, locked like a valuable possession in a tower block in Malmö, as a citizen, Lorna has some belongings of her own to protect. Keys and locks are recurring objects in the film, stressing the themes of confinement, safety and right of entry. *The Silence of Lorna* enacts a tension between freedom and entrapment, in terms of narrative and mise en scène. Lorna's marriage seems to signify liberty as it will grant her a Belgian identity card, but it also involves living in a small apartment and locking away her belongings every day. In the film's final sequence, Lorna runs to the woods (signifying the ideal of freedom). However, not only is the camera mostly centred on her rather than on the space around her, the end of this sequence also takes place in a locked and small shed, which stresses Lorna's continuing imprisonment. *The Silence of Lorna* can thus be seen to metaphorically represent Fortress Europe, which emerges as a highly guarded place where surveillance plays a determinant role. Lorna is constantly watched and constantly watches her belongings. Her new official European status signifies an apparent freedom, but she remains a second-class citizen because not originally 'European' and not a native speaker, in this specific case, of French.

Urban dystopias work as bookends to the second half of this chapter, from class and racial divisions in Glasgow and Paris, to the hellish lives of women like Lilya, Zulema and Lorna. These films show the difficulties those entering, leaving and living in Europe face in terms of bureaucracy, highlighting the prominence of passports, papers and certificates. The importance of language is equally stressed, especially in the sense of status; this is either official or non-existent, as in the simple dichotomy between the citizen and the illegal 'other'. However, while these remain strong motifs, legality and terminology are not the most pressing issues affecting Europe today, but rather the visible tip of a political iceberg that sees the actions of European institutions such as the EU preventing an increasing number of people from crossing its boundaries or doing so in humane conditions. The mobility of those depicted in the films discussed in the first section (whether European, like Xavier in *Pot Luck* or non-European – for instance, North American, like Carol in *Paris je t'aime*) is thus contrasted with the multiple obstacles faced by Lilya, Zulema and Lorna.

Urban space is a privileged lens through which to examine transformations in contemporary Europe. Cities emerge as part of Europe's heritage, at the same time as their importance is consistent with recent global changes. While the branding of European cities is not a new phenomenon (see, for instance, Shiel 2009), the link established between the contemporary European films examined here and the European integration process highlights the growing importance of the city at a time when the nation is increasingly questioned. Challenging Barber's (2002) suggestion, cities do not seem to be disappearing from European cinema; rather, they are becoming increasingly prominent, allowing for a reflection on Europe's current situation, including in relation to the continent's positioning in the world.

Cities such as Paris, London and Barcelona can indeed be 'walked' (Steiner 2006). However, the urban characters that populate them are no longer the *flâneur* and the poet. Artists still live in these cities (Pierre in *Paris*, Nola in *Match Point*, Huma Rojo in *All About My Mother*), but so do social workers (including in *Paris* and *All About My Mother*) and immigrants (*Paris je t'aime*, *Lilya-4-Ever*, *Princesses*), among many other figures. Contemporary European cinema overlaps positive and negative visions of European society, which thus emerges as complex and contradictory. It highlights Europe's contrasting nature, confirming Konstantarakos's (2000) point about the simultaneous importance of centrality and marginality as key tropes in European cinema's spatial configuration. While its cities are simultaneously dangerous and trendy (with the Glasgow of *Red Road* and that of *Ae fond kiss* a case in point), Europe is at the same time a destination for both tourists and migrants. The EU is simultaneously a political project defending multilingualism and a social reality discriminating against those who do not sound European. Europe is a borderless internal space that is also closed around its edges.

Tourists are often represented in contemporary European films. Most of these films, however, depict them in a negative light. Tourism is of course a crucial cultural activity, not to mention source of income, in today's Europe. Yet, the only form of tourism that is valued and accepted as 'good' is the one associated with art and culture. The connection between European cities and high art is particularly visible in *All About My Mother* and *Match Point* – in the latter, this becomes also a class issue, which is especially prominent in the British context. At the same time, both films testify to the extent to which cinematic auteurs, European or not, play a role in promoting and effectively 'selling' Europe, as well as its cities. Cinematic postcards further highlight the paradoxical nature of the idea of Europe in contemporary cinema, which is exclusive and inclusive at the same time. This middlebrow, consensual vision of Europe is also articulated on screen through the notion of universality. European cities appear in these films as cosmopolitan, global spaces. Through the idea of cosmopolitanism, the notion of Europeanness as universality gains strength, which highlights a desire by the EU to be perceived as a global actor that welcomes all. However, the visual representation of cosmopolitan Europe, especially in Klapisch's films, is in itself an optimist snapshot, a conceptual postcard. *Paris* and *Paris je t'aime*, for instance, highlight a dark and not just celebratory side of contemporary Europe and its urban sphere. Reading these films in relation to cosmopolitanism thus means questioning whether the universality of the European idea can ever be entirely inclusive.

Simultaneously, different areas and cultures emerge within the European metropolis, as ever more visible borders divide it into smaller units, in physical and symbolical terms. The two sides of Paris in *Hidden* testify to this, with CCTV offering a privileged tool to delimit and control these new micro spheres. The topics of surveillance and religion as well as the themes of silence and windows (among others) highlight a series of concrete boundaries – in contemporary cities and societies – despite the fact that theories of globalization, alongside the EU's adoption of the Schengen Agreement, construct a seemingly borderless Europe. If, as the EU claims, Europe has always been multicultural, new struggles are visible today, with immigrants such as those featured in *Paris* and *Princesses* being excluded from the continent.

This contradicts the positive attitude expressed by the European Commission in relation to multiculturalism and can be particularly observed in relation to language, as, in contrast with the English spoken in *Pot Luck* and *Russian Dolls*, new idioms become part of Europe's soundscape but are often ignored. Language is a seal of approval, important to terminology and legality too. These are especially important in a continent where definitions are key – for example, citizens and non-citizens. Who belongs to and who is not part of Europe becomes the central debate for the continent and the EU in the twenty-first century. A major goal of the European integration process is the opening of Europe's borders. However, this is only the case for the lucky few (the 'kinetic elite' discussed by Hannam, Sheller and Urry 2006). Seeking pleasure and desire for information can be contrasted with a parallel darker movement; the concept of borders (external and internal, rigid and porous) becomes particularly useful for an understanding of contemporary Europe in geographical, cultural and political terms. As the first sections in this chapter showed, Europe can never be completely closed because tourism is very valuable. These films highlight the emergence of a distinction between the 'right' and the 'wrong' kind of traveller.

A predominance of comedies in the first half of the chapter contributes to the positive and consensual tone of cinematic postcards. Most films considered in the second part of this chapter (crime films, melodramas and thrillers) can be seen as examples of European art cinema, traditionally seen as more committed than mainstream productions. Only by considering art and popular films can we have a comprehensive picture of Europe's current situation. These films draw attention to an economic, humanitarian (especially in relation to women and trafficking) and identity crisis (even for European citizens, as in the case of *Exiles*), as they incessantly problematize feelings of belonging. They are good examples of the convergence (especially in the first section) and, in some cases, divergence between cinema and EU policies, in cultural and other areas. As such, they probe and contribute to the definition of the idea of Europe that emerges on screen; they are prime examples of cinematic Euro-visions.

Conclusion: Cinematic Visions of Europe

As this book has shown, cinema is a rich field in which to look for the significance of the idea of Europe. Cinema tells the most varied tales of Europe, from the lives of historical figures, to wars, holidays and journeys of exclusion. It tells these stories in the most varied ways too, employing, for instance, camera movement, editing and aural transitions to make points about the fluidity of contemporary Europe, the similarities that exist between its spaces and the linguistic differences that separate those who inhabit it. Film is also a key maker of the idea of Europe because, by being produced at a transnational level and circulating beyond borders, it reaches people across the continent, presenting to different audiences the diverse aspects of the Europe it mirrors. But what idea of Europe does contemporary European cinema put forward? Confirming Edgar Morin's claim about Europe's dialogical essence (1987), Europe appears in contemporary European cinema as a space of contradictions and complexity. Its meaning can be found within three major oppositions, which will be explored in this conclusion: national versus transnational, art versus commerce and thought versus emotion.

National versus transnational

Because the focus of this book has been on the European Union (EU), the idea of Europe investigated here has a major institutional dimension. But Europe is also, and to begin with, a continent. The tension between the national and the transnational thus allows for a geopolitical understanding of Europe as well as of European cinema. The national has always been a prime way of exploring the issue of identity. When thinking about Europe, it is impossible to ignore the important role played by nation-states in the construction of this idea. Similarly, the understanding of film in Europe has been historically shaped by an attention to national cinemas. Yet, it is equally impossible to ignore the drive to go beyond borders that has developed with the expansion of globalization and, significantly, Europeanization, and that affects both the study of identities and of film.

It is important to note that the national and the transnational are not mutually exclusive; the national is, to start with, semantically, part of the transnational. This ostensible dichotomy should thus be better understood as a process, as the terms that constitute it are connected by an evolutionary line. This is a bidirectional path: it is not only the national that is 'transformed' into transnational, the latter also needs and often makes reference to the former. This is suggested, for instance, by the permanence of the national dimension in international co-productions, where we witness an apparent reverse shift from the transnational back to the national. In contemporary European films, including those oriented towards an international market (for instance, the North American market, as in the case of *La Vie en rose*), the idea of the nation is vividly present. However, it is as if national cultures (most often depicted through stereotypes, as in *Merry Christmas* or *Pot Luck*) are deliberately highlighted in order to be exploited; as if the national is precisely what allows film-makers to represent and audiences to potentially experience a transnational Europe. Somewhat paradoxically, it is the persistence and the solid grounding of the nation that allows many representations of Europe's past and present to go beyond borders.

As geopolitical terms, the 'national' and the 'transnational' are also related to other spatial spheres, namely, the globe and the city. Two major issues, which have appeared at different points in this book, problematize this dichotomy: universality on the one hand and the increasing urbanization of Europe on the other. Universality is a key characteristic of the history of Europe, the EU and European film. Europe is at once defined in opposition to others and welcoming to those beyond its borders. The EU wishes to be associated with, and promotes in its cultural policies and in the films it supports, general and undisputable values, such as tolerance, democracy and respect for human rights. Films such as *Merry Christmas*, *Sophie Scholl* and *Only Human*, for instance, foreground these kinds of incontestable ideals.

Tied to universality, and equally tied to the tension between the national and the transnational, is the rise of cosmopolitanism. Films about tourism and European travellers, from *2 Days in Paris* to *Pot Luck* and *Russian Dolls*, depict a positive perspective on an increasingly cosmopolitan, European and global society. Although the American tourists and European citizens presented on screen are alienated at the start of these filmic narratives, towards the end these characters realize they have benefitted from their encounters with other cultures.

Cosmopolitanism is also linked to the other key topic in the opposition between the national and the transnational in Europe: the growth in size and importance of the European metropolis. The EU has reinforced a number of policies crucial for the development of European cities, from a focus on Smart Cities, innovation and mobility, to the European Capital of Culture initiative. Similarly, and especially in the films analysed here that are set in the present, it is not so much the nation, but the city, that serves as the most significant sphere of identification. This is despite the fact that the city is the space where the nation lives, when we consider, for instance, the role of capitals in representing the state and consolidating the authority of political powers, as in the prominent shots of the Houses of Parliament and Westminster in European films set in London.

Contemporary cinema often depicts the story of a visitor arriving in a new place. *Paris je t'aime*, *Match Point* and *All About My Mother* highlight the importance of European cities – Paris, London and Barcelona, respectively – as cultural and touristic hubs, as well as strong markers of identification for the characters who live there or come to visit. The city is also where the nation is confronted with the transnational, or where the nation is at its most transnational, as it welcomes people from many different origins, as seen, for instance, in *Pot Luck*'s depiction of the Erasmus programme and in *Paris*'s focus on the multicultural status of the French capital. The city also plays a major role in shaping our understanding of the transnational framework as it offers a new sphere of reflection that is not just different from the nation, but also forms a key link between nations. Just as the European Capital of Culture initiative constitutes an institutional push to create a pan-European network of cities, so are many contemporary films set in different, but connected spaces. This is, for instance, the case of *Russian Dolls*, where similarities are drawn between London, Paris and St. Petersburg.

Art versus commerce – culture versus industry

The second major dialectical tension found in this book opposes art versus commerce; it can also be defined as culture versus industry. 'Art' and 'culture' are terms traditionally associated with Europe, the 'intellectual', highbrow continent, just as European cinema is generally – and despite invaluable academic work on popular European cinema (cf. Bergfelder 2015) – perceived as art cinema. But film is also an industry, not least because it is driven by transactions that often involve large sums of money. EU policies in support of the audiovisual industry have been characterized by a hesitation between wanting to increase the financial potential of European film and promoting its cultural aspects. These have encouraged a European cinema that, while always associated with quality, is simultaneously characterized by being popular (for instance, having many internationally successful stars) and highbrow (filmed by a long list of auteurs). We thus witness the emergence of an essentially middlebrow cinema as the cinema favoured by EU cultural institutions – a 'middlebrow-ness' that, through its inclusive guise (not too 'popular' to be disparaged, not too 'arty' to be alienating) echoes the notion of universality.

The representation of history on the one hand and the focus on contemporary Europe, in particular tourism and migration, on the other prove central to the definition of the idea of Europe in European cinema as two 'themes' that embody in a particularly clear way the tension between art and commerce. *Girl with a Pearl Earring*, *Becoming Jane* and *La Vie en rose*, for instance, present a series of important historical figures, especially artists, highlighting the link between history and art. However, as many critics have argued, the way in which these figures are represented suggests these films engage in a commodification of the past, which transforms 'serious' history into 'commercial' audiovisual spectacle. The notion of art is also associated with key European and international directors. This is despite the fact that some of these film-makers' work has been seen as a 'sell-out' (and therefore as commercial), as in the case of Woody Allen's box-office hit *Match Point*. Together with films such as *All About My Mother* and *Paris je t'aime*, *Match Point* explores the contrast between art and commerce also in the way in which it depicts European cities as visitor attractions. These emerge as profitable commodities, yet are spaces simultaneously defined by their culture, history and prestige.

The contrast between art and commerce also raises the issue of authenticity, which is a key point of debate in contemporary European films set in the past and in the present.

Critics of heritage cinema generally disparage costume dramas as unreal and fantastic tales. The narratives told in *Girl with a Pearl Earring* and *Becoming Jane*, for instance, are not received by reviewers as 'factual' history, but as romanticized accounts (see Rosenstone 2006). Authenticity is also relevant for our understanding of the cinematic presentation of tourism and the clichés this activity involves. The on-screen mockery of tourists emerging in *2 Days in Paris* and *Paris je t'aime* is a case in point, as visitors are disparaged because they engage in a seemingly superficial relationship with the spaces they see.

Originality and genuineness are also significant keywords in relation to the notion of European citizenship. Films such as *Ae fond kiss, The Class, Princesses* and others ask what people should be described as 'authentic' Europeans, as well as whether these can be defined by their race, religion and language. While EU foreign and security policy asks Europe to be 'serious' and build barriers, implementing tougher measures towards unwanted travellers, the films examined here seem to empathize with these excluded individuals. Adopting a more humanistic approach, films such as *Only Human, Lilya-4-Ever* and *Princesses* depict on screen stories of inclusion that invite viewers to identify with the victims of the enforcement of 'Fortress Europe'. By representing a vision of Europe that is not just defined by rational and apparently cold policies, but also by a warm desire to help, these films also show the extent to which the idea of Europe in contemporary European cinema is tied to both thoughts and emotions.

Thought versus emotion: Connecting with Europe

Throughout the history of Europe, intellect, reason and its association with high culture have been privileged to the detriment of emotion, which is seen as shallow and superficial. Enlightened Europe is serious and responsible – a vision replicated in the critiques voiced, for instance, by Morin (1987) and Derrida (1992), who question the relationship between Europe and the rest of the world in the postcolonial era. This is matched, in the realm of cinema, by the resurgence of committed film-making. *The Silence of Lorna*, by the Dardenne brothers, is an illustrative example of the contemporary political cinema that rationally engages with important and pressing issues facing Europe today – immigration in this particular case.

Reflection also emerges as a European idea with regard to the questioning of the value held by memory and history. For instance, *Good Morning, Night, Good Bye Lenin!* and *12:08 East of Bucharest* to some extent rewrite the history of different European nations on screen. There is in these films a recurring sense of having to challenge and rethink the past, as well as the way in which it has been written. Similarly, *Red Road* and *Hidden* testify to the prominence of thought in European culture by dramatizing the way in which the past often invades the present to settle accounts with it. In these films, Europe must reflect on its ongoing responsibility towards important but seemingly forgotten events.

European historical films frequently point to an idea of knowledge, and some have an accentuated didactic function. *Sophie Scholl*, which toured in schools, is one of the clearer examples of this trend. Equally, despite being disparaged by many (see, for instance, Neyrat 2006 in relation to *Sophie Scholl*), heritage films can also be seen as historical documents that contribute to the European citizens' knowledge of their own past. For instance, they work as museums, inviting the spectator to learn about European historical figures, such as Dutch painter Vermeer in *Girl with a Pearl Earring*. They talk about extraordinary individuals, as is the case of the biopics of Jane Austen and Edith Piaf, *Becoming Jane* and *La Vie en rose*. As reconstructions, these films often add details that are seen as secondary for the narrative or perceived to be there only for entertainment. Romantic plots, for instance, are used in *Girl with a Pearl Earring*, *Becoming Jane* and *La Vie en rose*. Heritage films thus vividly mirror the tension between thought (knowledge, facts) and emotion (spectacle, feelings), showing also that this tension does not necessarily need to be resolved, but actually works productively in terms of positioning European cinema as a quality *and* enjoyable product.

European films constitute a form of entertainment; the Europe they project on screen is also an object of passion. Films such as *Girl with a Pearl Earring*, *Merry Christmas* and *Sophie Scholl*, for instance, are characterized by spectacular images and overwhelmingly positive feelings that compel viewers to identify with the stories and characters represented on screen. Similarly, Europe's actual space, not just its stories and their protagonists, is also to be liked. Tourists visit and breathe in the European metropolis, sense its atmosphere and mood, for instance, in walks through cities such as Paris, London and Barcelona, in films including *Paris je t'aime*, *Match Point* and *Pot Luck*.

The meaning of Europe emerging in this book is therefore also tied to emotions. This is particularly clear from an analysis of the MEDIA 'clips', where joy, love and sadness in 2007 and passion in 2010 and 2011 encapsulate the EU's idea of Europe. Love, in particular, was presented by the European Commission as a theme and feeling for European cinema. European institutions put forward a wish for greater cinephilia (one that privileges films made in Europe) and a sense that to be European is also to *feel* European. This stress on emotion has to do with finding a balance between the idea of European unity and an increasingly individualistic society. Emotive Europe has been defined throughout this book by a sense of community, which paradoxically entails a focus on the individual too.

The idea of Europe depicted in contemporary European cinema is characterized by a sense of humanism (a value clearly expressed in the Declaration on European Identity signed in 1973), that is, by a focus on what constitutes human nature and what common values link individuals across the world. *Only Human*, *Ae fond kiss* and *The Class* highlight differences between individuals in Europe only to then suggest these differences can be overcome – that these films' characters are, after all, 'only human'. At the same time, while humanistic in tone, films such as *Merry Christmas*, *Sophie Scholl* and *Black Book* are concerned with the reactions of individuals in the face of adversity. The rising number of biopics emerging in Europe also testifies to the focus contemporary society places on singular human beings. Artists, heroes and anti-heroes feature in a cinema that adapts European history to personal memories. This personal dimension allows people to connect with Europe, while showing that individuals are, potentially, all the same. Just as the national is used to explore the transnational, the individual is here highlighted to represent humanity.

Cinematic Europe: Transnational, prestigious and emotional

The categories national and transnational, art and commerce and thought and emotion have been organized here into oppositional pairs. However, the disparities arising within these pairs are slightly imbalanced, as some terms have more weight than others. The transnational, for instance, appears as more important than the nation for the idea of Europe, especially as it is so highly valued in contemporary culture. Even if European states and national cinemas continue to play an important part in the definition of Europe and European film, it is undeniable that Europe is not a nation and that in fact a need to go beyond the nation is inherent to its essence.

In the opposition between art and commerce, despite the importance the economic and financial sectors have achieved in today's world (and the significance the euro-zone crisis, for instance, attained in the shaping of attitudes towards the EU), it is culture that appears as the most valued term. Quality, prestige and exclusivity have a greater weight in discussions about the idea of Europe and European cinema than economic success. The EU, criticized for its lack of legitimacy, reaches out to those it represents by moving the idea of Europe and the positioning of its cinema from a rational to an emotional dimension.

Historically, Europe has been labelled the continent of philosophy and of thinking. But in recent years, in order to bring its peoples together, the EU has been sponsoring a vague, albeit complex, idea of Europe that is essentially an emotional one. Instead of thought and reflection, emotion has been gaining currency. The MEDIA programme has essentially sponsored the circulation, rather than the production, of European cinema. Initiatives like the EU's MEDIA programme are rightly conceived if the institutional wish is to ensure the circulation of not only a larger number of European films, but also a wider variety, in terms of genre, budget and nationality. This insistence on diversity matches a cultural, not necessarily an industrial, aim. MEDIA's main goal appears to be not so much the financial development of the film industry, nor the establishment of a shared intellectual agenda for European film-makers, but more the creation of a transnational European audience. The major concern of contemporary EU initiatives in support of the audiovisual sector seems to be participation. This is a participation that relies on audiences *feeling* European and *liking* European cinema.

At the start of the twenty-first century, the EU's idea of Europe is not about thoughts but about feelings. Europe is transformed from a 'serious' into a 'passionate' continent, in the same way that the European integration process is to be appreciated rather than understood and European cinema should, from the point of view of European institutions, be experienced rather than examined. Testifying to a shift from the macro to the micro, from the social to the individual, the EU's idea of Europe that emerges in European cinema stresses Europe's transnational as well as prestigious character, at the same time as it grants space for a dialogical understanding of the continent, and especially, for an emotional connection to it.

Notes

Chapter 1

1 Data from the Standard Eurobarometer archives, which can be accessed online: http://ec.europa.eu/public_opinion/archives/eb_arch_en.htm (accessed 1 October 2014).
2 Available at http://ec.europa.eu (accessed 14 September 2014).

Chapter 2

1 The petition is available online at https://www.lapetition.be/en-ligne/The-cultural-exception-is-non-negotiable-12826.html (accessed 12 March 2014).
2 Data collected from the EAO's official website, www.obs.coe.int (accessed 12 March 2014).
3 Data collected from the MPAA's official website, www.mpaa.org (accessed 12 March 2014).
4 'Do not get confused', http://www.coe.int/aboutcoe/index.asp?l=en&page=nepasconfondre (accessed 12 March 2014).
5 Available online at http://eacea.ec.europa.eu/media/index_en.php (accessed 16 September 2014).
6 Results available through the EACEA's website, https://eacea.ec.europa.eu/creative-europe/selection-results_en (accessed 16 September 2014).
7 Data source: BFI – Statistical Yearbooks, http://www.bfi.org.uk/education-research/film-industry-statistics-research/statistical-yearbook (accessed 17 September 2014).
8 Data source: ICA – Instituto do Cinema e Audiovisual, Portugal, http://www.ica-ip.pt/pagina.aspx?pagina=434 (accessed 31 March 2014); and the UK Film Council (the UKFC closed in March 2011 and its website is no longer available; the data was accessed in 2009).
9 Available on YouTube, https://www.youtube.com/watch?v=5WVV5OSnwYU (accessed 21 September 2014).
10 Available on YouTube, https://www.youtube.com/watch?v=3kHoHH-05yI (accessed 21 September 2014).
11 Available on YouTube, https://www.youtube.com/watch?v=koRlFnBlDH0 (accessed 21 September 2014).
12 Available on YouTube, https://www.youtube.com/watch?v=_GccMzbgOrY (accessed 21 September 2014).
13 Available on YouTube, https://www.youtube.com/watch?v=4JlIFHsCz-Y (accessed 21 September 2014).
14 Available on YouTube, https://www.youtube.com/watch?v=fYMgx-p0l40 (accessed 21 September 2014).

Chapter 3

1 Similarly, the German film *Goethe!* (Philipp Stölzl, 2010) was released in the United Kingdom under the title *Young Goethe in Love*. With thanks to Paul Cooke for the reference.

2 Both stars had troubled lives marked by substance addictions; both died at the early age of forty-seven. More significantly, although working in different contexts, both were hugely talented performers, and massively popular not only in their countries, but also at an international level.

3 There is a long tradition of representing the First World War in this way, including in films such as *Dobrý voják Svejk/The Good Soldier Schweik* (Karel Steklý, 1957), an adaptation of Jaroslav Hašek's eponymous novel. With thanks to an anonymous reviewer for pointing me in the direction of this particular example.

Chapter 4

1 Arising in the 1980s, the *cinéma du look* has been primarily associated with directors such as Luc Besson, Leos Carax and Jean-Jacques Beinix. The genre is youth-oriented and characterized by its spectacular visuals, elaborate mise en scène and references to other films.

2 Literature on Paris and the cinema include: Dudley J. Andrew, *Mists of Regret: Culture and Sensibility in Classic French Film* (Princeton; Chichester: Princeton University Press, 1995) – on national cinema and on poetic realism; Alastair Philips, *City of Darkness, City of Light: Émigré Filmmakers in Paris 1929–1939* (Amsterdam: Amsterdam University Press, 2004); Tim Bergfelder, Sue Harris and Sarah Street, *Film Architecture and the Transnational Imagination: Set Design in 1930s European Cinema* (Amsterdam: Amsterdam University Press, 2007) – on European cinema; and Ginette Vincendeau, *La Haine* (London and New York: I.B. Tauris, 2005) – on *banlieue* cinema; among others.

3 All credited directors of *Paris je t'aime* are: Olivier Assayas, Frédéric Auburtin, Emmanuel Benbihy, Gurinder Chadha, Sylvain Chomet, Ethan Coen, Joel Coen, Isabel Coixet, Wes Craven, Alfonso Cuarón, Gérard Depardieu, Christopher Doyle, Richard LaGravenese, Vincenzo Natali, Alexander Payne, Bruno Podalydès, Walter Salles, Oliver Schmitz, Nobuhiro Suwa, Daniela Thomas, Tom Tykwer and Gus Van Sant.

4 *Paris vu par* was co-directed by Claude Chabrol, Jean Douchet, Jean-Luc Godard, Jean-Daniel Pollet, Eric Rohmer and Jean Rouch. *Paris vu par … vingts ans après* by Chantal Akerman, Bernard Dubois, Philippe Garrel, Frédéric Miterrand, Vincent Nordon and Philippe Venault.

5 *2 Days in Paris* was seen by 285,543 viewers in France and by 644,475 in the United States. *Paris je t'aime* had 434,183 viewers in France and 712,104 in the United States. Data source: the European Audiovisual Observatory's Lumière database, http://lumiere. obs.coe.int/ (accessed 16 September 2014).

6 Admission numbers listed on the Lumière database. According to the data compiled by the European Audiovisual Observatory, *Match Point* had over one million viewers in France, Spain and Italy, and only around five hundred thousand in the United Kingdom.

7 See, for instance, http://europa.eu/youth/article/erasmus-exchange-programme_en (accessed 8 October 2014).

8 A final instalment of the trilogy was released in 2013. *Casse-tête chinois/Chinese Puzzle* moves the characters from Paris to New York, and sees Xavier finding a home in Chinatown, seemingly confirming the global outlook of Klapisch's films.

9 For a discussion about the Paris of *Amelie*, see, for instance, Vanderschelden (2012).

10 This trend seemed to be inverting in 2012, with, for instance, an ever-growing number of Portuguese citizens migrating to Brazil because of the euro-zone debt crisis.

Bibliography

'Declaration on European Identity' (1973), in *Bulletin of the European Communities* (December), Luxembourg: Office for Official Publications of the European Communities, http://www.cvce.eu/content/publication/1999/1/1/02798dc9-9c69-4b7d-b2c9-f03a8db7da32/publishable_en.pdf (accessed 27 August 2014).

'Report by the Committee on a People's Europe Submitted to the Milan European Council (Milan, 28 and 29 June 1985)' (1985), in *Bulletin of the European Communities*, Luxembourg: Office for Official Publications of the European Communities.

Af Malmborg, M. and B. Stråth (2002), *The Meaning of Europe: Variety and Contention within and among Nations*, Oxford and New York: Berg.

Aitken, I. (2001), *European Film Theory and Cinema: A Critical Introduction*, Edinburgh: Edinburgh University Press.

Allinson, M. (2009), 'Mimesis and Diegesis: Almodovar and the Limits of Melodrama', in B. Epps and D. Kakoudaki (eds), *All about Almodovar: A Passion for Cinema*, Minneapolis, MN: University of Minnesota Press, 141–165.

Anderson, B. (2006), *Imagined Communities: Reflections on the Origins and Spread of Nationalism*, revised edition, London; New York: Verso.

Andrew, D. (1995), *Mists of Regret: Culture and Sensibility in Classic French Film*, Princeton; Chichester: Princeton University Press.

Anon (2003), 'Bellocchio, deluso, se ne va: "Il mio successo? Consenso di giovani e pubblico"', *La Stampa,* 7 September, http://archivio.lastampa.it/LaStampaArchivio/main/History/tmpl_viewObj.jsp?objid=4680558 (accessed 27 September 2010).

Anon (2007), 'It's red faces all round over EU's dirty movie', *Daily Mail*, 2 July, http://www.dailymail.co.uk/news/article-465509/Its-red-faces-round-EUs-dirty-movie.html (accessed 12 March 2014).

Anon (2010), 'Commission proposes "European Heritage" label', *EurActiv*, 10 March, http://www.euractiv.com/culture/commission-proposes-european-her-news-326066 (accessed 7 April 2014).

Appiah, K. A. (2007), *Cosmopolitanism: Ethics in a World of Strangers*, London: Penguin Books.

Balibar, É. (2003), *We, the People of Europe? Reflections on Transnational Citizenship*, Princeton, NJ; Oxford: Princeton University Press.

Barber, S. (2002), *Projected Cities*, London: Reaktion.

Barroso, J. M. D. (2009), 'Identidade Europeia/Identidades na Europa', in I. C. Gil (ed.), *Identidade Europeia, Identidades na Europa*, Lisbon: Universidade Católica Portuguesa, 17–25.

Barroso, J. M. D. (2014), '100 Years on from the First World War – lessons to learn and future of Europe', Speech to the European Parliament, Strasbourg, 16 April, http://europa.eu/rapid/press-release_SPEECH-14-330_en.htm (accessed 1 May 2014).

BBC (2014), 'Steve McQueen: *12 Years a Slave* is a "global tale" ', 7 January, http://www.bbc.co.uk/news/entertainment-arts-25632892 (accessed 15 September 2014).

Beardsworth, L. (2007), 'Becoming Jane', *Empire* 214, 56.

Beck, U. and E. Grande (2008), *Cosmopolitan Europe*, translated by Ciaran Cronin, Cambridge: Polity.

Bell, P. M. H. (2006), *Twentieth-Century Europe*, New York: Bloomsbury.

Bennett, R. (1999), *Under the Shadow of the Swastika: The Moral Dilemmas of Resistance and Collaboration in Hitler's Europe*, Basingstoke and London: Macmillan.

Berezin, M. (2003), 'Introduction: Territory, Emotion and Identity – Spatial Recalibration in a New Europe', in M. Berezin and M. Schain (eds), *Europe without Borders: Remapping Territory, Citizenship and Identity in a Transnational Age*, Baltimore, MA: The Johns Hopkins University Press, 1–30.

Berezin, M. and M. Schain (eds) (2003), *Europe without Borders: Remapping Territory, Citizenship and Identity in a Transnational Age*, Baltimore, MA: The Johns Hopkins University Press.

Bergfelder, T. (2012), 'Love beyond the Nation: Cosmopolitanism and Transnational Desire in Cinema', in L. Passerini, J. Labanyi and K. Diehl (eds), *Europe and Love in Cinema*, Bristol, UK; Chicago, USA: Intellect, 61–83.

Bergfelder, T. (2015), 'Popular European Cinema in the 2000s: Cinephilia, Genre and Heritage', in M. Harrod, M. Liz and A. Timoshkina (eds), *The Europeanness of European Cinema: Identity, Meaning, Globalization*, London: I.B. Tauris, 33–58.

Bergfelder, T., S. Harris and S. Street (2007), *Film Architecture and the Transnational Imagination: Set Design in 1930s European Cinema*, Amsterdam: Amsterdam University Press.

Berghahn, D. and C. Sternberg (eds) (2010), *European Cinema in Motion: Migrant and Diasporic Film in Contemporary Europe*, Basingstoke: Palgrave Macmillan.

Betz, M. (2009), *Beyond the Subtitle: Remapping European Art Cinema*, Minneapolis, MN; London: University of Minnesota Press.

Bingham, D. (2010), *Whose Lives Are They Anyway?: The Biopic as Contemporary Film Genre*, New Brunswick, NJ: Rutgers University Press.

Blaney, M. (2011), 'Top filmmakers sign petition to support future of MEDIA programme', *Screen Daily*, 23 February, http://www.screendaily.com/top-filmmakers-sign-petition-to-support-future-of-media-programme/5024114.article (accessed 12 February 2014).

Blum-Reid, S. (2009), 'Away from Home? Two French Directors in Search of their Identity', *Quarterly Review of Film and Video* 29:1, 1–9.

Bondebjerg, I., E. Novrup Redvall and A. Higson (eds) (2015), *European Cinema and Television: Cultural Policy and Everyday Life*, Basingstoke: Palgrave Macmillan.

Bradshaw, P. (2007), 'Missing in action', *Guardian*, 22 June, 9.

Brooks, X. (2007), 'What is the EU's sex film really selling?', *Guardian*, 5 July, http://www.guardian.co.uk/film/filmblog/2007/jul/05/whatistheeussexfilmreallyselling (accessed 12 March 2014).

Brooks, X. (2009), 'Can Cannes spring a late surprise?', *Guardian*, 21 May, http://www.theguardian.com/film/2009/may/21/cannes-film-festival-michael-haneke (accessed 2 May 2014).

Brown, T. and B. Vidal (eds) (2014), *The Biopic in Contemporary Film Culture*, New York and London: Routledge.

Brubaker, R. and F. Cooper (2006), 'Beyond Identity', in R. Brubaker (ed.), *Ethnicity without Groups*, Cambridge, MA and London: Harvard University Press, 28–63.

Brunsdon, C. (2007), *London in Cinema: The Cinematic City since 1945*, London: BFI.

Bruter, M. (2005), *Citizens of Europe? The Emergence of a Mass European Identity*, Basingstoke: Palgrave Macmillan.

Buch, E. (2003), 'Parcours et paradoxes de l'hymne européen', in L. Passerini (ed.), *Figures d'Europe. Images and Myths of Europe*, Brussels: P.I.E. – Peter Lang, 87–98.

Bugge, P. (2003), 'A European Cultural Heritage? Reflections on a Concept and a Programme', in R. S. Peckham (ed.), *Rethinking Heritage – Cultures and Politics in Europe*, London; New York: I.B. Tauris, 61–73.

Cameron, C. (2006), 'The London of "Match Point"', *The New York Times*, 7 February, http://travel2.nytimes.com/2006/02/07/travel/08weblondon.html (accessed 24 October 2010).

Casado, M. A. (2006), 'EU Media Programmes: Little Investment, Few Results', in L. Højbjerg and H. Søndergaard (eds), *European Film and Media Culture*, Copenhagen: Museum Tusculanum Press and University of Copenhagen, 37–61.

Castelli, L. (2007), 'Ecco EuTube, i video online della Commissione Europea', *La Stampa*, 3 July, http://www.lastampa.it/_web/cmstp/tmplrubriche/tecnologia/grubrica.asp?ID_blog=30&ID_articolo=2688&ID_sezione=38&sezione=News (accessed 12 March 2014).

Checkel, J. T. and P. J. Katzenstein (eds) (2009), *European Identity*, Cambridge: Cambridge University Press.

Cockrell, E. (2003), 'Good Bye Lenin!', *Variety* 390:1, 42.

Collins, R. (1994), *Broadcasting and Audio-Visual Policy in the European Single Market*, London: John Libbey.

Commission of the European Communities (1986), *Communication by the Commission to the Council: Action Programme for the European Audio-Visual Media Products Industry, 12 May 1986, (COM 86 25 final)*, Luxembourg: Commission of the European Communities.

Commission of the European Communities (1988), *The Audio-Visual Media in the Single European Market*, Luxembourg: Office for Official Publications of the European Communities.

Commission of the European Communities (1990), 'Conclusions of the Presidency – European Council', Rhodes, 2 and 3 December 1988, in *The European Community*

Policy in the Audiovisual Field – Legal and Political Texts, Luxembourg: Office for Official Publications of the European Communities.

Cooke, P. (2012), *Contemporary German Cinema*, Manchester: Manchester University Press.

Coopers and Lybrand (1993), *The Distribution Game: Can Europe Even the Score?* UK: Coopers and Lybrand.

Custen, G. F. (1992), *Bio/Pics: How Hollywood Constructed Public History*, New Jersey: Rutgers University Press.

D'Appollonia, A. C. (2002), 'European Nationalism and European Union', in A. Pagden (ed.), *The Idea of Europe: From Antiquity to the European Union*, Cambridge: Cambridge University Press, 171–190.

Dale, M. (1992), *Europa, Europa: Developing the European Film Industry*, Paris: Académie Carat and MEDIA Business School.

Daney, S. (2007), *Postcards from the Cinema*, translated by Paul Douglas Grant, Oxford; New York: Berg.

Darke, C. (2007), 'Paris je t'aime', *Sight and Sound* 17:7, 66–68.

Dave, P. (2006), *Visions of England: Class and Culture in Contemporary Cinema*, Oxford; New York: Berg.

De Valck, M. (2007), *Film Festivals: From European Geopolitics to Global Cinephilia*, Amsterdam: Amsterdam University Press.

Delanty, G. (1995), *Inventing Europe: Idea, Identity, Reality*, New York: St Martin's Press.

Delanty, G. (2005), 'What Does It Mean to be a "European"?', *Innovation: The European Journal of Social Science Research* 18:1, 11–22.

Deltcheva, R. (2005), 'Reliving the Past in Recent East European Cinemas', in A. Imre (ed.), *East European Cinemas*, AFI Film Readers, New York and London: Routledge, 197–211.

Derrida, J. (1992), *The Other Heading: Reflections on Today's Europe*, translated by Pascalle-Anne Bault and Michael B. Naas, Bloomington and Indianapolis: Indiana University Press.

Dickinson, M. and S. Street (1985), *Cinema and State: The Film Industry and the Government 1927-1984*, London: BFI.

Donald, S. H., E. Kofman and C. Kevin (eds) (2009), *Branding Cities: Cosmopolitanism, Parochialism and Social Change*, New York; London: Routledge.

Doyle, G., P. Schlesinger, R. Boyle and L. Kelly (2015), *The Rise and Fall of the UK Film Council*, Edinburgh: Edinburgh University Press.

Duchesne, S. and A.-P. Froigner (1995), 'Is There a European Identity?', in O. Niedermayer and R. Sinnott (eds), *Public Opinion and Internationalized Governance*, Oxford: Oxford University Press, 193–226.

Dyer, R. (1995), 'Heritage Cinema in Europe', in G. Vincendeau (ed.), *Encyclopedia of European Cinema*, London: Cassell, 204–205.

Eleftheriotis, D. (2001), *Popular Cinemas of Europe: Studies of Texts, Contexts, and Frameworks*, New York; London: Continuum.

Elsaesser, T. (1996), 'Subject Positions, Speaking Positions: from *Holocaust, Our Hitler* and *Heimat* to *Shoah* and *Schindler's List*', in V. Sobchack (ed.), *The Persistence of History: Cinema, Television and the Modern Event*, London and New York: Routledge, 145–186.

Elsaesser, T. (2005), *European Cinema: Face to Face with Hollywood*, Amsterdam: Amsterdam University Press.

Elsaesser, T. (2015), 'European Cinema into the Twenty-First Century: Enlarging the Context?' in M. Harrod, M. Liz and A. Timoshkina (eds), *The Europeanness of European Cinema: Identity, Meaning, Globalization*, London: I.B. Tauris, 17–32.

Erdoğan, N. (2009), 'Star Director as Symptom: Reflections on the Reception of Fatih Akin in the Turkish Media', *New Cinemas – Journal of Contemporary Film* 7:1, 27–38.

Esbenshade, R. S. (1995), 'Remembering to Forget: Memory, History, National Identity in Postwar East-Central Europe', *Representations* 49, Special Issue: Identifying Histories: Eastern Europe Before and After 1989 (Winter 1995), 72–96.

European Commission (2008), 'About the Year', http://www.interculturaldialogue2008.eu (accessed 13 January 2011).

European Commission (2009), 'Promoting Sustainable Urban Development in Europe – Achievements and Opportunities', Brussels: European Communities.

European Commission (2012), 'Myths and Rumours Debunked', http://ec.europa.eu/dgs/communication/take_part/myths_en.htm (accessed 13 April 2012).

Everett, W. (ed.) (2005), *European Identity in Cinema*, Bristol: Intellect.

Ezra, E. (ed.) (2003), *European Cinema*, Oxford: Oxford University Press.

Ezra, E. and A. Sánchez (2005), '*L'Auberge espagnole* (2002): transnational departure or domestic crash landing?', *Studies in European Cinema* 2:2, 137–148.

Ezra, E. and T. Rowden (eds) (2006), *Transnational Cinema: The Film Reader*, London: Routledge.

Fernandes, F. (2007), 'As Rapidinhas da Comissão Europeia', *Diário de Notícias*, 4 July, http://www.dn.pt/inicio/interior.aspx?content_id=660555 (accessed 18 September 2014).

Finney, A. (1996), *The State of European Cinema: A New Dose of Reality*, London: Cassell.

Forbes, J. and S. Street (eds) (2000), *European Cinema: An Introduction*, Basingstoke: Palgrave.

Fornäs, J. (2012), *Signifying Europe*, Bristol: Intellect.

Frasca, G. (2008), 'Dialoghi di Frontiera – Campo e Controcampo', in *Cineforum* 479 (November), 2–4.

Fuller, G. (2006), 'Court Jester', *Sight and Sound* 16:1, 14–18.

Galt, R. (2006), *The New European Cinema: Redrawing the Map*, New York, NY; Chichester: Columbia University Press.

Gant, C. (2006), 'The Power of Pedro', *Sight and Sound* 16:10, 8.

García, S. (1993), 'Europe's Fragmented Identities and the Frontiers of Citizenship', in S. García (ed.), *European Identity and the Search for legitimacy*, London; New York: Pinter for The Eleni Nakou Foundation and The Royal Institute of International Affairs, 1–29.

Gil, I. C. (ed.) (2009), *Identidade Europeia – Identidades na Europa*, Lisbon: Universidade Católica Editora.

Glasgow Development Agency (1992), 'Glasgow 1990 – European City of Culture', http://www.ecoc-doc-athens.eu/glasgow-home/the-organisation.html (accessed 10 July 2014).

Goldberg, D., T. Prosser and S. Verhulst (1998), *EC Media Law and Policy*, Harlow: Longman.

Güell, M. (2008), 'Barcelona según el cine', *ABC*, 17 February.

Guider, E. (2003), ' "Notte" opens eyes at Venice Fest', *Variety*, 5 September, http://www.variety.com/article/VR1117891950.html?categoryid=1236&cs=1 (accessed 26 September 2010).

Haastrup, H. K. (2006), 'Popular European Art Film: Challenging Narratives and Engaging Characters', in L. Højbjerg and H. Søndergaard (eds), *European Film and Media Culture*, Copenhagen: Museum Tusculanum Press and University of Copenhagen, 263–283.

Habermas, J. (2001), 'Why Europe Needs a Constitution', *New Left Review* 11, 5–26.

Halfyard, J. K. (2006), 'Screen Playing: Cinematic Representations of Classical Music Performance and European Identity', in M. Mera and D. Burnand (eds), *European Film Music*, Aldershot: Ashgate, 73–85.

Hall, S. (2003), 'In But Not of Europe: Europe and Its Myths', in L. Passerini (ed.), *Figures d'Europe. Images and Myths of Europe*, Brussels: P.I.E. – Peter Lang, 35–46.

Halle, R. (2006), 'German Film, European Film: Transnational Production, Distribution and Reception', *Screen* 47:2, 251–259.

Hannam, K., M. Sheller and J. Urry (2006), 'Editorial: Mobilities, Immobilities and Moorings', *Mobilities* 1:1, 1–22.

Harrod, M., M. Liz and A. Timoshkina (eds) (2015), *The Europeanness of European Cinema: Identity, Meaning, Globalization*, London: I.B. Tauris.

Hay, D. (1957), *Europe: The Emergence of an Idea*, Edinburgh: Edinburgh University Press.

Hayward, S. (2000), 'The City as Narrative: Corporeal Paris in Contemporary French Cinema 1950–1990', in M. Konstantarakos (ed.), *Spaces in European Cinema*, Exeter: Intellect Books, 23–34.

Hedling, O. (2009), 'Possibilities of Stardom in European Cinema Culture', in T. Soila (ed.), *Stellar Encounters: Stardom in Popular European Cinema*, Herts: John Libbey, 254–264.

Herold, A. (2010), *European Film Policies in EU and International Law: Culture and Trade – Marriage or Misalliance?*, Groningen: Europa Law Publishing.

Herrmann, R. K., T. Risse and M. B. Brewer (eds) (2004), *Transnational Identities: Becoming European in the EU*, Lanham, MD; Oxford: Rowman and Littlefield.

Higson, A. (1993), 'Re-presenting the National Past: Nostalgia and Pastiche in the Heritage Film', in L. Friedman (ed.), *Fires Were Started: British Cinema and Tatcherism*, Minneapolis and London: University of Minnesota Press and UCL Press, 109–129.

Higson, A. and R. Maltby (eds) (1999), *'Film Europe' and 'Film America': Cinema, Commerce and Cultural Exchange, 1920–1939*, Exeter: University of Exeter Press.

Hill, J. (1999), *British Cinema in the 1980s: Issues and Themes*, Oxford: Oxford University Press.

Hill, J., M. McLoone and P. Hainsworth (eds) (1994), *Border Crossing: Film in Ireland, Britain and Europe*, Belfast: Institute of Irish Studies in association with the University of Ulster and the BFI.

Hjort, M. (2010) 'Affinitive and Milieu-Building Transnationalism: The "Advanced-Party" Project', in D. Iordanova, D. Martin-Jones and B. Vidal (eds), *Cinema at the Periphery*, Detroit: Wayne State University Press, 46–66.

Hobsbawm, E. (1994), *Age of Extremes – The Short Twentieth Century, 1914-1991*, London: Abacus.

Holmes, D. and A. Smith (eds) (2000), *100 Years of European Cinema: Entertainment or Ideology?*, Manchester: Manchester University Press.

Hoskins, A. (2004), 'New Memory: Mediating History', *Historical Journal of Film, Radio and Television*, 21:4, 303–346.

Istanbul 2010 Agency, 'Why Istanbul?', http://www.en.istanbul2010.org/2010AKBAJANSI/hakk%C4%B1nda/index.htm (accessed 20 December 2010).

Jäckel, A. (2003), *European Film Industries*, London: BFI.

Kaiser, W. (2007), *Christian Democracy and the Origins of European Union*, Cambridge: Cambridge University Press.

Kirschbaum, E. (2007), 'Flying the Euro Film Flag', *Variety* 408, A11.

Kohli, M. (2000), 'The Battlegrounds of European Identity', *European Societies* 2:2, 113–137.

Konstantarakos, M. (ed.) (2000), *Spaces in European Cinema*. Exeter: Intellect.

Kourelou, O., M. Liz and B. Vidal (2014), 'Crisis and Creativity: The New Cinemas of Portugal, Greece and Spain', *New Cinemas* 12:1+2, 133–151.

Kumar, K. (2003), 'The Idea of Europe – Cultural Legacies, Transnational Imaginings and the Nation-State', in M. Berezin and M. Schain (eds), *Europe without Borders: Remapping Territory, Citizenship and Identity in a Transnational Age*, Baltimore, MD: The Johns Hopkins University Press, 33–50.

Lang, J. (1985), 'Letter [to Melina Mercouri]', Documentation Centre on European Capitals of Culture', http://www.ecoc-doc-athens.eu/athens-home/the-organisation.html (accessed 20 December 2010).

Le Galès, P. (2002), *European Cities: Social Conflicts and Governance*, Oxford; New York: Oxford University Press.

Le Goff, J. (1992), *History and Memory*, New York: Columbia University Press.

Lebas, E. (2005), 'Sadness and Gladness: The Films of Glasgow Corporation, 1922–1938', *Film Studies* 6 (Summer), 27–45.

Liz, M. (2014), 'From Europe with Love: Urban Space and Cinematic Postcards', *Studies in European Cinema*, 11:1, 3–13.

Liz, M. (2015), 'From European Co-productions to the Euro-Pudding', in M. Harrod, M. Liz and A. Timoshkina (eds), *The Europeanness of European Cinema: Identity, Meaning, Globalization*, London: I.B. Tauris, 73–86.

Loshitzky, Y. (2010), *Screening Strangers: Migration and Diaspora in Contemporary European Cinema*, Bloomington: Indiana University Press.

MacCannell, D. (1999), *The Tourist: A New Theory of the Leisure Class,* 2nd edition, Berkeley, CA; London: University of California Press.

Martin-Jones, D. (2009), *Scotland: Global Cinema: Genres, Modes and Identities*, Edinburgh: Edinburgh University Press.

Martin-Jones, D. (2012), '*Colombiana*: Europa Corp and the Ambiguous Geopolitics of the Action Movie', in *Senses of Cinema* 62, http://sensesofcinema.com/2012/feature-articles/colombiana-europa-corp-and-the-ambiguous-geopolitics-of-the-action-movie/ (accessed 3 January 2015).

Matloff, J. (2006), 'Woody Allen's European Vacation', in *Premiere* 19:5 (February), 98–101.

Mayer, F. C. and J. Palmowski (2004), 'European Identities and the EU – The Ties That Bind the Peoples of Europe', in *JCMS: Journal of Common Market Studies* 42:3, 573–598.

Mazierska, E. (2011), *European Cinema and Intertextuality: History, Memory and Politics*, Basingstoke; New York: Palgrave Macmillan.

Mazierska, E. and L. Rascaroli (2003), *From Moscow to Madrid: Postmodern Cities, European Cinema*, London: I.B. Tauris.

Merivirta, R., K. Ahonen, H. Mulari and R. Mähkä (eds) (2013), *Frontiers of Screen History: Imagining European Borders in Cinema, 1945–2010*, Bristol: Intellect.

Moran, A. (ed.) (1996), *Film policy: International, National and Regional Perspectives*, London: Routledge.

Morin, E. (1987), *Penser L'europe*, Paris: Gallimardi.

Morrison, A. (2007), 'Paris je t'aime', in *Empire* 217 (July), 49.

Mottram, J. (2004), 'In the Mood for Love', *Sight and Sound* 14:3, 22–23.

Mulvey, S. (2007), 'Sexy clip lifts EU YouTube debut', *BBC News*, 3 July, http://news.bbc.co.uk/1/hi/6263430.stm?lsm (accessed 12 March 2014).

Naremore, J. (2008), 'Films of the Year, 2007', *Film Quarterly* 61:4, 58.

Nathan, I. (2007), 'Black Book', *Empire* 212, 46.

Nesselson, L. (2005), 'Merry Christmas', *Variety*, 23–29 May, 32.

Neyrat, C. (2006), 'Sophie Scholl', *Cahiers du Cinéma* 611, 61.

Nora, P. (1989), 'Between Memory and History: Les Lieux de Mémoire', *Representations* 26, Special Issue: Memory and Counter-Memory, 7–24.

O'Leary, A. (2008), 'Dead Man Walking: The Aldo Moro kidnap and Palimpsest History in *Buongiorno, Notte*', *New Cinemas* 6:1, 33–45.

Pagden, A. (2002), *The Idea of Europe: From Antiquity to the European Union*, Cambridge: Cambridge University Press.

Passerini, L. (2002), 'From the Ironies of Identity to the Identities of Irony', in A. Pagden (ed.), *The Idea of Europe: From Antiquity to the European Union*, Cambridge: Cambridge University Press, 191–208.

Passerini, L. (2003), 'Dimensions of the Symbolic in the Construction of Europeanness', in L. Passerini (ed.), *Figures d'Europe. Images and Myths of Europe*, Brussels: P.I.E. – Peter Lang, 21–33.

Passerini, L., J. Labanyi and K. Diehl (eds) (2012), *Europe and Love in Cinema*, Bristol: Intellect.

Peckham, R. S. (2003), 'Mourning Heritage: Memory, Trauma and Restitution', in R. S. Peckham (ed.), *Rethinking Heritage – Cultures and Politics in Europe*, London; New York: I.B. Tauris, 205–214.

Petrie, D. (ed.) (1992), *Screening Europe: Image and Identity in Contemporary European Cinema*, London: BFI.

Philips, A. (2004), *City of Darkness, City of Light: Emigré Filmmakers in Paris 1929–1939*, Amsterdam: Amsterdam University Press.

Pinto, V. (2007), 'Interview with Daniel Burlac', 8 January, http://cineuropa.org/ffocusinterview.aspx?lang=en&treeID=1313&documentID=65820 (accessed 9 May 2014).

Powell, N. (1996), 'Foreword', in A. Finney (ed.), *The State of European Cinema: A New Dose of Reality*, London: Cassell.

Reding, V. (2003), Speech given at the 'Conference on the Future of Cinema and the Audiovisual Sector within the framework of European Union Enlargement', Thessaloniki, 25–27 May, in *From Cultural Diversity to a European Identity*, Athens: Hellenic Ministry of Culture, 13.

Retico, Alessandra (2003). 'Bellocchio: "Non è un film storico ho raccontato Moro e i terroristi"'. In *La Repubblica*, 4 September. Online. http://www.repubblica.it/2003/i/sezioni/spettacoli_e_cultura/cinema/venezia/bellocchio/bellocchio/bellocchio.html?ref=search Accessed 25/09/10.

Riding, A. (2007), 'On EU Tube (LOL!), Sex Sells (Duh!)', *The New York Times*, 11 July, http://www.nytimes.com/2007/07/11/arts/television/11ridi.html?_r=2 (accessed 12 March 2014).

Rinaldi, G. (2007), 'Paris je t'aime', *Cineforum* 456 (July), 62–63.

Riotta, G. (2012), 'Umberto Eco: "It's culture, not war, that cements European identity"', *Guardian*, 26 January, http://www.guardian.co.uk/world/2012/jan/26/umberto-eco-culture-war-europa (accessed online 31 March 2014).

Rivi, L. (2007), *European Cinema after 1989: Cultural Identity and Transnational Production*, Basingstoke: Palgrave Macmillan.

Roberts, L. (2010), 'Projecting Place: Location Mapping, Consumption and Cinematographic Tourism', in Richard Koeck and Les Roberts (eds), *The City and the Moving Image: Urban Projections*, Basingstoke: Palgrave Macmillan, 2010, 183–204.

Rosenstone, R. A. (2006), *History on Film/Film on History*, Harlow, UK: Pearson Education Limited.

Samuel, R. (1994), *Theatres of Memory. Volume 1: Past and Present in Contemporary Culture*, London; New York: Verso.

Sassatelli, M. (2009), *Becoming Europeans: Cultural Identity and Cultural Policies*, Basingstoke: Palgrave Macmillan.

Sassen, S. (2001), *The Global City: New York, London, Tokyo*, 2nd Edition, Princeton, NJ; Oxford: Princeton University Press.

Schlesinger, P. (1997), 'From Cultural Defence to Political Culture: Media, Politics and Collective Identity in the European Union', *Media, Culture & Society* 19, 369–391.

Schmitz, H. (2007), *A Nation of Victims? Representations of German Wartime Suffering from 1945 to the Present*, Amsterdam and New York: Rodopi.

Schwartz, V. R. (2007), *It's So French!: Hollywood, Paris and the Making of Cosmopolitan Film Culture*, Chicago, IL: University of Chicago Press.

Schwartz, V. (2009), Lecture on La Vie en rose to Graduate Seminar on 'French Cinema: History, Ideology and Politics', King's College London, 16 March.

Scicluna, N. (2012), 'When Failure Isn't Failure', *JCMS: Journal of Common Market Studies*, 1–16.

Scott, K. (2004), 'As the wealth and health gaps widen, Glasgow rebrands itself as city of style', *Guardian*, 10 March, http://www.theguardian.com/society/2004/mar/10/communities.britishidentityandsociety (accessed 10 July 2014).

Shiel, M. (2009), 'Branding the Modernist Metropolis: The Eternal City and the City of Lights in Cinema after World War II', in S. H. Donald, E. Kofman and C. Kevin (eds), *Branding Cities: Cosmopolitanism, Parochialism and Social Change*, New York; London: Routledge, 105–122.

Shiel, M. and T. Fitzmaurice (eds) (2003), *Screening the City*, London: Verso.

Shohat, E. and R. Stam (eds) (2003), *Multiculturalism, Postcoloniality, and Transnational Media*, New Brunswick, NJ; London: Rutgers University Press.

Shore, C. (2000), *Building Europe: The Cultural Politics of European Integration*, London: Routledge.

Shore, C. (2006), ' "In uno plures"(?) EU Cultural Policy and the Governance of Europe', *Cultural Analysis* 5, 7–26.

Smith, A. (1992), 'National Identity and the Idea of European Unity', *International Affairs* 68:1, 55–76.

Sørensen, G. (2004), *The Transformation of the State: Beyond the Myth of Retreat*, Basingstoke: Palgrave Macmillan.

Sorlin, P. (1991), *European Cinemas, European Societies 1939–1990*, London: Routledge.

Spencer, L. (2006), 'Russian Dolls', *Sight and Sound* 16:6, 67–68.

Spinelli, A. (1972), *The European Adventure: Tasks for the Enlarged Community*, London: Charles Knight & Co.

Steiner, G. (2006), *Una Certa Idea di Europa*, Milano: Garzanti.

Sternberg, C. (2013), *The Struggle for EU Legitimacy: Public Contestation, 1950–2005*, Basingstoke: Palgrave Macmillan.

Strode, L. (2000), 'France and EU Policy-Making on Visual Culture: New Opportunities for National Identity?', in E. Ezra and S. Harris (eds), *France in Focus: Film and National Identity*, Oxford: Berg, 61–75.

Taberner, S. and P. Cooke (eds) (2006), *German Culture, Politics, and Literature into the Twenty-First Century: Beyond Normalization*, Rochester, NY: Camden House; Woodbridge: Boydell & Brewer.

Tobin, Y. (2006), 'Paris je t'aime – L'auberge parisienne', *Positif* 545/546 (July/August), 133.

Trifonova, T. (ed.) (2008), *European Film Theory*, London: Routledge.

Urry, J. (2001), *The Tourist Gaze*, 2nd Edition, London: Sage.

Van Rompuy, H. (2012), 'From war to peace: a European tale', Acceptance of the Nobel Peace Prize Award to the European Union/Oslo, 10 December, http://europa.eu/rapid/press-release_SPEECH-12-930_en.htm (accessed 9 April 2014).

Vanderschelden, I. (2012), *Amélie*, London and New York: I.B. Tauris.

Vasconcelos, A. (1994), *Report by the Think Tank on the Audiovisual Policy in the European Union*, Luxembourg: Office for Official Publications of the European Communities.

Vasconcelos, M. (2011), 'The EU Heritage Label is a waste of taxpayers' money', 18 November, http://www.europeanfoundation.org/my_weblog/2011/11/margarida-vasconcelos-the-eu-heritage-label-is-a-waste-of-taxpayers-money.html (accessed 7 April 2014).

Vidal, B. (2012), *Heritage Film: Nation, Genre and Representation*, New York: Columbia University Press.

Vincendeau, G. (ed.) (1995a), *Encyclopaedia of European Cinema*, London: Cassell.

Vincendeau, G. (1995b), 'Cinéma du look', in G. Vincendeau (ed.), *Encyclopedia of European Cinema*, London: Cassell, 82–83.

Vincendeau, G. (2000), *Stars and Stardom in French Cinema*, London and New York: Continuum.

Vincendeau, G. (ed.) (2001), *Film/Literature/Heritage – A Sight and Sound Reader*. London: BFI.

Vincendeau, G. (2005), *La Haine*, London and New York: I.B. Tauris.

Vincendeau, G. (2009), 'The Rules of the Game', *Sight and Sound* 19:3, 34–36.

Vincendeau, G. (2015), 'Juliette Binoche: The Perfect European Star', in M. Harrod, M. Liz and A. Timoshkina (eds), *The Europeanness of European Cinema: Identity, Meaning, Globalization,* London: I.B. Tauris, 131–144.

Vivancos, P. (2000), *Cinéma et Europe – Réflexions sur les politiques européennes de soutien au cinema,* Paris: L'Harmattan.

Voigts-Virchow, E. (ed.) (2004), *Janespotting and Beyond: British Heritage Retrovisions Since the Mid-1990s,* Tübingen: Gunter Narr Verlag.

Wallström, M. (2008), 'Welcome to the EUROBAROMETER conference 2008', Paris, 21 and 22 November, http://ec.europa.eu/public_opinion/paris/paris_en/home.htm (accessed 19 September 2014).

Wayne, M. (2002), *The Politics in Contemporary European Cinema: Histories, Borders, Diasporas,* Bristol: Intellect.

Wheatley, C. (2008), 'Paris', *Sight and Sound* 18:8, 74.

Williams, L. R. (2007), 'Sleeping with the Enemy', *Sight and Sound* 17:2, 19.

Winter, J. and A. Prost (2005), *The Great War in History: Debates and Controversies, 1914 to the Present,* Cambridge: Cambridge University Press.

Wintle, M. (2009), *The Image of Europe: Visualizing Europe in Cartography and Iconography throughout the Ages,* Cambridge: Cambridge University Press.

Wood, M. (2000), 'Cultural Space as Political Metaphor: The Case of the European "Quality" Film', http://www.mediasalles.it/crl_wood.htm (accessed 18 September 2014).

Wood, M. (2007), *Contemporary European Cinema,* London: Hodder Arnold.

Zatterin, M. (2007), 'Sesso a volontà per il cinema europeo', *La Stampa,* 3 July, http://www1.lastampa.it/redazione/cmsSezioni/societa/200707articoli/23299girata.asp (accessed 12 March 2014).

Zelinsky, W. (1991), 'The Twinning of the World: Sister Cities in Geographic and Historical Perspective', *Annals of the Association of American Geographers* 81:1, 1–31.

Filmography

12 Years a Slave (Steve McQueen, 2013)

1492: Conquest of Paradise (Ridley Scott, 1992)

2 days in Paris (Julie Delpy, 2007)

25 degrés en hiver/25 Degrees in Winter (Stéphane Vuillet, 2004)

4 luni, 3 saptamâni si 2 zile/4 Months, 3 Weeks and 2 Days (Cristian Mungiu, 2007)

8 Femmes/8 Women (François Ozon, 2002)

A fost sau n-a fost?/12:08 East of Bucharest (Corneliu Poromboiu, 2006)

A Room with a View (James Ivory, 1985)

Adams æbler/Adam's Apples (Anders Thomas Jensen, 2005)

Ae fond kiss (Ken Loach, 2004)

Alatriste (Agustin Diaz Yanes, 2006)

Angel (François Ozon, 2006)

Astérix et les Vikings/Astérix and the Vikings (Stefan Fjeldmark, Jesper Møller, 2006)

Auf der anderen Seite/The Edge of Heaven (Fatih Akin, 2007)

Barbara (Christian Petzold, 2012)

Batalla en el Cielo/Battle in Heaven (Carlos Reygadas, 2004)

Becoming Jane (Julian Jarrold, 2006)

Belle de jour (Luis Buñuel, 1967)

Belle toujours (Manoel de Oliveira, 2006)

Bienvenue chez les Ch'tis/Welcome to the Sticks (Dany Boon, 2008)

Billy Elliot (Stephen Daldry, 2000)

Birdwatchers – La terra degli uomini rossi/Birdwatchers (Marco Bechis, 2008)

Brasileirinho (Mika Kaurismäki, 2004)

Breaking the Waves (Lars von Trier, 1996)

Bride and Prejudice (Gurinder Chadha, 2004)

Bridget Jones: The Edge of Reason (Beeban Kidron, 2004)

Brødre/Brothers (Susanne Bier, 2004)

Buongiorno, Notte/Good Morning, Night (Marco Bellocchio, 2003)

Caché/Hidden (Michael Haneke, 2005)

Camille Claudel 1915 (Bruno Dumont, 2013)

Caótica Ana/Chaotic Ana (Julio Medem, 2007)

Capitães de Abril/Captains of April (Maria de Medeiros, 2000)

Cashback (Sean Ellis, 2006)

Casino Royale (Martin Campbell, 2006)

Ceský sen/Czech Dream (Vít Klusák and Filip Remunda, 2004)

Closer (Mike Nichols, 2004)

Coco avant Chanel/Coco before Chanel (Anne Fontaine, 2009)

Coco Chanel & Igor Stravinsky (Jan Kounen, 2009)

Crossing the Bridge – The Sound of Istanbul (Fatih Akin, 2005)

Das Cabinet des Dr. Caligari/The Cabinet of Dr. Caligari (Robert Wiene, 1920)

Das Leben der Anderen/The Lives of Others (Florian Henckel von Donnersmarck, 2006)

Das weiße Band/The White Ribbon (Michael Haneke, 2009)

De battre mon coeur s'est arrêté/The Beat That My Heart Skipped (Jacques Audiard, 2005)

De ofrivilliga/Involuntary (Ruben Östlund, 2008)

Dear Wendy (Thomas Vinterberg, 2005)

Delta (Kornél Mundruczó, 2008)

Den brysomme mannen/The Bothersome Man (Per Schreiner, 2006)

Der Baader Meinhof Komplex/The Baader Meinhof Complex (Uli Edel, 2008)

Der Untergang/Downfall (Oliver Hirschbiegel, 2004)

Die Fälscher/The Counterfeiters (Stefan Ruzowitzky, 2007)

Die Höhle des gelben Hundes/The Cave of the Yellow Dog (Byambasuren Davaa, 2005)

Die Welle/The Wave (Dennis Gansel, 2008)

Direktøren for det hele/The Boss of It All (Lars von Trier, 2006)

Dobrý voják Svejk/The Good Soldier Schweik (Karel Steklý, 1957)

Doppo Mezzanotte/After Midnight (Davide Ferrario, 2004)

Du levande/You, the Living (Roy Andersson, 2006)

El laberinto del fauno/Pan's Labyrinth (Guillermo del Toro, 2006)

El secreto de tus ojos/The Secret in Their Eyes (Juan José Campanella, 2009)

El sueño de una noche de San Juan/Midsummer Dream (Ángel De La Cruz, Manolo Gómez, 2003)

Elementarteilchen/Atomised (Oskar Roehler, 2006)

Elle s'appelle Sabine/Her Name Is Sabine (Sandrine Bonnaire, 2007)

Emma (Douglas McGrath, 1996)

Emma's Glück/Emma's Bliss (Sven Taddicken, 2006)

En soap/A Soap (Pernille Fischer Christensen, 2006)

Entre les murs/The Class (Laurent Cantet, 2008)

Ex Drummer (Koen Mortier, 2007)

Exils/Exiles (Tony Gatlif, 2004)

Factotum (Bent Hamer, 2005)

Fish Tank (Andrea Arnold, 2009)

Forbrydelser/In Your Hands (Annette K. Olesen, 2003)

Franklin et le trésor du Lac/Franklin and the Turtle Lake Treasure (Dominique Monfery, 2006)

Frontière(s)/Frontier(s) (Xavier Gens, 2007)

Funny Face (Stanley Donen, 1957)

Funny Games (Remake) (Michael Haneke, 2007)

Gainsbourg (Joann Sfar, 2010)

GAL (Miguel Courtois, 2006)

Garage (Leonard Abrahamson, 2007)

Gegen die Wand/Head-on (Fatih Akin, 2004)

Girl with a Pearl Earring (Peter Webber, 2003)

Goethe!/Young Goethe in Love (Philipp Stölzl, 2010)

Gomorra/Gomorrah (Matteo Garrone, 2008)

Good Bye Lenin! (Wolfgang Becker, 2003)

Goodbye Bafana (Bille August, 2006)

Habana Blues (Benito Zambrano, 2005)

Hævnen/In a Better World (Susanne Bier, 2010)

Hannah Arendt (Margarethe von Trotta, 2012)

Happy Go-Lucky (Mike Leigh, 2008)

Home (Ursula Meier, 2008)

Hunger (Steve McQueen, 2008)

Il divo (Paolo Sorrentino, 2008)

Il Postino/The Postman (Michael Radford, 1994)

Ils (David Moreau, Xavier Palud, 2006)

Import/Export (Ulrich Seidl, 2007)

Irina Palm (Sam Garbarski, 2007)

It's All Gone Pete Tong (Michael Dowse, 2004)

Jane Eyre (Cary Fukunaga, 2011)

Johanna (Kornél Mundruczó, 2005)

Joyeux Noël/Merry Christmas (Christian Carion, 2005)

Kærlighed på film/Just Another Love Story (Ole Bornedal, 2007)

Kirikou et les bêtes sauvages/Kirikou & the Wild Beasts (Michel Ocelot, Bénédicte
    Galup, 2005)

L'Armée du crime/Army of Crime (Robert Guédiguian, 2009)

L'Auberge Espagnole/Pot Luck (Cédric Klapisch, 2002)

L'Enfer/Hell (Denis Tanovic, 2005)

La Haine/Hate (Mathieu Kassovitz, 1995)

La Mala Educación/Bad Education (Pedro Almodóvar, 2004)

La meglio gioventù/The Best of Youth (Marco Tullio Giordana, 2003)

La Môme/La Vie en rose (Olivier Dahan, 2007)

La Planète Blanche/The White Planet (Jean Lemire, Thierry Piantanida, Thierry
    Ragobert, 2006)

La Science des Rêves/The Science of Sleep (Michel Gondry, 2006)

La Vida Secreta de las Palabras/The Secret Life of Words (Isabel Coixet, 2005)

La vita è bella/Life Is Beautiful (Roberto Benigni, 1997)

La Zona/The Zone (Rodrigo Plá, 2007)

Lady Chatterley (Pascale Ferran, 2005)

Laitakaupungin valot/Lights in the Dusk (Aki Kaurismäki, 2005)

Las 13 Rosas/13 Roses (Emilio Martínez Lázaro, 2007)

Last Resort (Pawel Pawlikowski, 2000)

Le Fabuleux Destin d'Amélie Poulain/Amelie (Jean-Pierre Jeunet, 2001)

Le Fils/The Son (Jean-Pierre and Luc Dardenne, 2002)

Le Fils de l'épicier/The Grocer's Son (Eric Guirado, 2007)

Le premier jour du reste de ta vie/The First Day of the Rest of Your Life (Rémi Bezançon, 2008)

Le Serpent/The Snake (Eric Barbier, 2006)

Le Silence de Lorna/The Silence of Lorna (Jean-Pierre and Luc Dardenne, 2006)

Le Temps qui reste/Time to Leave (François Ozon, 2005)

Lemming (Dominik Moll, 2005)

Les Choristes/The Chorus (Christophe Barratier, 2004)

Les Poupées Russes/Russian Dolls (Cédric Klapisch, 2005)

Les triplettes de Belleville/Belleville Rendez Vous (Sylvain Chomet, 2003)

Lichter/Distant Lights (Hans-Christian Schmid, 2003)

Lilja 4-Ever/Lilya 4-Ever (Lukas Moodysson, 2002)

Lisbon Story (Wim Wenders, 1994)

Lola rennt/Run Lola Run (Tom Tykwer, 1998)

Los Lunes al Sol/Mondays in the Sun (Fernando León de Aranoa, 2002)

Love Actually (Richard Curtis, 2003)

Manderlay (Lars von Trier, 2005)

Mar Adentro/The Sea Inside (Alejandro Amenábar, 2004)

Maradona by Kusturica (Emir Kusturica, 2008)

Masjävlar/Dalecarlians (Maria Blom, 2004)

Match Point (Woody Allen, 2005)

Max & Co (Samuel Guillaume, Frédéric Guillaume, 2007)

Mies vailla menneisyyttä/The Man without a Past (Aki Kaurismäki, 2002)

Mio fratello è figlio unico/My Brother Is an Only Child (Daniele Luchetti, 2007)

Moartea domnului Lazarescu/The Death of Mr. Lazarescu (Cristi Puiu, 2005)

Molière (Laurent Tirard, 2006)

Mrs Henderson Presents (Stephen Frears, 2005)

My Beautiful Laundrette (Stephen Frears, 1985)

My Name Is Joe (Ken Loach, 1998)

My Summer of Love (Pawel Pawlikowski, 2004)

Niko – Lentäjän poika/Niko & The Way to the Stars (Michael Hegner, Kari Juusonen, 2008)

Nirgendwo in Afrika/Nowhere in Africa (Caroline Link, 2001)

No Body Is Perfect (Raphael Sibilla, 2006)

No Man's Land (Daniel Tanovic, 2001)

Nói albínói/Noi the Albino (Dagur Kári, 2003)

Nuovomondo/Nuovomondo – The Golden Door (Emanuele Crialese, 2006)

Nyöcker/The District (Aron Gauder, 2004)

O'Horten (Bent Hamer, 2007)

Obsluhoval Jsem Anglického Krále/I Served the King of England (Jirí Menzel, 2006)

Ocho apellidos vascos/Spanish Affair (Emilio Martínez-Lázaro, 2014)

Of Time and the City (Terence Davies, 2008)

Ondskan/Evil (Mikael Håfström, 2003)

Paisà/Paisan (Roberto Rossellini, 1946)

Paris (Cédric Klapisch, 2008)

Paris je t'aime (Olivier Assayas, Frédéric Auburtin, Emmanuel Benbihy, Gurinder Chadha,
    Sylvain Chomet, Ethal Coen, Joel Coen, Isabel Coixet, Wes Craven, Alfonso Cuarón,
    Gérard Dépardieu, Christopher Doyle, Richard LaGravenese, Vincenzo Natali,
    Alexander Payne, Bruno Podalydès, Walter Salles, Oliver Schmitz, Nobuhiro Suwa,
    Daniela Thomas, Tom Tykwer, Gus Van Sant, 2006)

Paris vu par (Claude Chabrol, Jean Douchet, Jean-Luc Godard, Jean-Daniel Pollet, Eric
    Rohmer, Jean Rouch, 1965)

Paris vu par … vingts ans après (Chantal Akerman, Bernard Dubois, Philippe Garrel,
    Frédéric Miterrand, Vincent Nordon, Philippe Venault, 1984)

Perfume: The Story of a Murderer (Tom Tykwer, 2006)

Persepolis (Marjane Satrapi, Vincent Paronnaud, 2007)

Phoenix (Christian Petzold, 2014)

Princesas/Princesses (Fernando León de Aranoa, 2005)

Quelques jours en Septembre/A Few Days in September (Santiago Amigorena, 2006)

REC (Jaume Balagueró, Paco Plaza, 2007)

Red Road (Andrea Arnold, 2005)

Renart, le renard/Renart the Fox (Thierry Schiel, 2005)

Requiem (Hans-Christian Schmid, 2006)

Retour en Normandie/Back to Normandy (Nicolas Philibert, 2005)

Revanche (Götz Spielmann, 2008)

Riparo – Anis tra di noi/Shelter (Marco Simon Puccioni, 2006)

RoboCop (Paul Verhoeven, 1987)

Rumba (Dominique Abel, Fiona Gordon, Bruno Remy, 2008)

Så som i himmelen/As It Is in Heaven (Kay Pollak, 2004)

Salvador (Manuel Huerga, 2006)

Savage Grace (Tom Kalin, 2007)

Secrets & Lies (Mike Leigh, 1996)

Sehnsucht/Longing (Valeska Grisebach, 2006)

Sense and Sensibility (Ang Lee, 1995)

Shakespeare in Love (John Madden, 1998)

Shirley: Visions of Reality (Gustav Deutsch, 2013)

Shooting Dogs (Michael Caton-Jones, 2005)

Skyfall (Sam Mendes, 2012)

Sliding Doors (Peter Howitt, 1998)

Slumdog Millionaire (Danny Boyle, 2008)

Somers Town (Shane Meadows, 2008)

Sommersturm/Summer Storm (Marco Kreuzpaintner, 2004)

Sophie Scholl – Die Letzten Tage/Sophie Scholl – The Last Days (Marc Rothermund, 2005)

Sorstalansag/Fateless (Lajos Koltai, 2004)

Starship Troopers (Paul Verhoeven, 1997)

Strings (Anders Rønnow Klarlund, 2004)

Svetat e golyam i spasenie debne otvsyakade/The World Is Big and Salvation Lurks around the Corner (Stephan Komandarev, 2008)

Sweet Sixteen (Ken Loach, 2002)

Sylvia (Christine Jeffs, 2003)

Sztuczki/Tricks (Andrjez Jakimowski, 2007)

Taxidermia (György Pálfi, 2006)

Terkel I Knibe/Terkel in Trouble (Stefan Fjeldmark, 2004)

The Artist (Michel Hazanavicious, 2011)

The Broken (Sean Ellis, 2008)

The Dreamers (Bernardo Bertolucci, 2003)

The Iron Lady (Phyllida Lloyd, 2011)

The King's Speech (Tom Hooper, 2010)

The Magic Flute (Kenneth Branagh, 2006)

The Mill and the Cross (Lech Majewski, 2011)

The Pianist (Roman Polanski, 2002)

The Road to Guantanamo (Michael Winterbottom, 2006)

The Ugly Duckling and Me (Michael Hegner, Karsten Kiilerich, 2006)

Tiro en la Cabeza/Bullet in the Head (Jaime Rosales, 2008)

Todo sobre mi madre/All About My Mother (Pedro Almodóvar, 1999)

Total Recall (Paul Verhoeven, 1990)

Transe/Trance (Teresa Villaverde, 2006)

Transylvania (Tony Gatlif, 2006)

Trilogia II: I skoni tou hronou/The Dust of Time (Theo Angelopolous, 2008)

Tvrdjava Evropa/The Fortress Europe (Zelimir Zilnik, 2001)

Ultimo Tango a Parigi/Last Tango in Paris (Bernardo Bertolucci, 1972)

Un conte de Noël/A Christmas Tale (Arnaud Desplechin, 2008)

Un héros très discret/A Self-Made Hero (Jacques Audiard, 1996)

Un long dimanche de fiançailles/A Very Long Engagement (Jean-Pierre Jeunet, 2004)

Vers le Sud/Heading South (Laurent Cantet, 2005)

Vicky Cristina Barcelona (Woody Allen, 2008)

Viva Zapatero! (Sabina Guzzanti, 2005)

Voksne mennesker/Dark Horse (Dagur Kári, 2005)

Volver (Pedro Almodóvar, 2005)

Vozvrashchenie/The Return (Andrey Zvyagintsev, 2003)
Waltz with Bashir (Ari Folman, 2008)
Wesele/The Wedding (Wojciech Smarzowski, 2004)
Zwartboek/Blackbook (Paul Verhoeven, 2006)

Index